SECOND EDITION

SIBLING ABUSE

Books Under the
General Editorship of Jon R. Conte

Hate Crimes: Confronting Violence Against Lesbians and Gay Men
edited by Gregory M. Herek and Kevin T. Berrill

Legal Responses to Wife Assault: Current Trends and Evaluation
edited by N. Zoe Hilton

The Male Survivor: The Impact of Sexual Abuse
by Matthew Parynik Mendel

The Child Sexual Abuse Custody Dispute Annotated Bibliography
by Wendy Deaton, Suzanne Long, Holly A. Magana,
and Julie Robbins

The Survivor's Guide
by Sharice Lee

Psychotherapy and Mandated Reporting of Child Maltreatment
by Murray Levine and Howard J. Doueck

*Sexual Abuse in Nine North American Cultures:
Treatment and Prevention*
by Lisa Aronson Fontes

The Role of Social Support in Preventing Child Maltreatment
by Ross A. Thompson

*Intimate Betrayal: Understanding and Responding to the Trauma of
Acquaintance Rape*
by Vernon R. Wiehe and Ann L. Richards

*Violence Against Women Research: Methodological and Personal
Perspectives*
by Martin D. Schwartz

Sibling Abuse: Hidden Physical, Emotional, and Sexual Trauma
by Vernon R. Wiehe

SECOND EDITION

SIBLING ABUSE

Hidden Physical, Emotional, and Sexual Trauma

Vernon R. Wiehe

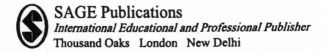

SAGE Publications
International Educational and Professional Publisher
Thousand Oaks   London   New Delhi

For information:

SAGE Publications, Inc.
2455 Teller Road
Thousand Oaks, California 91320
E-mail: order@sagepub.com

SAGE Publications Ltd.
6 Bonhill Street
London EC2A 4PU
United Kingdom

SAGE Publications India Pvt. Ltd.
M-32 Market
Greater Kailash I
New Delhi 110 048 India

Printed in the United States of America

Library of Congress Cataloging-in-Publication Data

Wiehe, Vernon R.
  Sibling abuse: Hidden physical, emotional, and sexual trauma/
Vernon R. Wiehe.—2nd ed.
    p. cm.
  Includes bibliographical references (p.   ) and index.
  ISBN 0-7619-1008-5 (cloth).—ISBN 0-7619-1009-3 (pbk.)
    1. Sibling abuse—United States.   2. Adult child abuse victims—
United States.   3. Adult child sexual abuse victims—United States.
4. Incest victims—United States.   I. Title.
HV6626.52.W54   1997
362.76—dc21   97-4600

This book is printed on acid-free paper.

01 02 03 10 9 8 7 6 5 4

Acquiring Editor: C. Terry Hendrix
Editorial Assistant: Dale Grenfell
Production Editor: Sherrise M. Purdum
Production Assistant: Denise Santoyo
Typesetter/Designer: Marion Warren
Indexer: Teri Greenberg
Cover Designer: Candice Harman
Print Buyer: Anna Chin

Contents

To my wife, Donna, whom I admire, respect,
and deeply love, and who has struggled so bravely
from a debilitating stroke.

1

Sibling Abuse:
An Undetected Problem

Please tell others that there is such a thing as sibling abuse, so that children don't experience what I did from my sibling.

A sibling abuse survivor

I was raped when I was 13 years of age—not by a stranger in a dark alley but by my own brother in my own home when he was baby-sitting me and my younger siblings. He threatened to kill me and make it look like an accident if I ever told my parents. I didn't tell, and he used me sexually from then on whenever he wanted.

I would tell my parents about how my brother would hit me. "You must have done something to deserve it," they would say. I didn't do anything. He constantly was beating me. If I tried to protect myself or hit him in return, it was proof to them I deserved it. I spent a lot of time hiding from him to protect myself.

Recently, I was with a group of friends and we were telling about nicknames we had as children. I said I didn't have any nicknames, but all the while we were laughing and talking, the name I was called by my sister kept going around in my head—*lard ass*. I wouldn't tell them that is how I was known in my house to my sister when I was a child. My parents used to laugh about it. I wasn't laughing; I was crying. My childhood

was a nightmare. I don't even want to look at pictures of when
I was a child. I threw my school pictures away. The memories
hurt so much. At the age of 42 I have finally found the courage
to seek counseling. Maybe I can come out of my shell and enjoy
the remaining years of my life.

These are neither quotations from the script of a play nor words of
characters of a novel. They are the comments of adults who as
children were victims of a type of abuse that has largely remained
undetected—sibling abuse. While considerable progress has been made
in the field of family violence in detecting, treating, and preventing
different types of abuse—child, spouse, or elder—one type of abuse
remains largely undetected. This is the physical, emotional, and sexual
abuse of one sibling by another.

During past years, parents have excused sibling abuse in various ways.
Some have looked the other way. Other parents have ignored the
problem, or they wouldn't believe their children when they were told
what was happening. Some have blamed the victims for the abuse they
experienced—as if they were asking for it or deserved what they experienced. Still others have said it was normal behavior, simply sibling
rivalry, and that this was a normal part of growing up.

Ask the survivors if they would agree that sibling abuse is typical
behavior of children when they are growing up, that it is merely sibling
rivalry, or that they deserved what happened to them. A resounding *No*
would be heard from around the country, as it was from the 150
survivors of sibling abuse who tell their stories in these pages.

Ignoring sibling abuse, pretending it doesn't exist, believing the problem will solve itself, or blaming the victim for the abuse are inappropriate ways of coping with this problem. In the pages that follow, survivors
will describe how their parents handled their abuse from a sibling in
these ways. The adult lives of these survivors are scarred both from their
abuse from a sibling and from their parents' response to the abuse: They
are fearful of others; feel they can trust no one; have very low self-
esteem; are having problems with drugs and alcohol; and exhibit serious sexual problems.

■   Historical Perspective

During the past several decades, various types of family violence —
child abuse, spouse abuse, elder abuse—have been brought out into the

open from behind the closed doors of the family home. As these types of abuse have become known and understood, organizations and resources have developed to combat them.

While progress has been made in detecting, preventing, and treating these types of family violence, sibling abuse has largely remained unrecognized. Several reasons may be cited for this. First, there has been a reluctance for the government through its legislative bodies, the courts, police, and social service agencies to concern itself with what happens in the privacy of the home. Americans value highly their freedom. This includes the freedom to raise their children according to their religious and social values. Thus, historically the philosophy has developed, "What happens at home is the family's business." The published findings of an initial study of violence in American families, based on a sample of over 2,000 families, was aptly titled, *Behind Closed Doors* (Straus, Gelles, & Steinmetz, 1980).

However, the philosophy that the home is a man's castle and what happens behind the closed front door is no one else's business has been challenged, and rightly so, by individuals who have been victims of abuse in their own homes—children abused by their parents, women battered by their husbands, senior citizens mistreated by their adult children. Adult survivors of child abuse, for example, have worked through the media to bring to public attention the malnutrition, beatings, sexual molestation, and death of innocent children. Legislation was passed by Congress in 1974 in the form of the Child Abuse Prevention and Treatment Act (Public Law 93-247) that among other things provided funds to the states for combating and preventing child abuse. This legislation made the reporting of incidents of child abuse mandatory and provided protection to the individual doing the reporting. Spouse abuse likewise has come to public attention in part through the efforts of the feminist movement and through the criminalization of domestic violence cases, beginning in the 1970s. States have formed adult protective service agencies for the reporting and adjudication of incidents of elder abuse. Consequently, the *closed door* of the family home is now open to the scrutiny of the court and allied agencies when the abuse of any family member is suspected. A better understanding has arisen regarding limitations to the authority of parents and other caregivers.

Unfortunately, this has not been true for sibling abuse. This problem has not yet been brought out into the open. Its symptoms go unrecognized, and its devastating effects continue to be ignored. Generally, violent acts between siblings do not come to the attention of the courts unless a parent or the victim is willing to file assault charges against the perpetrating sibling. The latter rarely occurs.

There is a second reason why sibling abuse has been ignored. The abusive behavior of one sibling toward another is often excused by parents as normal behavior: "Kids will be kids"; "All kids call each other names"; "Didn't you ever play doctor when you were a child?"; "It's just normal sibling rivalry." Professionals in the field of mental health, too, have been guilty of viewing abusive behavior between siblings as part of the normal process of growing up. The behaviors to which these statements refer do occur in many families. However, these statements are inappropriate when they are used to excuse the physical, emotional, or sexual *abuse* of one sibling by other. A differentiation must be made between *sibling rivalry* and *sibling abuse*.

Approximately four decades ago child abuse was recognized. This doesn't mean that there was no child abuse before that time. It was occurring, but it was not recognized as abuse. In 1962, an article titled "The Battered Child Syndrome" was published by Dr. C. Henry Kempe and his colleagues at the University of Colorado Medical Center (Kempe, Silverman, Steele, Droegemueller, & Silver, 1962). This article, which would prove to have a historical impact in the field of family violence, was written by physicians who had seen many victims of child abuse. They coined the phrase *battered-child syndrome* as a clinical condition to describe the fractures, burns, wounds, and bruises they saw in their young patients as a result of physical abuse.

John Demos (1986), a historian of the family, commented on the historical impact of this article:

> Child abuse evoked an immediate and complex mix of emotions: horror, shame, fascination, disgust. Dr. Kempe and his coauthors noted that physicians themselves experienced "great difficulty . . . in believing that parents could have attacked their children" and often attempted "to obliterate such suspicions from their minds, even in the face of obvious circumstantial evidence." In a sense the problem had long been consigned to a netherworld of things felt but not seen, known but not acknowledged. The "Battered Child" essay was like a shroud torn suddenly aside. Onlookers reacted with shock, but also perhaps

> with a kind of relief. The horror was in the open now, and it
> would not easily be shut up again. (p. 69)

The time has come for the shroud to be torn aside on yet another type
of abuse—the physical, emotional, or sexual abuse of one sibling by
another. Professionals may have seen this abuse in families with whom
they have worked; they may have seen the effects in adults who have
sought help for their problems-in-living, but they were not able to link
the effects to the cause. Perhaps they remain unsure of how to recognize
this form of abuse or how to prevent it.

▪ The Purpose of This Book

The purpose of this book is to bring sibling abuse out into the open. This
will be done by allowing adult survivors who experienced this problem
when they were growing up to tell their experiences of how they were
abused physically, emotionally, or sexually by a sibling, their parents'
reaction to the abuse that was occurring, and how the abuse has affected
their lives. The book also will discuss why sibling abuse may occur in
some families and how this social problem may be prevented. Implications for the treatment of sibling survivors will be presented for mental
health professionals.

The book was written with several audiences in mind. Primarily, the
book is directed to professionals working in the field of family violence,
to mental health professionals engaged in therapy in counseling centers, as well as to students preparing to become professionals in the field
of mental health. Mental health professionals include individuals leading self-help groups for those who have experienced abuse, child protection workers, and persons such as parent life educators, clergy,
nurses, and others who are teaching families how to effectively live
together. Those preparing to become professionals may include individuals preparing for careers in the field of mental health, such as
students taking courses in family violence and related subjects in college and university departments of social work, sociology, psychology,
and family studies. The survivors' accounts of the abuse they experienced from a brother or sister will assist professionals and students in
understanding the problem of sibling abuse, in diagnosing the problem
in families with whom they may be working, in treating those who are

attempting to cope with the effects of such abuse on their lives, and in preventing this problem from occurring in other families.

A second audience to whom the book is directed are adult survivors of sibling abuse. The author has received numerous comments and letters from adult survivors of sibling abuse who have read an earlier edition of this book or who have heard the author discuss the subject of sibling abuse on television and radio programs. Repeatedly, these comments and letters state that the author's discussion of sibling abuse has "validated" for them that what they experienced from a sibling as a child was not sibling rivalry but sibling abuse. The last chapter, "A Final Word," is directed to persons who may have been abused by a sibling as a child. This book may help these readers realize that they are not alone in the abuse they experienced from a sibling, and that the nightmare of abuse in their childhood is not their fault. Perhaps, as the survivors in this book speak about their abuse, their comments will encourage these readers to seek help if they are having problems struggling with the effects of sibling abuse on their lives now as adults.

Although the book was not written specifically for parents, some parents may find the book helpful. The accounts of the survivors—how they were physically, emotionally, or sexually abused by a sibling—may sensitize parents to the subtle and not-so-subtle forms of sibling abuse that may be occurring within their own families. Becoming sensitive to sibling abuse may prompt parents to take action to stop such abuse or to prevent the problem from occurring.

Throughout the book, the findings from the author's research on sibling abuse will be related to the larger body of research on family violence, especially child abuse, since most sibling abuse survivors were children at the time of their victimization. Numerous references to the literature in the field of family violence are cited that may be helpful to readers in pursuing in greater depth specific areas of interest.

* The Research

During the past several decades, when the author would speak to audiences on the subject of child abuse, repeatedly someone at the end of the lecture would comment, "I think I was abused as a child but not by my parents. Rather, I feel I was abused by a sibling. Have you ever heard of that?" After this repeatedly occurred, the author initiated a study on the subject of sibling abuse that forms the basis of this research.

Research Subjects

Individuals participating in the research responded to ads in several major newspapers and newsletters of professional associations, as well as notices sent to organizations working in the field of family violence. These notices asked that individuals who had been physically, emotionally, or sexually abused by a sibling when they were growing up write for a questionnaire to which they could respond anonymously. The 14-page questionnaire included both open- and closed-ended questions about their earliest memory of abuse by a sibling, their typical experience of abuse, their reactions to the abuse, their parents' response to the abuse, how the abuse has affected their lives as adults, and their suggestions for preventing sibling abuse. Participants could respond to identical questions for each type of sibling abuse that they experienced—physical, emotional, or sexual.

The information presented in this book is based on 150 responses. (Completed questionnaires as well as requests for questionnaires continued to come to the author long after the closing deadline for gathering data.) Descriptive information on the respondents will help to understand their responses.

Eighty-nine percent (134) of the respondents were female; 11% (16) were male. The average age of those responding was 37 years. Eighty-five percent (127) were white; 13% (20) were African American, and 2% (3) represented other racial or ethnic backgrounds.

Twenty-seven percent (41) of the respondents were single. Forty-seven percent (73) were married and 3% (4) identified themselves as cohabiting with someone. Twenty-one percent (31) were divorced. Only one person who was widowed responded to the research.

The respondents represented a well-educated group of persons: 16% (24) having a high school education or less, while 50% (75) had attended college or completed an undergraduate degree. An additional 34% (51) held a graduate degree.

The educational level of the respondents' parents was examined as a way of characterizing their families. Fifty-seven percent (85) of the respondents' mothers had a high school education or less. Forty-three percent (65) had attended college, completed college, or held graduate degrees. The educational levels of the respondents' fathers was almost identical with only one more father having attended or completed college.

It was not possible to control for the socioeconomic status of the respondents' parents because of the absence of information on the parents' income and the different times when the respondents were children. The average educational level, one index of socioeconomic status, for the parents was at least a high school education. Thus, the respondents appear on the average to come from at least middle-income families.

Seventy-one percent (107) of the respondents provided their names, addresses, and phone numbers at the end of the questionnaire, indicating their willingness to be contacted for a possible follow-up letter or phone call.

Data Analysis

Research data are generally analyzed by quantitative methods that rely on counting or measuring following the use of standardized instruments and scales. Data of this nature may then be analyzed through the use of descriptive and inferential statistics. But research on topics about which little is known—exploratory research—lends itself to qualitative rather than to quantitative analysis. The goal of qualitative analysis is to understand the research topic from the perspective of the participants involved—their thoughts, emotions, or first-hand experiences (Royse, 1995).

Qualitative data analysis is descriptive in nature, with little to no use of statistics. Anecdotal accounts form an important part of the findings. Qualitative analysis tries to catch the emotions and moods of the respondents to learn about the problem from *their* perspective and to discover their reaction to the problem. Thus, qualitative analysis was the form of data analysis chosen for this initial study in sibling abuse. The survivors' descriptions of sibling abuse in their own words form an essential component of this book. While it was not possible to include the comments of all respondents, a deliberate effort was made to avoid sensationalism in selecting the comments to illustrate the major themes. The comments are reproduced with only limited editing to correct the grammar. The respondents' written comments were content-analyzed for major themes and subjects. These themes form the major chapter divisions.

Application of the Findings

No claim can be made that the sample responding to this research is representative of the larger population. The number of persons who were in therapy or support groups, and the number of professionals working in the area of family violence who were survivors of sibling abuse, may cause a bias in the direction of individuals who were acutely aware of their abuse and have either sought help or have chosen to work in the area of treating and preventing family violence. Eighty-seven percent (130) of the respondents indicated that they had received counseling for emotional problems. The sample may also represent a bias toward individuals who were abused by a sibling more severely than other survivors of sibling abuse. The geographical dispersion of the respondents, however, and the fact that they received treatment from a variety of resources, rather than just from one type of mental health agency, helps to reduce the bias and enhance the representativeness of the sample.

Researchers in the field of family violence, especially in the area of sexual abuse, are encouraged to secure survivor-participants as soon as possible after abuse is reported. But this is not possible for sibling sexual abuse, which is generally not reported and for which help is not sought until many years after the abuse occurred. Longitudinal research could accomplish this, but such research is costly and difficult to implement because of methodological issues, such as the influence of intervening variables, as well as sample mortality. Individuals who have been in treatment for their abuse for a significant period of time or who have been involved in a support group for abuse survivors, however, may have a greater awareness and sensitivity of how their abuse has affected them than survivors who are just realizing that they were victimized as children. This may be regarded as a bias, but since the intent of this initial research on sibling abuse is to sensitize professionals and parents to the problem, the sensitivity and awareness of these individuals adds strength to their message.

The use of a control or comparison group is an important component of research methodology. It was not possible to use such a group in this research, nor was it deemed appropriate because of the exploratory nature of the research. When further research of a more rigorous nature is done, the use of control and comparison groups will be important in advancing knowledge about sibling abuse.

▪ Readers' Response to the Research

Some readers may find the comments of survivors harsh, crude, and in reference to sexual abuse even vulgar. Those readers should remember that these are the comments of *survivors* of sibling abuse—physical, emotional, or sexual. They are telling their stories not to entertain or please but to describe what happened to them, the pain and emotional suffering they experienced as children at the hands of a sibling that made their childhood a nightmare, and the effects of a victimization that continues to haunt them as adults.

Other readers may react to the survivors' stories with disbelief and deny the validity or truthfulness of their statements. However, logically, why would someone go to the trouble of writing a letter requesting a copy of the research questionnaire only to falsify a response? If subjects had been paid to respond, this might be a legitimate criticism, but there were no rewards. It even cost the respondents their time and energy to complete the research instrument, 14 pages in length. To deny the validity of the survivors' comments is to respond to sibling abuse as Freud and Kinsey historically responded to the sexual abuse of women; with reference to Freud, to discount the reality of incestuous abuse or to blame the child for being the one who wanted the sexual contact in the first place, and in the case of Kinsey, to discount the seriousness of the consequences of the sexual abuse of children (Herman, 1981; Masson, 1984; Rush, 1977; 1980; Russell, 1986).

▪ Terminology

Several terms and phrases should be clarified. The term *survivor* rather than *victim* will be used to refer to individuals who experienced sibling abuse when they were growing up. Individuals who have been victims of various forms of abuse prefer to call themselves survivors. Being a victim implies helplessness. A victim of an automobile accident may be trapped in the wreckage or may be unconscious. The victim needs someone to act as a rescuer. Being a survivor, however, implies survival, persistence, recovery, despite the abuse that has occurred. In subsequent chapters, the term *survivor* will generally be used to refer to the individual who was the target of aggression from a sibling; however, at times the designation *victim* may be used when referring to the individual at the time the abuse was occurring. The individual engaging in the abusive behavior against a sibling will be referred to as the *perpetrator.*

Throughout the pages that follow, reference will be made to abuse that occurs "*between* siblings." The use of the word *between* suggests that only two siblings were involved; that the abuse did not occur *among* three or more siblings. The phrase "*between siblings*" was deliberately chosen because although sibling abuse may occur among several siblings in a family, the survivors who described their experiences in this research generally did so as the victims of a single sibling.

▪ Format of the Book

In Chapters 2, 3, and 4 the survivors tell how they were physically, emotionally, and sexually abused by their siblings, respectively. Chapter 5 describes the parents' reaction to the abuse. Chapter 6 presents theoretical frameworks for understanding sibling abuse. The effects of sibling abuse on the survivors is the focus of Chapter 7. Chapter 8 identifies criteria for distinguishing normal interactive behaviors between siblings from abusive behavior. Based on an understanding of why sibling abuse occurs and what distinguishes abusive behavior from normal sibling interactions, Chapter 9 focuses on strategies for preventing sibling abuse. Chapter 10 discusses implications of sibling abuse for mental health professionals who may be treating survivors. A final word to the readers is found in Chapter 11.

▪ A Challenge

Sibling abuse may be happening in many families across the nation. Just as efforts successfully have been made through education and legislation to prevent other types of family violence, the challenge faces society now to recognize that abuse in families can occur not only between adults or between adults and children, but also between children in the same family in the form of sibling abuse. Efforts must be made to recognize this form of abuse so that it can be prevented and the survivors treated for the effects of the abuse on their lives. One respondent to the research made a plea for this:

> Thanks for being interested in sibling abuse. Those of us who have been victims of this have had to live with it as if we deserved it or it was our fault. My childhood was horrible because of what my brother did to me. I recently met someone whose sister abused her. It was only because I finally sought therapy for my problems that I could talk to her about the abuse both of us experienced from our siblings. Please get the message out that there is such a thing as sibling abuse.

▪ Summary

During the past decades, several types of family violence have been recognized by society—child, spouse, and elder abuse. Legislation has been passed and organizations have been formed for detecting, treating, and preventing these problems. One type of family violence—sibling abuse—largely remains unrecognized but often is excused as part of the normal process of growing up or as sibling rivalry.

2

Physical Abuse

My childhood was terrible. My older brother was repeatedly hitting, slapping, beating me up.

A sibling abuse survivor

Picture the following scenario. A child is taken into the emergency room with bruises and a bleeding wound on the face. The parents are questioned regarding how these injuries occurred. If the mother were to state that the father hit the child, legislation requires that a report be filed with the local child protective service agency by an attending staff member in the emergency room. This report would initiate an investigation of the parents for child abuse by child protective services that could end in prosecution of one or both of the parents.

Let's go back to the scenario in the emergency room. The same child is brought into the emergency room with the same injuries. The parents are questioned as to how the injuries occurred. If the mother were to state that the child was fighting with a sibling, no further investigation probably would take place. The case would be considered closed. Why would this happen? The injuries would not be considered as child abuse but would be viewed as normal sibling rivalry that got out of hand.

As the survivors speak in this chapter about the physical abuse—at times even life-threatening—that they experienced from siblings, two facts become obvious. First, while society recognizes the physical abuse of children by adults, it ignores the same type of abuse that occurs between siblings in the same family. Second, steps must be taken by

13

states across the nation to provide children the same type of protection from their siblings that they receive from their parents or adults who might physically mistreat them.

▪ Incidence of Physical Abuse

What is meant by the physical abuse of one sibling by another? Physical abuse was defined for the purposes of this research in the following way: Physical abuse consists of willful acts resulting in physical injury such as slapping, hitting, biting, kicking, or more violent behavior that may include the use of an instrument, such as a stick, bat, gun, or knife.

The individuals who completed the research questionnaire used this definition as a guide for their response. The responses indicate that the physical abuse the survivors experienced from a sibling while they were growing up at home constituted a wide range of behaviors.

How frequently does sibling abuse occur? Several studies in the literature give some indication. In a survey of 57 randomly selected families, a high level of physical violence between siblings was found, as reported in families' comments and in diaries they kept for a week (Steinmetz, 1977). Similarly, in a nationwide survey of 2,143 families regarding violence among any of the family members, researchers concluded that violent acts between siblings occurred more frequently than parent-child (child abuse) or husband-wife (spouse abuse) violence (Straus et al., 1980). The survey data indicated that 53 out of every 100 children per year attack a brother or sister. Likewise, a study reported by *U.S. News & World Report* found that 138,000 children ages 3 to 17 used a weapon on a sibling during a one-year period ("Battered Families," 1979). If these attacks had occurred outside the family, they would have been considered assaults. However, because these attacks occurred between children in the same family, they were basically ignored. Unfortunately, current national or state data on incidents of sibling abuse are not available because abusive behavior between siblings is excused as sibling rivalry and mandatory reporting of these incidents is not required.

Physical abuse does not appear to occur alone but rather in conjunction with emotional and sexual abuse by a sibling. Physical abuse occurred along with emotional and sexual abuse for 64% (96) of the respondents.

The following comments from survivors demonstrate the way in which physical, emotional, and sexual abuse interact:

> Along with the name calling there were the beatings I got from my brother.

> My brother would try to get me to do things to him sexually and when I refused he beat me 'till I did.

> I remember the physical abuse—hitting, choking, rough force, hitting my head against things, and tearing at my clothes—that he used to force me to engage in sexual activities.

■ Forms of Physical Abuse by a Sibling

The nature of physical abuse that the respondents received from their siblings may be divided into three forms:

1. Most common—hitting, biting, slapping, shoving, and punching
2. Unusual—tickling
3. Injurious or life-threatening—smothering, choking, and being shot with a BB gun

These categories are not necessarily mutually exclusive. Also, although a separate category of sibling physical abuse has been labeled as "injurious or life-threatening," this is not meant to imply that other forms of physical abuse may not have potentially serious consequences for the victim's life.

■ Most Common Forms

The most common forms of physical abuse reported were hitting, slapping, pushing, punching, biting, hair pulling, scratching, and pinching. Respondents reported having been hit by a sibling with objects such as a broom handle, rubber hose, coat hanger, hairbrush, belt, and sticks, and being threatened and stabbed with broken glass, knives, razor blades, and scissors.

A 40-year-old woman from Kentucky described her earliest memory of physical abuse by her sibling:

When I was 3 or 4, my brother pushed me down some stone steps. I had approximately 30 stitches in my knee.

This same respondent experienced continual physical abuse as she was growing up with two older brothers:

My brothers typically slugged me in the arm. I was not to cry or everyone went to their rooms. The other favorite activity was to play scissors, paper, and stone. My wrist would be stinging from the hits when I lost. My older brother would usually hit me in the stomach, push me down on the floor, and hold me down while he continued to hit me in the stomach and on the arms.

A female survivor from New Mexico described the abuse she experienced from an older brother:

He would engage me in wrestling matches daily, typically punching me in the stomach until I could not breathe, torturing my joints, wrists, and knees, spitting on me, putting his knees on my arms, and pinning me down and beating on my chest with his knuckles.

A 42-year-old woman from Wisconsin retains this vivid memory of the childhood abuse she suffered from two older brothers:

I remember frequently being curled up in a living room chair with my hands over my face being hit over and over. I usually ended up on the floor and not moving or making noises so they would go away.

Another survivor wrote:

My sister would hit, kick, or spit on me. Although she was only one year older, she was always much stronger and bigger than me.

A survivor from Maine wrote:

I can't ever remember not being physically abused by my brother. He beat on me every day. It was just part of existing to me. He would punch, pinch, and kick me. Sometimes he would pull out my hair. Sometimes he would use weapons or anything else close.

A female survivor from Kansas wrote about the physically abusive behavior of her older brother:

> He would start by taking jabs at my face and force me into a corner or until I fell over something and was down. Then he would pound at my shoulders until I cried or pleaded for him to stop, usually telling him I would do his work for him.

A male Missouri respondent described the physical abuse he received from an older brother and identified the source from which the brother learned this behavior:

> Usually the abuse would consist of getting beat up by my brother with his fists or being slapped around with the inside of his hands—a practice he learned from our parents—along with being kicked in the rear.

Often, the abuse escalated, as a survivor from Massachusetts described:

> The abuse consisted usually of my brother punching me in the arms, stomach, back, etc. Usually it started out with a verbal fight, but sometimes he just began punching me if I wouldn't do what he told me to or if he wanted to watch something different on TV. Sometimes things were worse. Once he tried to hit me with an aluminum baseball bat. When I ran away and locked myself in the bathroom, he kicked a hole in the door.

Another survivor:

> A minor argument would erupt into violence when I wouldn't do what my brother wanted me to or I wouldn't agree with his opinion. I was shaken, hit, kicked, and slapped. I was never badly hurt, but the level of my brother's rage was such that I was always afraid of it. I knew what was happening was wrong, but I don't think I thought of it as abuse at the time. I have blocked out my memories of these events for many years and still do not have all of them back.

A survivor described how the abuse she suffered from an older brother increased in intensity over the years:

> It was mostly my brother who is 5 years older than me that did all the abuse. I would usually be playing by myself somewhere. He would barge in mad or drunk or both and he'd want me to either get something for him or cook for him. When I would say

"No," he'd get extremely angry and start hitting me, cursing at me, kicking me, pushing me around in a total frenzy of violence. It started out by slapping, pushing, cursing. The older we got, the more severe it became. I have suffered from a broken nose and collarbone, countless bruises and scratches. I still have a BB in my leg where he shot at me with a BB gun. He kicked me with steel-toed boots on my upper arm, and it was red and purple for weeks. I thought he had broken it.

■ An Unusual Form of Abuse

An unusual form of physical abuse by a sibling that respondents reported was tickling. Tickling generally is not regarded as a form of physical abuse, but in fact it can become physically abusive under certain conditions.

Tickling involves two persons—a perpetrator engaging in the behavior, and a victim. Tickling can be pleasant—even erotic—or it can be painful. The unpleasantness often associated with tickling may be due to the fact that the nerve fibers that respond to tickling are the same ones that respond to pain (Farrell, 1985). Tickling can be pleasant when it occurs in a context of trust and mutual respect. In such a context, the victim trusts that the perpetrator will stop the behavior at the victim's request.

But tickling becomes painful and abusive if the victim has no control over the situation. When the victim requests that the tickling cease, but the perpetrator continues to engage in the behavior, it is abusive. As reported by survivors in this research, some perpetrators even restrained their victims, such as pinning them to the floor. Often, there was little the victim could do because of their smaller size or weaker strength in relation to their perpetrator.

Several survivors described having serious reactions to the tickling they experienced from a sibling. A 48-year-old Ohio woman reported that a sister, 3 years older, would physically abuse her by punching, slapping, and pinning her down on the floor. Most disturbing, however, was the fact the sister would tickle her to the point that she would vomit.

Another respondent described the repeated, abusive tickling that she suffered at the hands of her older brother. The brother, who was very strong, would restrain her arms on the floor with his knees and slap and tickle her. She was powerless to resist. As an adult, she described her reaction to this physical abuse in a symbolic way, feeling as if she were still in that position on the floor:

> I became a doormat in my other relationships with men. It made me very timid and shy and left me with no self-esteem.

Another adult woman wrote that she had recently attended a seminar on child abuse where tickling was mentioned as a form of abuse. She became aware that she had been a victim at the hands of her siblings, not only through this form of abuse, but through other behaviors that were upsetting to her. But she felt she was expected by her parents and society to accept these behaviors as the typical way children play. She recalled experiencing this type of abuse throughout her childhood from a sibling and foster brother, both of whom were 8 years older.

> I was unmercifully tickled by my brother who held down every limb and body part that wiggled and covered my mouth when I cried and yelled for help. He pulled my hair after I pulled his, thinking that would hurt him and he would stop.

This survivor said her mother ignored what her brother did, calling it playing, even though she tried to convince her mother that it was not playful activity. The survivor reported that this abuse affects her even now as an adult. She does not like to be touched by other people, especially when they hug her or hold her in any way reminiscent of being restrained.

A survivor from Missouri who was abusively tickled by an older brother and sister received a similar reaction from her mother when she told her of it:

> My brother and sister would hold me down and tickle me until I cried. They considered this play and would usually do it when my parents were gone. They would finally let me go and then laugh because I was a "crybaby."

▪ Injurious or Life-Threatening Physical Abuse

Play among siblings can escalate into aggressive behavior that may result in injury to one of the participants. All children probably at some time or another are injured while playing, even accidentally, by a

sibling. To distinguish the incidents reported in the following para-
graphs from what generally happens to children, the events must be
viewed in context.

First, the experiences were typical or repetitive of what occurred for the
victim from a brother or sister. Although many people may report at
some time having suffered some type of physical injury while playing
with a sibling, generally it is an isolated or single incident. In some
instances, the particular abusive behavior experienced by the survivors
may have only occurred once, but it was *typical* of injurious abuse they
experienced repeatedly from a sibling.

Second, the event must be seen in terms of the perpetrator's reaction to
the injury the sibling suffered. In most instances, the perpetrator
laughed at the victim. This reaction further "injured" the victim by
giving the message that the behavior was not accidental but had an
intentional element to it.

Finally, the abusive behavior also must be understood in the context of
the parents' reaction to what occurred. Normally, when children are
injured by a sibling when playing, their parents comfort them, take care
of their injuries, and discipline the sibling who perpetrated the injury.
At the very least, parents make an attempt to determine what happened.
The survivors of sibling physical abuse reported that their parents'
reaction to the injurious or life-threatening incident was one of noncha-
lance, a denial of the suffering they were experiencing, and in some
instances even blaming them for what happened.

An adult woman described an incident that happened to her when she
was approximately 6 or 7 years of age and that was typical of the abusive
behavior she experienced from her siblings. This was the earliest memory in a long series of abusive events, but it remains vivid in her
memory. She reported that her two brothers grabbed her by her legs and
arms, swung her around three times and released her into a hedge of
bushes with thorns.

A 55-year-old woman described a similar physically abusive incident
in childhood from a sister that resulted in injury. The scars from this
injury remain today as a reminder to her of the physical abuse she
experienced from this sister as a child:

> I climbed on the chicken coop and a nail penetrated my foot. It
> went all the way through my foot. I was literally nailed to the

coop. My older sister saw me and laughed and told me that's what I deserved. She left and wouldn't help me down. After a long time my older brother came by, helped me get down, and took me to the hospital for help and a tetanus shot. I was so afraid I would get lockjaw. I still have the scar on my foot.

Once my sister was ironing. She was a teenager. I was between 4 and 5. I was curious as to what she was doing. I put my hands flat up on the ironing board and she immediately put the hot iron down on my hand. She laughed and told me to get lost. I still have the burn scar on my left hand.

Another life-threatening or injurious form of abuse reported was the use of BB guns.

My younger brother was playing April fools jokes so one of my older brothers aimed a BB gun at him and shot him. He said "April fools," and started laughing. My younger brother was lying on the ground in a lot of pain.

Another survivor commented:

My brothers would chase me into an open field and shoot BBs from a gun at me. I was hit in the ankle.

A Nevada survivor said she had been deliberately shot in the face with a BB gun by her brother, who repeatedly physically abused her throughout her childhood. This survivor lost an eye as a result of this incident.

A woman in her late 40s described the injurious abuse she suffered from an older brother as a child and her parents' response to it:

When I was 2 or 3, my mother went to visit my father, who was in the Army, and my brother and I were left in the care of my grandparents. My brother was helping my grandfather paint a fence, and he painted me from head to toe with dark brown paint. I remember the paint was in my hair, face, clothing, etc., and I had to be scrubbed down with turpentine and repeated baths. Some of my hair had to be cut to get the paint out. My brother laughed and teased me about all of this. Later, during another incident, my brother wrote his name on my bare back with his woodburning kit. He seemed to treat me as an object rather than as a person with any feelings. My abuse continued through high school. My brother would twist my arms or pin me down and bend my arms or legs to get me to do things he wanted me to do, such as his chores or to cover for him by lying to my parents. These incidents usually happened when my parents weren't home. When I reported them to my parents, he would say I was making it up to get him in trouble. Then we would both be punished. I knew my parents didn't know how to handle the problem, so I quit reporting to my parents. I would just arrange to go to a friend's house or have a friend over when my parents were going to be out.

A survivor from California wrote:

My brother discovered that hitting in the solar plexus caused one to black out. So he would hit me and watch me pass out.

The physical abuse some siblings experienced may not have actually resulted in injury, but it certainly had a life-threatening quality. Numerous respondents reported having been "playfully" strangled by an older sibling. While the behavior may have occurred in jest, the survivor spoke of the terror, fright, and anxiety experienced while it was happening. Some respondents still suffer from the effects of the abuse many years after it occurred. A 40-year-old woman from Texas reported:

I have photographs of my brother pushing me down and trying to "playfully" strangle me when I was an infant.

This same woman remembers that as a child of 4 to 6 years old, her brother would restrain her and in a threatening but supposedly playful manner put his hands around her neck, as if to choke her to death. She indicated that as an adult she remains very frightened of men and has a phobia about anyone touching her neck. She also stated that because of her experience with her sibling, she is not willing to have more than one child.

A respondent from Texas who described herself as being extremely afraid of people—especially men—also experienced life-threatening abuse from an older brother:

My oldest brother would put his arms around my chest tight and not let me inhale any air while I had to watch in the mirror as he laughed and explained how I was going to die.

Similarly, another survivor:

Under the guise of "play-fighting," my older brother would choke me until I was gagging. As he got older and stronger, this got more vicious. He also brutalized other kids smaller than he was.

Respondents told of siblings smothering them with a pillow, another form of life-threatening physical abuse, when they were growing up. This particular behavior seems to have occurred when siblings were playing together on a couch or bed. The frightening response of the victim to what initially might be described as a playful activity became a clue for some siblings of the power and control they could exert over their sibling.

> I remember my brother putting a pillow over my head. He would hold it and laugh while I struggled to get out from under him and the pillow. I remember being *terrified*. I honestly thought he would smother me to death. This occurred frequently.
>
> Once all three of my brothers put a pillow over my face and I couldn't breathe. I struggled as much as I could to get away. What stopped them was my Mom was coming up the driveway.

One respondent reported the following abusive, life-threatening behavior from an older brother:

> He put a pillow over my face and smothered me until I almost died. He was twice my size and very big. One time I did pass out and I came to when he gave me mouth-to-mouth resuscitation.

A male survivor from Oregon described the abuse he experienced from an older brother:

> Sometimes he would choke me with his hands or pin me down with a pillow over my face. The first time he did this was when I was 4 years old.

A survivor from Washington wrote:

> My brother forced me to the bottom of my sleeping bag and held the top closed so I couldn't get out or breathe. When I realized I couldn't get out, I became panic-stricken and thought I was going to die. Even as I write this, I am taken back to that moment and feel just the way I felt then. As an adult, I'm claustrophobic and can't have my face covered without panic setting in.

A survivor of sibling abuse from Louisiana, the youngest of four children, described another form of injurious or life-threatening physical abuse:

> I don't remember when it started but my brothers and sisters used to hit me in the stomach to knock the breath out of me because I had asthma and they thought it was funny to see me wheeze. I was around 4 or 5 years of age. Also, my sister and brothers would hit me in the nose to make me sneeze and count the number of times I would sneeze. Whoever made me sneeze most was the winner. Once I sneezed 17 times. On another occasion I bled from my nose all over a new chair my parents had bought, after my brother hit me in the nose.

Another form of life-threatening abuse was reported by a respondent from New York, who had one sibling, a brother 3 years older:

> My brother made several serious attempts to drown me in local pools and later laughed about it. These attempts continued until I was strong enough to get away and could swim.

A survivor from Iowa who described vicious attacks by older siblings throughout her childhood reported her earliest memory of physical abuse:

> I was 3 or 4 years old. My family went camping often. We were out at a little lake. I was walking with my two brothers. We walked out on a dock to see the ducks closer and my brother pushed me into the water. I couldn't swim! They just stood on the dock and laughed at me. I was gasping for air. I thought I was going to die! Then the next thing I remember is someone pulling me out. It was a farmer driving by on his tractor. He took us all back to the camp and he told my parents he had pulled me out. I told my parents that my brothers had "pushed" me and they said I "fell" in.

■ The Theme of Power and Control in Sibling Abuse

After reading these accounts of the various types of abuse children experienced from their siblings, a common reaction might be to ask the question, "Why would brothers and sister do these kinds of things to each other?" This will be discussed more fully in a later chapter, but a theme that runs throughout the abusive incidents should be identified here. This same theme can be seen in child sexual abuse and especially in spouse abuse. This is the theme of power and control. Abuse as a means of achieving power and control over another person is evident not only in sibling physical abuse but can be noted in the chapters that follow on sibling emotional and sexual abuse. A survivor from Illinois described this theme of power and control when discussing the abuse she experienced from her brother:

> He would punch me with his closed fists in the arms or back. Usually this occurred around issues of him dominating me. He would resort to physical abuse to dominate me.

The perpetrator abuses a sibling as the means to dominate or have power and control. The perpetrator does this because he or she feels powerless for a variety of reasons; for example, the perpetrator may think that the sibling receives more attention because of good grades in school, friends, or physical attractiveness. The perpetrator may also be exhibiting his or her own insecurity and uses abuse as a means to bolster self-esteem.

A survivor from Indiana described how physical force was used by her sibling to gain control over her:

> My sister would be instantly angry over seemingly little incidents. If her assault of words didn't bring about what she thought was a submissive response, she became violent with her hands and fists. She would slap my face, arms, and shoulders.

In many of the abusive incidents reported in this research, the perpetrator was a male. It would appear the male abusers felt that being male equaled being in control and having power over their female siblings.

In American society today power and control often are gender related. The mistaken notion is held by many males that they must dominate and control females. They feel that they must satisfy the perceived expectation that as men they should be powerful. These males attempt to achieve a sense of power (a false sense) by putting females—in sibling abuse, their sisters—in a powerless situation by means of abuse. By this behavior, they make their sisters their victims, and they become perpetrators. The feeling of power and control over a victim that a perpetrator experiences as a result of the abusive behavior serves as a reinforcement for repeating the abusive behavior. It meets a need for the male, but unfortunately, it is an insatiable and pathological need. In subsequent chapters, we will see that male siblings gained power and control over their sisters by means of emotional and sexual abuse as well as physical abuse.

■ The Survivors' Response

How did the survivors who experienced physical abuse from a sibling respond to what was happening?

Protecting Themselves

As one would expect, the most typical response was that the survivors attempted to protect themselves. A young woman from New York described how she tried to protect herself from a sister who was a year older:

> My sister would beat me up, and I would sit on my bed with my knees up guarding myself until she stopped.

Screaming and Crying

Another typical, natural reaction was that the victim screamed or cried out for help. Unfortunately, this reaction often provoked the perpetrator to intensify the physically abusive behavior. Following is a typical scenario: An older brother is beating on a younger sibling. If the younger sibling cries or screams for help, the beating intensifies under the warning, "Take it like you should!" or "If you cry, I'll give you more." Unfortunately, some children learn or model this behavior from their parents and the way in which they have been disciplined by them. This scenario is often played out between parents and children in the context of discipline. A parent is attempting to discipline a child by spanking. After the child has been spanked, the parent warns the child not to cry: "If you don't stop crying, I'll really give you something to cry about."

Analyze for a moment the interaction that is occurring, both in the incident between the two siblings and between the parent and child. The victim's reaction to the abuse or punishment is a natural reaction—

crying, hurt, or perhaps even calling for help. But the victim is told by the perpetrator to deny their feelings or else they will receive further abuse or punishment. The victim is in a no-win or catch-22 position.

One survivor described this dilemma:

> My brother was very violent—quick to anger, quick to strike out. He would slap, hit, kick, or trip me. If I reacted negatively, he would become more violent and use his size and strength to hurt me, that is, punch me in the face or shove me.

A survivor from Tennessee wrote:

> My brother would begin by hitting, biting, or placing a pillow over my face. He would demand that I say uncle or beg him to stop. When I did so he only hurt me more. If I didn't do what he said, he'd hurt me more. I was in a *no-win* situation. I felt helpless because I *was* helpless.

A survivor from Indiana attempted to run away from her abusive brother, which only provoked more physical abuse:

> When I tried to run away, he would chase me until he could grab my hair and pull me to a stop.

Separating Themselves From the Abuser

The position of powerlessness in which the survivors of physical abuse often found themselves with siblings prompted many of them to respond in the only way they could; namely, to separate themselves from the perpetrator and literally hide themselves to avoid being abused. The victims would lock themselves in their bedroom, if they were fortunate to have their own room, or they would spend as much time as possible away from their home with friends.

A survivor described her efforts at self-protection from an abusive brother:

> I became a very withdrawn child. I would retreat to my room and read. If my brother was involved in a game, I wouldn't play. If he was in a particular room, I would go to a different one.

An adult woman recalled her experiences as a young girl and that of her younger siblings who experienced physical abuse from an older sister when they were growing up. These young girls finally discovered a way of controlling the abuse.

> She would yell and scream and chase us around. She would swing her arms at us and hit any part of us she could. I'd curl up in a ball and cover my head in my arms when she caught me. Often I was lucky enough to run away from her and hide. One day I was playing in the basement with a small snake when she came after me. She saw the snake and ran away in fear. After that I really liked snakes and tried to have one with me as often as I could for protection against her rage.

A 44-year-old woman who was a frequent victim of physical abuse from an older brother coped with the abuse in this way:

> I would try to stay away from him, but if he caught me, I wouldn't say or do anything. I was afraid he would just get angrier if I made a fuss. I tried telling my parents, but they always believed my brother. I didn't tell them anymore.

Another woman described the abuse she experienced on a daily basis from an only sibling, a brother 4 years older:

> My brother would hit me, bite me, wrestle me, etc., anytime my parents were out of sight. The times that were most frightening for me were after school—the period between the time we arrived home from school and my parents came home from work, about 2 to 3 hours. I would run to my room and lock the door or go to a friend's house so he wouldn't terrorize me.

A survivor of physical abuse from an older sister reported:

> I didn't dare cry because no one believed me anyway. Most of the time I just got away from her and hid.

A Montana survivor who was physically abused by a brother reported that her brother, 7 years older, was always playing games in which she became his victim. One game he repeatedly played, that readers may remember from their childhood, was "Flinch." Her brother would thrust his hand at her face, and if she blinked, he would hit her on her arm. If she didn't flinch the first time, he would keep doing it until she did, and then he would hit her twice because he felt he got bonus points. Obviously, from the way he set up the game, she was always the loser or the victim. He also invented the game "Tickle Torture," in which he would tickle her until she wet her pants or couldn't breathe. Still another game was "Crab People," in which he would pinch her, leaving bruises on her body. The survivor attempted to handle her abuse this way:

> My brother was so much bigger it was impossible to retaliate. He would hurt me and it would make me angry. I tried to hurt back but it was useless. I was too small. My hits were nothing and he was likely to try something else. It was better to hide.

In general, the survivors of physical abuse by a sibling appeared to live in constant fear of further abuse. Attempts to scream or cry out for help often resulted only in further abuse. The only way some of the survivors could cope with the abuse was to stay away from the sibling. As children, life involved sensing the mood of an abusive sibling as a means of self-protection. A 39-year-old woman from Maine, a survivor of physical abuse from an older brother, reported:

> I learned to sense his bad moods and dreaded being left alone with him at any time, as he seemed always to find some reason to hurt me.

Abusing a Younger Sibling in Turn

One type of victim response reported was to inflict the same abuse they themselves were experiencing on a younger sibling. This behavior can be understood in two ways. One, the victim used the older sibling's behavior as a model and in turn became a perpetrator. Social learning theory states that violence or abuse is often a learned behavior. The behavior may be learned from adults—parents, for example, if they are abusive to each other, from an older sibling who may be abusive, from peers, or from television, movies, and videos (Eron, Huesmann, Lefkowitz, & Walder, 1972; Eron & Huesmann, 1985; Irwin & Gross, 1995). A continuing pattern is set up, and unless the parents intervene in this behavioral pattern, abuse can potentially become a normal way for older siblings to interact with younger siblings. Secondly, the behavior may be understood as a psychological defense. Anna Freud (1946), in her well-known book *The Ego and the Mechanisms of Defense,* called the reaction of a victim who in turn abuses another victim a psychological defense and labeled the behavior as "identification with the aggressor." The victim assumes the characteristics of the aggressor by shifting from a passive victim role to an active aggressive role and inflicting the same behavior on another victim. The end result is that the siblings are in a constant state of conflict. A young adult woman described the process in this way:

> The worst fights started around the time I was in third grade. I got a lot of abuse from my older brother. Then I would turn around and abuse my sister. I would get her twice as hard as what I received. As we got older, it got worse. I would have knives pulled on me. Then I would turn around and pull a gun on one of the others. I would take my anger out on my sister or younger brother. I became very violent, especially toward my sister.

Telling Their Parents

Many of the survivors of sibling abuse told their parents about the abuse, but the parents' responses were often such that they did not help the survivor. Indeed, reporting the physical abuse often resulted in the victim's being further victimized. A typical parental response to a victim who reported physical abuse by a sibling was to blame him or her for it. "You must have done something to deserve it," a parent would respond. Obviously, such a response provided a victim with no protection from future physical assaults and discouraged the victim from ever again telling the parents about the abuse. Another common parental response was to become very angry and discipline both the perpetrator and the victim with corporal punishment. This response also led the victim to conclude that it did not pay to report the physical abuse.

Undoubtedly, many children who are physically abused by a sibling do report the behavior to their parents, and the parents do effectively intervene. The parents' intervention may involve examining the incident with the siblings, determining what provoked the abuse, perhaps identifying the contribution of each sibling to the conflict that escalated to abusive behavior, and helping the siblings consider other ways the altercation could have been handled. This "problem-solving approach" is an effective way for parents to intervene in potentially abusive sibling interactions. (The approach is discussed more fully in a later chapter.) This approach teaches siblings to effectively handle interpersonal problems without resorting to abuse or violence, and the parents give a clear message that abusive behavior will not be tolerated. Obviously, many parents try to use this or other methods for dealing with abusive interactions between siblings. But for the respondents to this research, some parents' interventions were ineffective, and as a result, they were a *victim* of sibling abuse. Even as adults, years after the abuse occurred, many of them continue to cope with the effects of their abuse on their psychosocial functioning.

■ Summary

In this chapter, survivors reported the various ways they were physically abused by a sibling as they were growing up at home. These survivors are aware of the abuse they suffered, and many have sought professional help for the problems they experience in their daily living. Emotional suffering and pain remains in other persons who were physically abused by a sibling but who have shut off that part of their life.

The various types of physical abuse have been identified here as a way of sensitizing mental health professionals, parents, and even survivors of sibling abuse to the forms this abuse can take. Repeated patterns of the behaviors such as physical assaults, tickling, or life-threatening abuses (smothering with a pillow, being shot by a BB gun) indicate abusive behavior. When physically abusive behavior is occurring between siblings, parental intervention is necessary. If such behavior is ignored, the behavior will continue and further abuse may be expected to occur.

3

Emotional Abuse

The names I was called by my older sister still hurt today as an adult.
A sibling abuse survivor

When children are being teased, they often respond with the following jingle: "Sticks and stones may break my bones, but words
will never hurt me." The source of this jingle is unknown, but it has been
passed down through generations as a statement of truth. Its message
is that physical assault may hurt but verbal attacks do not. But is this
true?

In this chapter the survivors of emotional abuse from a sibling will give
their answer to the question. They will tell of the names they were called
and the ridicule and degrading comments they received from a sibling.
They will relate how their personal possessions were destroyed or their
pets tortured or killed. The emotional abuse they experienced from a
brother or sister as children still affects them as adults. Their stories
indicate that the old jingle is not true, and that it carries a false message.

■ Terminology

Researchers in the field of child abuse have identified emotional abuse
or psychological maltreatment as a form of child abuse along with
physical and sexual abuse. Emotional abuse also occurs between siblings, but as compared to child abuse, the perpetrator is not an adult
but, rather, a brother or sister. Emotional abuse, as the child abuse
literature states, is more prevalent and potentially even more destruc-

tive than other forms of child abuse and it often precedes and accompanies physical and sexual abuse (Claussen & Crittenden, 1991; Hart & Brassard, 1987). This form of abuse is difficult to document because of the absence of physical evidence that often can be found in physical abuse and sometimes in sexual abuse. Some researchers, however, identify emotional abuse as the core component and major destructive force in all types of child abuse, with its most damaging effects impacting on the victim's self-esteem, interpersonal relationships, and psychosocial functioning in general (Brassard & Gelardo, 1987; Garbarino & Vondra, 1987; Hart & Brassard, 1987).

Despite the absence of consensus on a precise definition of the term *emotional abuse*, it was included under the category "mental injury" in the federal Child Abuse Prevention and Treatment Act of 1974. Emotional abuse often is associated with the term *teasing*. Individuals who identified themselves as survivors of emotional abuse by a sibling frequently reported that they were "teased" by their sibling. While the word *teasing* can denote a behavior that often occurs among siblings, it has also become a catchall word to denote a number of other behaviors. Synonyms for the verb *tease* indicate the specific types of actions that comprise this behavior: *belittle, ridicule, intimidate, annoy, scorn, provoke,* and *harass*. Generally, *emotional abuse* refers to rejection; to coercive, punitive, and erratic discipline; to scapegoating, ridiculing, and denigration; to unrealistic behavioral expectations; to chaotic family environments; or the use of excessive threats in an attempt to control a child (Hart, Germain, & Brassard, 1987).

Teasing should be distinguished from joking. Teasing and joking are two different types of behavior. Teasing, and the synonyms associated with it, implies that one person engages in the activity as the perpetrator while another person serves as the object of the behavior or the victim. There is a "one down" relationship between the person doing the teasing (perpetrator) and the targeted individual (victim). Thus, teasing occurs at the expense of the victim. Joking, by contrast, implies more of a mutual relationship between two persons and the result of the behavior is often not harmful, such as laughter. (This is not to deny that joking can be very vicious when one person becomes the target or victim of the other.)

Emotional abuse was defined in the research questionnaire as verbal comments aimed at ridiculing, insulting, threatening, or belittling a sibling. Also included in the definition was the destruction of personal

property, such as a sibling who deliberately destroys a prized posses-
sion or pet of another sibling.

※ Interaction of Emotional, Physical, and Sexual Abuse

Eleven persons or 7% of the sample indicated that they had *only*
been emotionally abused. Although the three forms of sibling abuse—
physical, emotional, and sexual—were treated separately in the research questionnaire, the responses of the participants indicated that
one form of sibling abuse rarely occurred in isolation. (The only exception was that some survivors did not report being sexually abused by a
sibling.) Generally, several forms of abuse occurred in interaction with
each other. Thus, 71% (107) of the sample indicated that they had been
emotionally, physically, *and* sexually abused. Combined with the eleven
persons who indicated that they had been *only* emotionally abused, this
means that 78% or 118 of the 150 persons in the sample had been
emotionally abused. Thus, emotional abuse was a very prevalent form
of sibling abuse and, as the comments of the survivors indicate, a very
destructive one.

The interaction of emotional and physical abuse is demonstrated by the
following comments of a respondent from Maine, a survivor of abuse
from a brother 3 years older:

> I can't remember a time when my brother didn't taunt me,
> usually trying to get me to respond so he would be justified in
> hitting me. Usually he would be saying I was a crybaby or a
> sissy or stupid or ugly and that no one would like me, want to
> be around me, or whatever. Sometimes he would accuse me of
> doing something and if I denied it, then he would call me a liar.
> I usually felt overwhelmingly helpless because nothing I said
> or did would stop him. If no one else was around, he would
> start beating on me after which he would stop and go away. I
> felt helpless to stop any of it.

A 38-year-old woman from an eastern state wrote:

> It's impossible to separate the emotional abuse from the physi-
> cal abuse. I put this questionnaire aside for a week trying to
> think about how to separate them. I can't. I remember my older

sister saying mean things to me all my life. She would call me names and tell me I was in trouble, then go to my parents to complain and I would be in trouble.

A survivor from Massachusetts experienced a similar interaction of emotional and physical abuse:

It's impossible to separate out the physical and emotional abuse for me. In particular, it was emotionally abusive to be waiting for the physical abuse to start again.

Respondents also reported on the interaction of emotional and sexual abuse. A survivor from New Jersey described how her brother, 9 years older, used emotional abuse in connection with sexual abuse:

The emotional abuse stemmed directly from the sexual abuse. The earliest memory was when I was about 5 years old. It is difficult for me to be specific about a single event since it is hard for me to remember many instances. I've blocked a lot out of my mind. But I always remember being afraid of being rejected by my parents. My brother was the oldest and he made me believe that my parents would always believe him over me since I was only 5 and he was 13. So, you see, he always had some sort of power over me emotionally and physically. As a child and adolescent I was introverted and never really shared my inner feelings with *anyone*. I felt like dirt and that my needs, concerns, and opinions never mattered, only those of other people. I was always in fear of both forms of abuse (emotional and sexual). I learned to prepare myself for both. I'm so resentful that I had to do this to survive mentally in my home. My brother would always present himself in these situations as being perfect—mature, responsible, brave—a model brother. Then, I'd feel like an immature, not-credible child. He'd say things like how my parents thought he was so special, being the oldest. And that if I told on him, I would destroy the entire family; my parents would divorce; I would be sent to a foster home. He had such emotional control over me in that sense that I "obeyed" him and never told. He had control over my self-image *and* my body.

Although emotional abuse is distinguished from physical and sexual abuse in this research, in reality it is difficult to separate them. The ultimate impact of abuse of any kind is on the psychological well-being of the child. The wounds from a physical assault may heal rather quickly and *physically* there may be little or no damage. The ultimate damage in emotional abuse, as well as other types of abuse, is psychological, as the survivors attest when they describe the impact of the abuse on their adult lives (Hart & Brassard, 1987).

■ Identifying Emotional Abuse

Emotional abuse is difficult to identify. Accepted legal standards are not available either for proving that emotional or behavioral problems resulted from emotional abuse or for determining the seriousness of emotional abuse (Corson & Davidson, 1987; Navarre, 1987). Nor does emotional abuse leave physical evidence, such as abrasions, wounds, bruises, or staining of clothing, as physical and sexual abuse may do. Thus, on the surface or from the outside, a family may appear to be functioning well psychosocially. But within the family one sibling may be emotionally abusing another.

Detecting emotional abuse by a sibling is complicated by the fact that professionals and parents have tended to accept emotionally abusive behavior as a phenomenon that occurs with all children as they interact with their peers and their siblings. The teasing and verbal put-downs in which siblings engage with each other and with children in general, although disliked by parents, are often accepted as normal behavior, and between siblings, are simply excused as sibling rivalry.

When parents excuse or overlook emotional abuse that occurs between siblings, however, the victims are given the message that this abusive behavior is really not abusive. Different child-rearing practices and cultural values may reinforce a denial that certain behaviors or styles of communication between siblings are emotionally abusive. Thus, there is a tendency for victims of emotional abuse themselves to deny this form of abuse.

A similar phenomenon happened historically with the physical abuse of children by adults. Pediatricians for years saw children with wounds that they could not explain. Dr. John Caffey (1946), a New York pediatrician, published an article in 1946 in a radiology journal in which he shared his observations on six infants who had multiple fractures of long bones and chronic subdural hematoma. Dr. Caffey attempted to explain these observations from a medical perspective, on the basis of factors such as injury that may have occurred from convulsive seizures, scurvy, or various skeletal diseases. He ruled out these reasons for the fractures and concluded that "the fractures appear to be of traumatic origin but the traumatic episodes and the causal mechanism remain obscure" (p. 173). Dr. Caffey obviously was suspicious but seemed reluctant and fearful to admit that the injuries could possibly have resulted from child abuse. It was not until almost two decades later that Dr. C. Henry Kempe and colleagues at the University of Colorado Medical Center published an article in the *Journal of the American Medical Association* in which they labeled what they had been seeing in their medical practices "the battered children syndrome" (Kempe et al., 1962). Also, historically, the physical abuse of children was overlooked because children were viewed as the property of their parents and what occurred behind the closed doors of the family residence was the business of that family. Children who experienced severe beatings by their parents and other forms of physical assault were forced to conclude that they must have deserved this behavior, despite their physical and emotional suffering. Only as adult-child physical abuse became recognized by society as a social problem have its victims been able to seek help for its effects on their lives, and has society taken steps to prevent it. Only within the last decade have serious efforts been made to identify how parent-child physical abuse occurs, its tragic effects on its victims, and ways in which it can be prevented.

But the emotional abuse of one sibling by another remains largely undetected. As a 42-year-old woman from Kentucky put it:

> When asked if I was emotionally abused by a sibling, my inclination is to say No, that it was not significant. However, I used to say the same thing about sexual abuse.

▪ Frequency of Emotional Abuse

The research questionnaire asked respondents to identify how frequently emotional abuse occurred in their family while they were growing up. Their responses revealed that emotional abuse—name calling, ridicule, and degradation—was a common pattern in the relationship between siblings and in some instances between the siblings and their parents. One survivor of emotional abuse commented that she was aware all siblings use verbal put-downs with each other but "the frequency and intensity of these" made her relationship with an older brother different. Respondents repeatedly used words like *constant* and *always* to describe the emotional abuse they experienced from a sibling in the form of name calling, ridicule, or being degraded. Many of the respondents spent their childhood years in a climate of name calling, ridicule, and mockery.

An Illinois respondent stated:

> I was constantly being told I was no good, a pig, whore, slut, all sexually oriented negatives. I was constantly emotionally being degraded.

A survivor from Maine:

> I can't remember a time when I was growing up when my brother didn't taunt me.

A respondent from Virginia wrote:

> He constantly teased me about my appearance—every aspect of it—and everything I did.

A 38-year-old woman:

> I don't ever remember not being teased or made to cry. I was always called names.

A respondent from Ohio:

> From my earliest memories, age 5 or so, my siblings called me names and said degrading things to me.

A 44-year-old mother of several children recalled her childhood with an older brother:

> He constantly berated me verbally, calling me names like worthless, slut, pig.

Many respondents said their earliest memories of emotional abuse dated from age 4 or 5. This may not necessarily be the earliest occurrence of sibling emotional abuse in their life; it may only be as far back as they can actually remember. For some, emotional abuse by a sibling was a way of life; they could not remember a time when they were not emotionally abused by a sibling. Mary described the emotional abuse she experienced from a brother, Sam:

Let me put it this way. In my baby book, my mother wrote, "Mary's first words were—Sam, don't!"

She said that her brother hated her from the day she was born and behaved accordingly.

■ Forms of Emotional Abuse

The respondents described numerous ways they had been emotionally abused by a sibling. The various forms of emotional abuse can be classified in a variety of ways. One group of researchers have classified the various behaviors comprising emotional abuse or psychological maltreatment as *rejecting, isolating, terrorizing, ignoring,* and *corrupting* (Garbarino, Guttman, & Seeley, 1986). In the present research, the behaviors constituting emotional abuse by a sibling will be classified into the following categories: *name calling, ridicule, degradation, exacerbating a fear, destroying personal possessions,* and *the torture or destruction of a pet.* This list is not exhaustive but reflects the most common forms of emotional abuse identified by the respondents. Nor does this categorization in any way imply that one form of emotional abuse is more serious than another. Rather, each form is serious since all forms of emotional abuse by a sibling can affect the victims' adult lives.

The first three types of emotional abuse—name calling, ridicule, and degradation—are commonly referred to as "teasing." But for the purposes of this research, they will be identified individually in order that readers may be sensitized to the various ways emotional abuse can occur.

Name Calling

Name calling was the form of emotional abuse most frequently reported by the respondents. Nearly every individual who was emotionally abused made some reference to being called names. The perpetrator appeared to use name calling as a way to belittle or degrade the victim. (Degradation, discussed later, also occurred without name calling.) The name calling generally focused on some attribute of the victim, such as his or her height, weight, a physical characteristic, intelligence, inability to perform a skill, and the like. For example, a survivor from Arkansas wrote that her older brothers had called her "fatso" and "roly-poly" because of her weight. A dry skin problem of another survivor prompted her siblings to call her "snake" and "crocodile."

A survivor of the emotional abuse of name calling from her brothers wrote:

> When I was 6, my mother realized I needed glasses. For the next several years my brothers told me I was ugly and taunted me with a lot of names referring to being unattractive.

Another stated:

> I was told by my siblings that I was stupid and ugly and usually called "ugly" as a name.

A respondent from Montana also experienced name calling by her siblings while she was growing up:

> I was heavy as a young child, about 7 or 8 years old. My brother called me, "Cow." He was asked to mark all the children's socks with our names so for mine he drew the face of a cow. He would take a mistake I made and turn it into a nasty word game that he would call at you for years. I once put on a halter top and due to the design, I put it on sideways. Then, he called me, "the sideways girl." He called me a Spanish word that I understood meant "whore." A mistake was for a lifetime.

A person from a western state wrote:

> My brother, 4 years older than me, would tease, taunt, and call me names. He often did this in front of my or his friends, the latter of whom were encouraged to join in.

For many respondents, their competency as individuals was the target of the emotional abuse. These survivors reported being called "stupid" and "dumb" by siblings both older and younger than the victim. A survivor of emotional abuse by two older sisters wrote:

> I would be told by one or both of my sisters I was dumb and ugly and that's why I didn't have many friends to play with like they did.

A Washington respondent:

My sister would verbally harass me—you're ugly, stupid, fat, etc. If I did accomplish something, she would turn things around and prove that I had failed or been a fool.

An adult male survivor from Ohio:

I was left-handed and could not throw a ball very well. When we played softball in our neighborhood, my older brothers never wanted me to play on their teams. I was called names because of this. When they chose sides, they would never want me. Many times I would be left out of the game and would go home because they didn't want me. Of course, neither my brother nor anyone else would help me learn to properly throw a ball. The same was true for coaches who taught gym classes. Their only concern was to win, win, win! To this day I hate sports! I thought a coach's job was to help you learn sports. When I hear the word *sports* or *coach* today, I want to puke.

Ridicule

Ridicule appeared to be a sport to some siblings and a form of emotional abuse that survivors recalled with painful emotions. *Ridicule* may be defined as words or actions used by a perpetrator to express contempt, often along with laughter directed against the victim. A young woman wrote:

My sister would get her friends to sing songs about how ugly I was.

Another survivor wrote that her older sister composed a song about her and the fact that she was overweight. The song, which rhymed, was sung by the older sister whenever she was in the presence of the victim. This survivor spoke of the humiliation she experienced at school when her sister sang the song in front of her friends and the friends would join in the laughter and fun.

A 33-year-old survivor of emotional abuse from a sibling stated:

My brother would tease me about not saying certain words correctly. Some words I could not pronounce correctly, so he would get me to say them and then would laugh at me.

This respondent wrote that as an adult, she does not speak up when she should.

> I feel like people will laugh at what I have to say or they will think it's dumb.

The ridicule she experienced as a child from her brother continues to affect her as an adult.

A survivor from Massachusetts described her emotional abuse by an older brother in this way:

> It consisted mostly of mindless ridicule—"You're ugly." "Your hair is frizzy." "You're going to go to school looking like *that*?" The abuse usually occurred when we were alone or in front of the family.

A woman from Indiana described the ridicule she suffered from a sister who was 2 years older. She related that her high school years were the worst years for the abuse:

> If we were riding around town and a boy or boys would wave, I'd wave back and she would begin a battery of insults. "Why did you wave? Never wave at anybody when I'm in the car. They wouldn't wave at you anyway. You are scar face, crooked tooth, dumpy, and ugly. No one wants to wave at you," and on and on she would go. She would criticize me in front of her friends—not simple verbal attempts but a battery of verbal assaults as if my living on earth was enough to deserve it. Her friends laughed, which brought on more despair for me. I internalized this incessant criticism as something for which I was responsible.

Often a sibling's name was used as the means to ridicule the victim. One respondent wrote that she was called "Sewer" because her first name was Sue and her last name began with a W. Something that was not her choosing—the name she was given by her parents—became a repeated object of ridicule by her own siblings.

Emotional abuse in the form of ridicule often had sexual overtones. A survivor from Kentucky wrote:

> There was much teasing of a sexual nature from my brothers as I was going through puberty. Great fun was made of my wearing a bra and putting cotton in it.

> When I started menses, I would hide used Kotex in my
> radio so they would not tease me.

A 48-year-old female from Idaho still vividly remembers the emotional
abuse she experienced in her family of 13 children. She was repeatedly
emotionally abused by means of ridicule during her childhood. When
she was 8 years old, she lost a front tooth and the new tooth came in
crooked and diseased. At age 12 she gained weight.

> Between the two, I was under fire constantly—ugly, fat, rotten
> tooth, etc. and freckles didn't help.

Another respondent wrote:

> Life as a child consisted of constant taunts and ridicule on issues
> such as things I said, clothes I wore, my friends, etc.

A survivor from Washington summarized her abuse:

> I was ridiculed by my older brothers and sisters for just being.
> Ridicule and put-downs were "normal" for our family.

Degradation

Another form of emotional abuse aimed at depriving individuals of
their sense of dignity and worth is degradation. Many respondents
reported that siblings who were emotionally abusing them told them
that they were "worthless" and "no good." Degradation, as a form of
emotional abuse, appears to have been emotionally devastating to the
survivors, both at the time it occurred and even years later as adults.
The survivors' comments indicate that the degrading messages they
received as children from their siblings seemed to haunt them into their
adult years. This may have been especially true for the respondents
whose parents did not intervene in the abusive behavior but ignored it,
accepted it as normal behavior, or, worst of all, joined in.

Children who degrade their siblings or peers do not appear to realize
how this form of emotional abuse can harm another individual. Reinforcing this, the victim may appear as if the degrading comments have
no effect. Perhaps this is why the jingle "Sticks and stones may break
my bones but words will never hurt me" was coined. Although the
victim suffers from the verbal assault, he or she takes a defensive stance,
denying the emotional pain of being the butt of the degrading comments.

Imagine you are a small child again. Your world and the security you feel in it is centered in your relationships with family at home and with your peers in your neighborhood and at school. You are aware of what others think of you. You want to be liked, to be valued by your siblings and your peers. But a sibling repeatedly tells you that you don't belong in the family and that no one really likes you—your friends or anyone else who really knows you. Obviously, your sense of self-worth, self-esteem, and personal dignity are attacked, both at the time and for years to come, if such verbal assaults continue and your parents do not intervene.

Children are especially vulnerable to degrading remarks because it is during their childhood that they are developing a positive sense of self-worth and self-esteem. Unfortunately, interactions with peers, in play and at school, often do not facilitate the development of self-worth and self-esteem. Verbal put-downs among siblings as well as peers become so commonplace that there is a tendency for parents and others in authority to accept this as normal behavior. The failure of parents to stop such behavior sends a message to perpetrators that this is acceptable behavior and a message perhaps to the victims that in some way they deserve it. The abusive behavior can be expected to continue unless some action is taken to discontinue it.

A survivor from Washington described the message she repeatedly received from an older sister when she was growing up:

> I was being constantly told how ugly, dumb, unwanted I was. Already about 2 years of age I was told, "No one wants you around. I wish you were dead. You aren't my *real* sister, your real parents didn't want you either so they dumped you with us." I grew up feeling if my own family doesn't like me, who will? I believed *everything* my sister ever told me—that I was ugly, dumb, homely, stupid, fat—even though I always was average in weight. I felt no one would ever love me. When you're little, you believe everything you're told—it can last a lifetime.

A man in his mid-40s is in therapy for the emotional abuse he experienced from two older brothers:

> I was told that I was no good, that no one loved me, that I was adopted (which was not true), that my parents did not really want me. My parents were always gone and emotionally un-

available, partially due to alcohol abuse, so that I was often left in the care of my two older brothers.

A survivor from California:

> When we were kids, my brother would tell all his friends how ugly I was. He belittled me as long as I can remember.

A young adult male who identified himself as gay experienced degrading comments from a brother when he was growing up:

> My brother would tell me what a sissy or faggot I was, that I wasn't a man, and then would laugh. He would tell others to taunt me, to bait me. He would bring me to tears.

Another survivor's emotional abuse continued throughout her childhood years:

> I was about 5, and my father was fussing at me about not knowing how to tie my shoes. But no one ever taught me. My brother started laughing at me, telling me I was stupid and dumb and I was not his sister. He said my mother and father found me in a trash can and felt sorry for me and took me to their house. He wished I would go back to the trash can.

To be told you are not really part of your family and to see that your physical characteristics are different from those of your siblings can add to the trauma of the emotional abuse, as a respondent from Louisiana wrote:

> My brothers and sisters would tell me I was adopted because I had blonde hair and fair skin and they were dark-skinned and dark-haired. They would tell me Mom and Dad wouldn't love me if I told on them.

A survivor from Kansas wrote about her emotional abuse from an older brother:

> I would cry and feel deeply wounded after he emotionally abused me by calling me names. I felt for many years that I was adopted because we looked so different and he was treated so very different than me. I soon adapted my life to do and be the exact opposite of him. He made A's, I got by on C's.

In a few short sentences, a respondent from Tennessee reported the emotionally devastating comments she received from her two older brothers regarding their mother's mental illness:

> She went crazy after she had you. If it weren't for you, she'd be all right.

A Kentucky resident experienced a constant pattern of emotional abuse while growing up with two older brothers:

> My brothers loved to tease me to tears. They were ruthless in their teasing and did not let up. They teased me for being ugly. They teased me for being sloppy. They teased me for just being. This was the worst.

One respondent received verbal messages that she shouldn't exist, and in addition, this message was acted out by her siblings:

> My brothers and a cousin tied me to a stake and were preparing the ground around me to set it on fire. They were stopped and built a dummy of me instead and burnt that.

Many survivors said that their emotional abuse continued into their adulthood. The pattern of degradation established in childhood continued, even though they were no longer children. *Labeling theory* explains that one child in a family may be labeled as a scapegoat or as outside the mythical family circle, and the pattern continues even as the family members move into adulthood. This may be seen also in nicknames that children acquire from their siblings that often remain with them as adults. Similarly, descriptive labels a child acquires, often focusing on a specific personality trait or physical characteristic that distinguishes them from their peers, may continue to haunt them into adulthood.

A woman from South Carolina, who has formed a support group for adults abused as children, experienced emotional abuse from an older brother and sister that continues in her adult life:

> They would tell me things like I was stupid and call me other names, make fun of me, make me do things I did not want to do, beat me up when I didn't do what they wanted. They made me feel I was not part of their family. They showed they loved each other but not me. And they still do this to me the same way, even at the age of 35.

A female physician in her forties who was emotionally abused by an older brother as a child writes about how the emotional abuse from her brother persists:

> I can't recall a specific instance of emotional abuse. It was more of an attitude that still continues today. There is no sensitivity or openness from my brother. As a child I always felt I had to be "nice" and agree or I would be yelled at or not accepted. As a child he wouldn't think of me as a person. Even now there is no acknowledgment of me as an adult. But now I pity him more than anything because I see through his macho front and see a very insecure, immature, selfish, weak man who is threatened by my success and assertiveness. He still has a superior attitude. I do see him. Our interactions are not meaningful or supportive—more formal or "proper." But he still calls me names if he doesn't get his way.

A 43-year-old woman from Massachusetts wrote:

> My relationship with my brothers and sisters is still somewhat strained. I am out of place with them. Their humor is sarcastic. They make insulting, negative remarks.

Although some survivors of emotional abuse experienced repeated instances of name calling, ridicule, and verbal degradation over a period of time, a single occurrence of such abuse can also be devastating, especially if the perpetrator means for the statement to be accepted as true and if the victim's parents do not intervene. The survivor who was blamed for her mother's mental illness is an example of this. The victim of a comment of this nature may experience it as being as emotionally injurious as a wound is physically injurious. A physical wound may heal, but the pain of an emotionally abusive incident can linger a lifetime.

Another way one sibling degrades another is to "use" the sibling. Frequently, this occurred along gender lines when a brother "lorded it over" a sister. Specifically, an older sibling would command a younger sibling to do things on his behalf, such as household chores that he was expected to do. The failure of the victim to comply with the perpetrator's demands at times resulted in physical abuse.

Such respondents reported how they felt they existed only to do things for an older sibling, as if they were a servant to an older sibling. This was especially true when the abuse occurred along gender lines. A survivor who was raised on a farm in North Dakota in a very religious family of eight children had to wait on her older brothers in the house, even if she had been working all day in the fields. Her parents instructed her to obey her older brothers in their absence. "It was as if my brothers could do no wrong." The older brothers took advantage of her, not only by demanding that she do tasks for them but by tricking her out of her allowance and eventually by sexually abusing her.

A survivor from Iowa was degraded by an older brother in a similar manner:

> He'd come home drunk and wake me up in the middle of the night and make me cook for him. I was his personal slave. He'd have a party and make a hell of a mess. I'd have to clean it up.

A general theme that recurs throughout the comments of the survivors of sibling abuse—physical, emotional, or sexual—is the false assumption of the superiority of males and the "rightness" of their domination over females. This represents again the theme of power and control of males over females, a theme referred to earlier. Only as this insidious assumption is extinguished in the socialization of males—at home, in school, at work, in play, in commerce, in government, in religious organizations, and in any other places where it overtly or covertly appears—can the abuse of girls and women by boys and men be prevented, whether in sibling relationships or among persons in general.

A survivor from New Mexico, for example, received attention from an older brother, but emotional abuse often accompanied this attention. The emotional abuse focused on her gender and implied a lack of competency and worth:

> He would tease me for being a weak girl. He would taunt me about being sissy. He would take delight in teasing me, make me laugh sometimes and then discard me. It was confusing because I liked the special attention, but it hurt so much.

This survivor reported that the emotional abuse she experienced has severely affected her adult life:

> I felt guilty bonding with other males and wasn't sure I could trust them. I felt crippling shame. I drank and acted out.

Another form of degradation experienced by respondents to the research was that they were ignored by a sibling. A survivor from the West Coast was ignored by her older and younger brothers:

> They totally ignored me. They did not want me along or around
> for anything ever. They would not talk to me or play with me.

This survivor stated that her brothers treated her this way because she was a girl—another instance of abuse associated with gender. She felt that the message she received from her brothers was that she was supposed to take care of them but not to play with them or have fun with them. The brothers tried to force her to stay at home and serve them.

Another survivor who was emotionally degraded through being ignored by siblings is an adult woman from Maine:

> The worst kind of emotional abuse I experienced was if I
> walked into a room, my brother would pretend he was throw-
> ing up at the sight of me. As I got older he most often would
> pretend I wasn't there and speak as if I didn't exist even in front
> of me and my mother.

Survivors who experienced emotional abuse in the form of degradation had a pervasive feeling during their childhood that they should not exist, like the survivor whose older brothers teased her "for just being." The transactional analysis (TA) school of psychology refers to this as the game "Don't Be," a game parents often play with their children (Berne, 1967). In a variety of ways a subtle message is given to a child that life would be much better if the child were not around; the parents would have fewer financial expenses, or there would be less tension in the home. When this "game" is analyzed from a reality perspective, its extreme psychological destructiveness can be understood. A child is not responsible for his or her existence. The parents brought the child into existence. Realistically, what can a child do to fulfill the parents' overt or covert wish that he or she not exist? Obviously, this vicious game sends a message of self-destruction.

Although this destructive and emotionally damaging game is often played by parents, it is also played by siblings. One survivor reported that her younger and older brothers treated her as if she didn't exist and even verbalized this wish to her. Her parents' reaction to the brothers' behavior was:

They just never thought about it or thought that it was harmful.
They denied the evidence of my unhappiness and depression.

A 36-year-old woman from Texas also received a message from a sibling
that she shouldn't exist:

> I was 2 or 3 years old, and my parents and my brothers had
> gone somewhere. I had fallen asleep in the back window of the
> car. I woke up and was alone in the car. It was raining. I was
> scared to get out so I just sat and waited. My oldest brother
> came out of the house and ran to the car. When he opened the
> door he laughed at me because he knew I was scared. He told
> me my parents hated me and they left me there hoping someone
> would come and kill me. He said he hoped he would get to kill
> me. Then he told me over and over how he would do it.

Exacerbating a Fear

Some respondents to the questionnaire wrote of another form of emotional abuse by a sibling. The sibling would exacerbate a fear that the
victim had, such as a fear of being lost, a fear of the dark, or a fear of
strangers. The perpetrators would use fear as a means of controlling the
victim and getting him or her to do what they wanted. Perhaps the
perpetrators were modeling their behavior after that of their parents
because some parents coerce a child to comply with their wishes by
manipulating the child with a fear the child has.

One respondent described her intense fear of a parakeet that the family
kept as a pet.

> When we were in elementary school, my sisters would get the
> parakeet out of the cage and bring it near me. They would put
> it by my head so it would scratch me.

The victim panicked when the bird came near her while her sisters
delighted in teasing her about it. Her only recourse at the time would
be to hide until they grew tired of the activity.

Another fear that older siblings exacerbated to emotionally abuse a
younger sibling was the fear of becoming lost and unable to find the
way home again. A respondent from Virginia wrote that her older
brothers would take her to the woods near their home and leave her so
that she had to find her own way home. She experienced extreme fright
when this occurred.

Another fear that older siblings played on was their younger siblings' fear of being eaten by wild animals or mysterious creatures—themes found in fairy tales and children's stories. One survivor wrote that her earliest memories of emotional abuse date from the first grade, when her oldest brother threatened to tie her to a tree and let the wolves eat her. He threatened her repeatedly with being locked out of the house so that the "bogeyman" would kill her.

A survivor from Virginia, now in her 40s, also experienced this form of emotional abuse:

> They would take my sister and me out into the field to pick berries. When we would hear dogs barking, they would tell us they were wild dogs and then they'd run away and make us find our own way home. We were only 5 or 6, and we didn't know our way home.

An older sibling manipulated and controlled a younger sibling by exacerbating a fear of being taken away from the family.

> I remember *very clearly* that my older sister, who was 7 years older, would go to the telephone and pretend to call a man she called "Mr. Krantz." He ran an institution, she said, for "bad children" and my sister said she was going to send me there, banishing me from the family. I was terrified.

One woman wrote that an older sister played on her fear of the dark to force her to do the older sister's household tasks and in general to dominate and control her. The victim was afraid of the dark, but her older sister would not allow her to sleep with her unless she did her older sister's bidding. The victim was caught in a bind. The parents were not aware of this arrangement; but she knew if she told her parents about it, her sister would not allow her to sleep with her and she would be alone with her fear of the dark. The survivor indicated she acquiesced in her sister's domination and repeatedly became the victim of her emotional abuse.

Destroying Personal Possessions

A child's possessions—such as a bicycle, toys, or clothing—are valued and have special meaning for a child. Everyone remembers a favorite toy, book, or blanket from their childhood. As adults we may still have these objects. A perpetrator of emotional abuse may use these treasured objects as the instrument for abuse.

While the abuse may be directed at objects, the actual target of the abuse is the sibling who owns the object. In Freudian terms, these objects become *cathected* or invested with the emotions and feelings of the owner. Thus, harming the object is actually harming the individual who treasures these objects.

The emotional investment in a favorite toy, in this example a tricycle, is evident in the way a 29-year-old woman described her earliest memory of emotional abuse from a brother 3 years older:

> My earliest memory of being emotionally abused occurred when I was about 4 years of age. My brother took apart my tricycle and hid some of the pieces so it could not be put back together. I loved my tricycle and rode it practically every day. I was so hurt at the loss of this tricycle and at seeing my brother's sense of satisfaction that he got away with it.

This survivor's brother also damaged her doll, ridiculed her, and called her hurtful names.

A respondent from Texas experienced similar abuse from two older brothers:

> They called me names. I was told my parents hated me. If my brothers found out I cared about something—for example, toys—they were taken and destroyed in front of me.

The personal possessions of this survivor from Massachusetts were also destroyed by a sibling:

> My sister used to take my things and wreck them, cut my clothes up to fit her and blackmail me to do her housework.

A survivor from Maine:

> My brother would cut out the eyes, ears, mouth, and fingers of my dolls and hand them to me.

An adult male who was abused by an older brother reported:

> A typical experience of abuse I suffered was my older brother would take whatever I had and destroy it. Then he would give it back, broken.

One adult male, who as a small child experienced emotional abuse from an older brother, related how this sibling took his Mickey Mouse ears, deliberately broke them, and then laughed about it. Initially, one might see this as humorous: Why should an adult care that his older brother destroyed his Mickey Mouse ears when they were children 25 or more years before?

The destruction of the toy per se is not the point. To understand what the survivor is saying and to empathize with what he is expressing in his statement, several factors must be considered. First, the destructive behavior was only one in a series of abusive incidents directed at the survivor; it was not a one-time event. (Although a single abusive incident *may* be harmful, as it was for the survivor who was told that she was responsible for her mother's mental illness. A survivor may experience a single abusive incident as harmful, depending on the circumstances. This is especially true for sexual abuse by siblings.)

Second, the destruction of the Mickey Mouse ears must be viewed in the context of the *deliberateness* of the perpetrator's actions. Respondents to the research repeatedly wrote of the delight perpetrators took in destroying something that was meaningful to the sibling. The incident was not an accident; the deliberateness with which it occurred makes it abusive.

Finally, the incident must be considered in the light of its impact on the survivor. The survivor was deeply hurt by his brother's behavior. Again, the destruction of the Mickey Mouse ears per se was not the point, but its impact on the survivor, who was the real target of the abusive behavior. The statement people often make when something like this happens indicates how they experienced its impact; namely, "How could someone do this to *me!*" They are verbalizing in this statement that the abuse actually was not directed at the object but at them personally.

An analogy may help clarify this. A house is burglarized. Nothing of value is taken, and little damage is done to the property. But the victims of the burglary say that what bothers them most about the break-in is that someone violated *their* privacy, *their* property, and the special meaning it has for *them*. Similarly, the survivor of the incident of the Mickey Mouse ears is expressing his hurt that his brother thought so little of him or despised him so much that he would deliberately destroy something meaningful to him.

Torture or Destruction of a Pet

Although the torture or destruction of a pet may resemble the destruction of prized possessions, it involves the abuse of life—an animal's life. This implies an even greater degree of cruelty toward the object, although the emotional pain the human victim experiences may be the same.

Respondents reported the torture and destruction of their pets by a sibling as examples of emotional abuse. A woman from Tennessee's worst and earliest experience of emotional abuse was at the hands of an older brother over 25 years ago:

> My second oldest brother shot my little dog that I loved dearly. It loved me—only me. I cried by its grave for several days. Twenty years passed before I could care for another dog.

The torture of the survivor's pet often occurred in conjunction with other forms of emotional abuse, such as name calling:

> My older brother would come to my room and tear up my toys. He would beat my dog after tying his legs together and wrapping a cloth around its mouth to tie it shut. My brother would tell me I was stupid and say, "Why me, why me? Why did I get a sister so stupid and dumb?" My brother also would tell me he hated me and wished I was dead.

A 37-year-old male experienced as a child the following abusive incident from an older brother:

> He took my pet frog and stabbed it to death in front of me while I begged him not to. Then he just laughed!

■ The Victims' Responses

In the previous chapter, the following ways were identified that victims responded to physical abuse: (a) by protecting themselves; (b) by screaming and crying; (c) by hiding or separating themselves from the perpetrator; (d) by abusing a younger sibling; and (e) by telling their parents. Victims of emotional abuse responded to their abuse in these and other ways. They also responded by fighting back or internalizing the abusive message.

Fighting Back

Unlike survivors of physical abuse, survivors of emotional abuse reported that they fought back and in turn emotionally abused the perpetrator by name calling, ridicule, and degrading comments. (Victims of physical abuse did not respond this way because generally they were younger then their abusers and did not have the strength to effectively fight back.)

A survivor from California reacted to an older brother's abusive teasing, taunting, and name calling by fighting back. (The emotional abuse generally occurred when she and her brothers were among their peers.)

> Often I became so mad that I would hit him, but with him being 4 years older and much larger, he would hit me back twice as hard. I would then end up crying, feeling totally humiliated.

A survivor from Pennsylvania wrote that an older sister would "yell swear words and names" at her as one aspect of her verbal abuse. At the age of 8 or 9, she was shocked by her sister's language but she soon "gave as good as I got, swear-word-wise." Another respondent reported, "I retaliated with equally mean words." It is possible that fighting back in this manner established a style of interpersonal relations that created difficulty for these survivors as adults. That several respondents seemed to relate to other adults as if they were dealing with their emotionally abusive perpetrator appears to support this possibility. But there is a healthy aspect to this also. The victim resisted the verbal attacks of her sibling and learned to be assertive, to stand up for herself.

Internalizing the Abusive Message

A response unique to the survivors of emotional abuse was to accept and internalize the abusive messages they were receiving. That is, the survivors accepted the name calling, the ridicule, and especially the degrading comments as if they were true. But by internalizing the messages or accepting them as if they were true, the perpetrator's abuse became a self-fulfilling prophecy for the victim. Accepting the message as reality further confirmed the victims in their role as victims into which the perpetrators had initially put them. As quoted earlier, a survivor from Washington wrote:

I believed *everything* my sister ever told me. I was dumb, homely, stupid, fat. No one would ever love me.

Still, at 41, as a reasonably bright adult woman, she believes her abusive sister's comments—that she is no good, dumb, and ugly. She still feels now that her worth as a person is only as good as what she does. As she describes it, in her adult life she is constantly trying to prove with her actions that she is worth something.

* Summary

Children are often heard to repeat the jingle: "Sticks and stones may break my bones, but words will never hurt me." But the comments of survivors of emotional abuse discredit the truth of this jingle. Words can and do hurt.

By contrast, a line written several thousand years ago, from the Apocryphal portion of the Bible, more aptly portrays the effect words can have:

> The blow of a whip raises a welt, but a blow of the tongue crushes the bones. Many have fallen by the edge of the sword, but not so many as have fallen because of the tongue. (Ecclesiasticus, Sirach, 28:16-18)

Sexual Abuse

*My brother touched me in places he shouldn't have, but I couldn't
tell my parents because he threatened to hurt me if I did.*
A sibling abuse survivor

The term *sexual abuse* provokes many different responses in people.
A frequent response from parents is, "This could never happen in
my home," or "This occurs only in certain kinds of families"—meaning
families that are highly dysfunctional. But research on sexual abuse
indicates that these statements are incorrect.

Two researchers, Finkelhor and Baron (1986), reviewed several surveys
focusing on the demographic backgrounds of individuals who were
sexually abused as children. Although certain high-risk factors could be
identified, they concluded that "sexual abuse is prevalent in remarkable
large quantity in individuals from virtually all social and family circumstances" (p. 44).

▪ Research on Sibling Incest

The term *incest* is generally thought of as referring to sexual relations
between fathers and daughters. Most of the literature on incest focuses
on this parent-child relationship, even though many researchers feel
sibling incest is more common (Finkelhor, 1979; Justice & Justice, 1979;
Meiselman, 1978). The lack of attention to this type of abuse may be due

to the reluctance of families to report to authorities the occurrence of sibling incest, the threat under which victims are placed when it occurs, and the perception that sexual contact between siblings is within the normal range of acceptable sexual play or exploration between siblings (Adler & Schutz, 1995).

Studies on sibling incest have been hampered by their small sample size that makes it difficult to generalize the data from the sample to the general population and the absence of comparison or control groups. For example, Adler and Schutz (1995) studied 12 male sibling incest offenders who had been referred for evaluation and treatment to a hospital-based, outpatient clinic. The sample of sibling sexual offenders came from middle- to upper-middle-class, suburban, primarily Caucasian families where the majority had parents married to each other and living in the home. The offenders had no previous records with juvenile justice offenders. Other studies on sibling incest, however, report previous offender contact with the juvenile system, the physical absence of a parent, and low socioeconomic status (Becker, Kaplan, Cunningham-Rathner, & Kavoussi, 1986; Finkelhor, 1979; O'Brien, 1991). Although none of the Adler and Schutz (1995) sample reported that the perpetrators had a history of being sexually abused, the presence of a history of intrafamilial physical abuse by one or both parents was present. Other studies of sibling sexual abuse, however, report rates of prior sexual victimization on the part of the perpetrators ranging from approximately 25 to 50% of the sample (Becker et al., 1986; O'Brien, 1991; Smith & Israel, 1987). Although the perpetrators denied using verbal threats to intimidate their victims, 75% of the victims reported that they had been verbally threatened to maintain silence about the sexual abuse.

O'Brien (1991) studied the characteristics of 170 adolescent male sexual offenders who had been referred for evaluation and/or treatment to an outpatient mental health clinic. The offenders were subdivided into three groups: sibling sexual abusers, child molesters (nonfamily child victims), and nonchild offenders. Compared with the child molesters and nonchild offenders, the sibling sexual abusers admitted committing more sexual crimes, had longer offending careers, and generally engaged in more intrusive sexual behavior, such as vaginal penetration. O'Brien concluded that this was because the sibling victim is easily available to the perpetrator, and the context of secrecy in which the sexual abuse occurs in the family prevents early disclosure.

The sexual abuse of siblings was defined in the research questionnaire in the following manner: inappropriate sexual contact such as unwanted touching, fondling, indecent exposure, attempted penetration, intercourse, rape, or sodomy between siblings.

▪ Incidence of Sexual Abuse

Adults are generally assumed to be the perpetrators of child sexual abuse, and most likely an adult closely known to the victim. There is evidence, however, that brother-sister sexual relationships may be five times as common as father-daughter incest (Gebhard, Gagnon, Pomeroy, & Christenson, 1965). Although specific statistical data on the number of cases of sibling sexual abuse occurring annually are not available, research on the extent to which sexual abuse in general occurs from a perpetrator within the family (including a sibling) and from perpetrators outside the family gives some notion of the extent of this problem.

Finkelhor (1984) reported that the incidence of sexual abuse by adults is basically unknown. Estimates are that 35% of all girls have been sexually abused. The perpetrators generally are males and may include siblings. A survey of 796 undergraduates of six New England colleges found that 15% of the females and 10% of the males reported some type of sexual experience involving a sibling (Finkelhor, 1980). Fondling and touching the genitals were the most common activities in all age categories. Twenty-five percent of the incidents could be regarded as exploitative because force was used and because of the large age disparity between the individuals involved. Forty percent of the students reported that they had been less than 8 years old at the time of the sexual experience. But 73% of the experiences occurred when at least one partner was older than 8, and 35% occurred when one was older than 12 years of age.

In a sample of 930 women residents of San Francisco who were 18 and older, Russell (1986) found that 16% of the sample (152 persons) reported at least one experience of incestuous abuse before the age of 18. Twelve percent of these women (108) had been sexually abused by a relative before reaching 14 years of age. Abuse by a nonrelative was even more prominent, with nearly one third of the sample (31% or 290 persons) reporting at least one sexual abuse experience before reaching the age of 18. Before these women had reached their 14th birthday, 20% (189) had been sexually abused by a nonrelative. Combing the two categories of incestuous and extrafamilial child sexual abuse, 38% (357) of the 930 women in the sample reported at least one experience of sexual abuse before reaching 18 years of age; 28% (258) identified at least one such experience before the age of 14. If the findings reflect the prevalence of sexual abuse in the United States, then one woman in eight is incestuously abused before the age of 14, and one in six before the age of 18. The data also indicate that more than 25% of the population of female children have experienced sexual abuse before age 14 and more than one third by age 18.

Using a national sample of adult men and women, researchers (Finkel-hor, Hotaling, Lewis, & Smith, 1990) found that 27% of the women and 16% of the men reported a history of childhood sexual abuse. Nearly half of these men and a third of the women never disclosed their abuse to anyone.

Cole (1990) studied a volunteer sample of 122 adult women from 28 states who had been sexually abused by a brother and 148 women sexually abused by their father. The mean age of the onset of the sexual abuse for the brother-sister survivors was 8.2 years compared to 5.2 years for the father-daughter survivors. Approximately one third of both groups experienced the sexual abuse for 4 to 10 years and did not disclose the abuse for 20 years or more. The sibling sexual abuse survivors reported feeling more responsible for their abuse as compared to their father-daughter survivor counterparts.

Yet these studies probably grossly underestimate the extent of sibling sexual abuse because feelings of embarrassment and shame connected with the event prevent both perpetrators and victims from talking about it. Many adults, too, may no longer remember childhood sexual incidents with a sibling. The information on sibling sexual abuse that is available frequently comes from reports filed in court against a perpetrator. But these cases barely represent the tip of the iceberg, since most incidents of sexual abuse by siblings go not only unreported but undetected by parents.

Studies on the incidence of child sexual abuse by adults indicate that most incidents are never disclosed. The cases that come to the attention of the courts, mental health clinics, and support groups for victims of sexual abuse appear to be the exception rather than the norm. As the comments of respondents to the present research reveal, the same is true for victims of sexual abuse by a sibling.

Sixty-seven percent (100) of the respondents in this research indicated that they had been sexually abused by a sibling while they were growing up, compared with 33% (50) who had been physically and/or emotionally abused. Those having been sexually abused represent the largest proportion of the individuals responding to the research questionnaire.

Why were so many more of the respondents survivors of sexual abuse as compared to survivors of physical and emotional abuse? One reason may be that many of the people who participated in the research were already in treatment for their abuse at counseling centers or were affiliated with support groups for people who have experienced abuse. Survivors of sexual abuse may seek treatment for their abuse more readily than survivors of physical or emotional abuse. Even between siblings, sexual abuse is recognized by society as *abuse* unlike physical and emotional abuse, which are often ignored and overlooked. For example, the meaning of the term *incest* is commonly understood to mean illicit sexual activity between family members, including between brothers and sisters. But the meaning of the terms *emotional abuse* or *physical abuse* between siblings is not commonly understood. Thus, it may be easier for persons who have been sexually abused to acknowledge their victimization than it is for those who have been physically and emotionally abused. Also, the trauma from sexual abuse may be more severe than the trauma from physical or emotional abuse, and it may cause victims to more readily seek treatment for its impact on their lives.

Sexual abuse did not occur in isolation for the survivors responding to this research. Three percent (5) indicated that they had been both physically and sexually abused; 11% (16) said they had been both emotionally and sexually abused; and 37% (55) reported that they had been physically, emotionally, and sexually abused. Other research has found similar results. For example, Goodwin (1982) found that in 50% of incest cases reported to a protective service agency, there was also evidence of physical abuse or neglect.

The interaction of sexual and physical abuse can be seen in the survivors' comments. Some survivors were threatened with physical harm and even death by their sibling perpetrator if they reported the sexual abuse to their parents. The interaction of sexual and emotional abuse is exemplified by the comment of a respondent from Kansas, whose sexual molestation by a brother 10 years older, including forceful vaginal penetration, began when she was 3 or 4 years old:

> Later, when I was about 7 or 8 years old, he would tease me by asking me if I was a virgin and laughing at me when I said no. It was humiliating.

Although far more females than males reported having experienced sexual abuse from a sibling, males also are sexually abused. In their review of eight random-sample community surveys that had interviewed both men and women regarding sexual abuse during childhood, Finkelhor and Baron (1986) found a much higher percentage of males who had been sexually abused than the present study. Approximately 2.5 women were sexually abused for every man; among all victims of sexual abuse, 71% were females and 29% males. A study of boys and girls who were sexually abused revealed that although the majority of all victims were sexually abused within the family, boys were more likely than girls to be victimized by someone outside the home (36.7% versus 10.9%). Researchers found in a sample of 375 individuals who had been physically or sexually abused before age 18 that females were almost 3 times more likely than males to experience any type of abuse and were over 11 times more likely than males to report sexual abuse (Silverman, Reinherz, & Giaconia, 1996). Clinicians agree that the sexual abuse of boys is underreported due to stereotypical expectations regarding masculinity and the fear that disclosure on the part of victims may give them the appearance of being homosexual.

■   Earliest Memories of
     Sexual Abuse by a Sibling

Respondents to the present research generally reported that, as they remember it, the earliest incident of sexual abuse by a sibling occurred when they were 5 to 7 years old. The most frequently reported age when the abuse began was 5 years old. Again, this may be merely the earliest incident that survivors can recall, and their sexual abuse may have actually begun at a much earlier age. Some respondents reported that they were aware they had been sexually abused as infants, but they do not indicate how they had become aware of this. One respondent, for example, wrote:

> Sexual abuse was a part of my life from the time I was an infant. The age of 3 months is the earliest memory I have.

Many parents think of children as beginning to engage in sexual activity when they reach adolescence or become sexually mature, not at age 4 or 5. Parents often think that their children are not interested in or knowledgeable about sex at such an early age. Even though a child may not be sexually mature at this age and does not exhibit any interest in sex, the child may become a victim of sexual abuse. Prevention efforts against child sexual exploitation whether by siblings or adults must begin early in a child's life. (Chapter 9 focuses on strategies for preventing sibling abuse.) A study found that only 29% of 521 parents of children aged 6 to 14 in the Boston metropolitan area discussed sexual abuse with their child (Finkelhor, 1984). Only 22% mentioned possible abuse by a family member. Most of the parents believed that the optimal age for discussing sexual abuse with a child was around 9. Unfortunately, many children by that age already have been victimized. Also, parents mistakenly assume that any potential perpetrators would be strangers rather than family members, including a sibling. A researcher found from interviewing 20 sexually abused girls, ages 10-15, that they were provided with little or no sex education or information about sexual abuse (Gilgun, 1986). Neither parents nor schools provided this information. The researchers described their abuse as occurring in a knowledge vacuum. In order to prevent sexual abuse by a sibling, parents must empower their children with the ability to say no to inappropriate touches at a very early age.

In most of the cases reported in this research, the perpetrator of the abuse was an older brother or sister, generally 3 to 10 years older. The younger sibling may have become a victim of the older sibling because of a lack of knowledge regarding how to prevent sexual abuse.

The data provided by respondents indicated that it may be appropriate to coin a new adage, "You are never too old to be a victim." Several respondents continued to be victims of their siblings' sexual advances throughout their teen years and into adulthood. One person who had been a frequent victim of her older brother's sexual abuse when she was growing up at home assumed the abuse would stop when he went away to college. But one weekend she visited her brother at college. In the dormitory he attempted to force her to have sex with him again. Another survivor's older brother attempted to rape her after she was married and the parent of several children. The perpetrators in these incidents thus continued to view their sisters as sexual objects, even into adulthood.

How does the sexual abuse of one sibling by another begin? In the following pages the survivors will recount their earliest memories of being sexually abused by a sibling. In many instances the initial episodes of sexual molestation escalated into more and different kinds of sexual abuse. If the victims had been empowered—given the permission and ability to say no to the perpetrator—some of the trauma could possibly have been avoided. Most certainly the abuse would not have continued. This is not to blame the survivor but to support the case for parents instructing children about how to prevent sexual abuse—even from members of their own family.

The survivors describe abusive incidents from when they were 4 years old through adolescence. The sexual abuse occurred in a variety of settings and under various circumstances. The accounts of the survivors' initial incidents of sexual abuse are arranged by the age at which the incident occurred, whenever such information was available.

A survivor from Michigan wrote:

> I was 3 years old and I remember my oldest brother being in bed with me and rubbing against me in a way that I knew he shouldn't.

A story with a tragic ending was told by a survivor from California:

> About age 3, my older brother started fondling me, which progressed to full sexual intercourse over the next years, starting when I was about 9 or 10 and continuing to age 15, when I ran away and became a hooker.

A woman from Maryland:

> I was 4 years old and my older brother told me that he wanted to show me something that Mom and Dad did. I refused. Then he offered to pay me a quarter and said that I would like it. If I turned him down, it was clear that he would hurt me. So I gave in and he made me perform oral sex with him.

Another survivor recalled her first sexually abusive incident with an older brother:

> At approximately the age of 4, my older brother made me take my clothes off and get into his toy box where he fondled me and pretended to take pictures with a play camera.

A woman recalled that her first sexually abusive encounter had occurred at the age of 4. Like many of the survivors, the pain of the trauma made it difficult for her to remember what happened:

> It's difficult to pinpoint the first time or close to it that the sexual abuse occurred. After being in therapy, I still cannot remember. The earliest possibly was when I was 4. It could have been earlier. It was mainly my brother making me touch his erection through his underwear and touching my vagina in my underpants.

A 34-year-old mother from Ohio wrote:

> My brother sat on his lower bunk and made me suck his penis. He urinated in my mouth. I was in kindergarten, he must have been in the fourth grade then. I remember I became very angry. He laughed. It seems my parents were not at home at this time or in another part of the house.

Another survivor from Ohio reported being initially sexually abused at the age of 5. Her comment indicates that vaginal bleeding in a child should be an important clue for parents in detecting sexual abuse:

> I was sexually abused at the age of 5. I remember experiencing vaginal bleeding, but I have no memory of what happened.

A survivor from Washington described her first sexually abusive incident, abuse that continued three to five times per week:

> When I was 5 years old, my older brother, then 12 or 13, took me out into the woods by our house and pulled my pants down and looked at me. I don't remember if he touched me or not. The next day or so he did it again and touched me.

A respondent from Texas found it difficult to separate the physical, emotional, and sexual abuse she experienced as a child.

> I know there was abuse before this but I can only remember pieces of it. This is the first one where I can remember a lot of

it. I am 5 years old. My brothers and I and two other boys were there. My brothers sold me to the two boys and they sexually abused me. When the oldest brother forced me to touch him and put his penis in my mouth, I got sick. This made him mad. He hit me and put his pocket knife at my throat and sexually abused me. Then the other brothers repeated the same acts as did the oldest brother. Then both urinated on me and locked me under the house where I was tied to a pole with no clothes on. They let me out before my parents arrived. This is all I can remember.

A survivor from Alabama:

I was about 6 years old. My brother persuaded me to lie down on the bathroom floor. There were some neighbor boys in the house. He promised not to let them in. He got me on the floor with my pants down and then opened the door. He laughed about it.

A Colorado woman in her 40s recalled that an older brother sexually abused her under the guise of informing her about sex:

I was 6 or 7 and my parents were at work. My brother, age 11 or 12, persuaded me to stay home from school and smoke cigarettes. He talked to me about other secrets from parents and introduced me to sex.

A young woman was first abused sexually by a brother who was 8 years older:

I believe the first time was when I was 6 years old. He was baby-sitting me because the rest of my family was out somewhere. He came to my aunt's house to pick me up and he walked me home. I knew something felt different. He was holding my hand in a protective sort of way. It felt nice to have my brother taking care of me. We got home and he showed me his penis and wanted me to touch it. After that I don't remember much except he started masturbating and he ejaculated into the trash can. I was scared because I didn't know what was happening to him.

Numerous respondents also reported that their sexual abuse by a sibling occurred when they were under the care of an older sibling, for example, an older brother who was baby-sitting.

He was baby-sitting for me and our younger sister. She was in the tub. We were watching TV. He offered me money. He did oral sex on me.

An adult male described how his older brother sexually abused him when their parents were away from the home. He related that the abuse continued to occur three to four times per week:

I don't remember when it began but it started with me giving him oral sex. I usually masturbated him. I remember this happening on Sunday mornings because Mom and Dad would be gone to Grandma's.

Frequently, the sexual abuse occurred in the context of a threat from the older sibling:

I was 7 and my eldest brother took me into the woods while my mother was working. He wanted to "play dirty" with me. He touched me on my nipples, then touched me on my vagina. Then he made me touch his penis. After it was all over he said, "If you tell anyone, I will kill you!" I believed him and was frightened and yet, I didn't even realize what he was doing. To me it was like brushing my hair.

Another survivor was threatened by a brother who was 13 years older:

My brother threatened to kill me if I told our parents about him molesting me. I was 3 or 4 years of age at the time; he was about 18. He showed me the butcher block we kept in the cellar with the ax and blood. He said he'd kill me there if I told.

These comments describe a difference in the way sexual abuse by an adult (relative or nonrelative) occurs in comparison to sexual abuse by a sibling. Adult sexual abuse of children generally occurs in the context of the perpetrator telling the victim that he or she is special, that the sexual activity will be a secret that they will share with no one. Sibling sexual abuse generally occurs in the context of a threat with the perpetrator (brother) threatening harm or even death to the victim (sister).

Several survivors reported that their first incident of sexual abuse by a sibling ended with their being blamed for what happened. Such survivors are revictimized when they themselves are blamed for the abuse.

I was about 8 years old. My mother and stepfather had gone out for a few hours, and my brother told me he wanted to

imitate something he had seen between adults. He took my
skirt off and was kissing and fondling me. He then laid on top
of me and was rubbing himself against me mimicking intercourse. This went on for about an hour until my mother came
home and caught us. As was the usual case in my home, she
didn't say anything to my brother and pinned all the blame on
me for what happened.

Another survivor who was blamed for what happened was a man from
Missouri, who was sexually abused by two older brothers:

About age 4 or 5, my older brother performed oral sex on me,
made me available to his older peers, and threatened me with
physical violence if I told my parents. He showed me pornographic pictures, invited little girls over, and forced me into
sexual play. I felt I had absolutely no control. I felt I was inferior,
bad, and that there was something very wrong with me. I
doubted I would be able to have a normal sex life and had fears
about homosexuality and of becoming insane. Fortunately, at
age 13 my grandmother found out about the molestation and
she rescued me and became my legal guardian. My parents
were happy to relinquish me because they felt I was weird and
had initiated these sex acts.

For another survivor, pornography played into the sexual abuse she
experienced from a teenage brother:

I was 9 and my brother was 16. I remember him showing me
pictures from magazines like *Playboy, Oui, Screw,* etc. and rubbing my back. I can't remember what happened next. I just
know after that it went on for 2 years. I was felt all over my
body. I looked at lots of pictures. I was instructed on what felt
good for my brother. The first time I ever saw him ejaculate, I
almost vomited.

A survivor from Indiana described her initial incident of sexual abuse:

When I was about 9, my brothers and I and some of their friends
were watching TV. My brother was under a blanket on the floor
and invited me and a friend to join him. When I did, he fondled
my genitals. Then he went over to his friends on the couch and
bragged about what he had done.

The perpetrators frequently used trickery to involve the victim in an initial sexual encounter. A woman from Kansas wrote:

> About age 10 my brother approached me to engage in "research" with him. He told me he was studying breast feeding in school and needed to see mine. He proceeded to undress me and fondle my breasts.

Another woman was tricked by an older sibling into a sexual encounter as a child:

> I was about 6 to 8 years old. My oldest brother called to me to come up the street to his best friend's house. They told me they had a new game to play. They told me to pull my pants down and then they told me to lay down under a table that was covered with a sheet so no one could see. They took turns rubbing their penises all over my lower body. I don't remember if there was penetration. They told me not to tell. I said okay.

She then described her reaction to what occurred:

> I don't remember much about it. I did not tell anyone. I remember the vague feeling that my brother was more important than me and I should keep quiet and do what he wants.

This survivor, now the parent of a 3-year-old-daughter, stated she has instructed her daughter on the difference between good touches and secret touches.

A Kentucky survivor's older brother initially sexually abused her when he was baby-sitting his younger siblings. Older siblings baby-sitting younger siblings often inappropriately used the authority given to them by their parents in the latter's absence to sexually abuse a younger sibling. (This occurred also with physical and emotional abuse.)

> My oldest brother was baby-sitting me and my other brother who was outside one day after school. The abuser told me to come to a bed in the living room—we were crowded up where we lived. He told me to lay down. I was taught to do as people told me. I laid down, he raised my dress, lowered my panties, put his fingers on my genitals. Then he spit on me there and exposed his penis, which he then put on me down there, too. I remember a white sticky stuff and a smell and slimy feel, but I don't remember any emotions at the time. When he was done,

he pulled my pants up and lowered my dress. I was 6 years old. He was 12 the first time this happened. My mother was seldom gone, but she was gone that day.

Generally, the sexual abuse continued beyond the initial occurrences. But a survivor who did not identify herself reported a single incident of sexual abuse about which she is still very angry. She feels that this incident has affected her sexuality in her marriage.

There was only one instance of sexual abuse. I was 11 years old. The upstairs in our house had two bedrooms and one bath. My older brother and I always slept late on Saturday mornings. One Saturday morning I woke up but did not open my eyes because he was unbuttoning my pajamas. He was very careful as if he was trying not to wake me. I feigned sleep. He attempted to lie on me and penetrate me. I rolled over as if stirring to avoid this. He left the room. That morning when we were alone preparing breakfast, he did not mention anything. I told him I had had a strange dream. He smirked at me. We said no more about it. Later I received a note from him. He wanted us to share the bathroom together when we showered. I wrote back *NO* to this.

This survivor reported that shortly after this incident, her parents moved her to a downstairs bedroom and put her two younger brothers in the room she had been occupying.

A survivor from Kansas wrote that it is very "painful to dig out of my repressed childhood" her memory of sexual abuse. She described her older brother, the perpetrator of the sexual abuse, as her parents' "golden-haired" son, their favorite child:

I was about 10 or 11, fifth or sixth grade. My parents were out of the house. My brother came into the bedroom saying, "Do you want to feel something good?" Remember, this guy was *GOD* around the house and here he was paying attention to me. So we went to bed. I remember it hurting. I was a virgin and he said it wouldn't hurt for long. He climaxed and I was left hurting physically and mentally.

Another survivor recalled her first sexually abusive encounter with a brother:

> I was 11 and was taking a bath. My brother came in and forced
> his way into the tub and sexually assaulted me.

Perpetrators frequently used violence to force their sibling to comply
with their sexual wishes. A survivor from Ohio was threatened with
further violence if she did not go along with the already violent act of
sexual abuse:

> I was about 12 years old. My brother told me if I didn't take my
> clothes off, he would take his baseball bat and hit me in the head
> and I would die. I knew he would do it because he had already
> put me in the hospital. Then, he raped me.

A woman from Arizona who has been in counseling for several years
described her earliest memory of sexual abuse, abuse that continued
throughout her teenage years:

> My stepbrother and I were just goofing around in our den. He
> grabbed me from behind between my legs. He kept his hand
> there longer than necessary for our game and rubbed my clito-
> ris through my pants. I was 13 and he was about 15.

Another survivor from Arizona recalled that the first time she was
sexually abused was on vacation, when she and her brother, a year older,
shared a bedroom. The sexual encounters continued when they returned home with her brother coming into her bedroom during the
night when their parents were asleep.

> My earliest memory is of my brother sneaking into my bed
> while we were on vacation and were sharing one bedroom. This
> happened while my parents were still out on the town. I pre-
> tended I was asleep and it was very difficult to determine what
> to do about it because of the physical pleasure but inappropri-
> ate and selfish behavior on his part.

The victim often experienced some physical pleasure of an autonomic
nature when being sexually abused by a brother, as the previous comment indicates. This pleasurable feeling is often used by the perpetrator
as a defense for his behavior when he is confronted about having
sexually abused his sister. The perpetrator will say, "You enjoyed it; you
could have stopped it, if you had wanted to." This comment of the
perpetrator partially shifts the blame for the abuse away from himself
to the victim. The comment also often adds to the guilt the victim

experiences seen in self-blame for engaging in the sexual behavior and not stopping it.

In a single, brief sentence, an adult woman told her story of her initial incident of sexual abuse by a sibling:

> I was 14—my brother pushed me down and raped me.

A 42-year-old woman described the feelings she remembered from the initial abusive incident by a brother. Her brief but poignant statement expresses the feeling that many of the respondents shared as victims of sexual abuse by a sibling.

> I remember waking up as my brother was touching me. I was so scared!

※ Typical Experiences of Sexual Abuse

As stated earlier, only a few respondents indicated that their sexual abuse by a sibling was a single or one-time event. In most instances the episodes continued and proceeded to other and different kinds of sexual abuse, often accompanied by physical and emotional abuse. The repetitious nature of the sexual abuse for siblings resembles that of children who are victims of sexual assault by an adult such as their father or other close family members. The sexual assault is generally repeated and continues in a compulsive or addictive manner until the child becomes old enough to forcibly prohibit the behavior or the sexually abusive behavior is discovered and appropriate interventions occur (Benward & Densen-Gerber, 1975).

A survivor wrote:

> I can't remember exactly how the sexual abuse started but when I was smaller there was a lot of experimenting. He would do things to me like putting his finger in my vagina. Then, as I got older, he would perform oral sex on me.

Another respondent wrote:

> Initially, I was forced to masturbate him one night, but from then on it moved quickly to oral sex on him and eventually rape.

Clarification should be made about the use of the term *rape*. In most states, *rape* is legally defined as the penetration of the penis into the vagina under force or the threat of force. Because of the growing understanding of sexual abuse and its effect on victims, *rape* is now being defined more broadly, consistent with feminist thought (Russell, 1986). The word *rape* is now being used to refer to any sexual activity between a perpetrator and a victim in which force, the threat of force, or threats in general are used. (An example of a "threat in general" would be a perpetrator warning a victim not to tell anyone about his sexual activity with the victim because he may be sent to jail.) If both parties do not consent to the sexual activity or if one party is not able to because of developmental constraints, then the act becomes a violation of the privacy and dignity of the individual who is the target or victim of the behavior, even if the perpetrator and victim know each other. The act becomes rape.

This broadening of the meaning of the term *rape* has important implications both for the prosecution of perpetrators and for the treatment of sexual abuse survivors. In terms of prosecuting perpetrators, a perpetrator's use of aggression, force, or threats brings his or her behavior into the realm of rape, regardless of the nature of the activity. For example, fondling a victim's genitals can no long be labeled as less harmful than sexual intercourse (although pregnancy could occur as a result of the latter but not the former) because the consequences are essentially the same: the victim's rights to privacy have been abused by means of an aggressive act. In other words, the victim has been raped. Likewise, the implications for the treatment of sexual abuse are that regardless of the nature of the activity, a victim of sexual abuse is a victim of an aggressive act. The survivor quoted earlier used the word *rape* in the legal sense: sexual intercourse under the threat of force. But actually, she had already been a victim of rape when she was forced to engage in masturbation and oral sex against her wishes.

What was the nature of the sexual abuse that followed the initial abuses? Again, the survivors themselves answered this, describing the nature of the sexual activity, the setting, and the context in which the abuse continued.

A 48-year-old woman from Idaho wrote:

> It began as games and grew to "look and feel." As I became older, he played with my breasts and then fondled my genitals

always wanting but never achieving intercourse. He showed
me with his fingers how it would feel.

A perpetrator approached his younger sister on the grounds that his
sexual abuse was an "experiment":

> He made it into an experiment. He would have me undress and
> he would look and touch me—especially my vagina. I was
> frequently required to touch him on his penis. He would have
> me in the playhouse or basement room. At age 9 or 10, he started
> penetrating me—again as an experiment. No emotions or feel-
> ing. I was told not to tell because it was an experiment and if I
> told it would fail. There was more to his convoluted logic, but
> that was the gist of it.

Another survivor stated the sexual abuse she experienced occurred
whenever her parents went out, which was at least once per week. After
the initial incident, the abuse progressively increased:

> It became *much* more frequent as he got older. It mostly hap-
> pened when I was in sixth to ninth grade, ages 11 to 15. I knew
> he would try so I would lock myself in my room. He would pick
> the lock and force me to the floor or bed. I can remember yelling
> at him, or crying, or begging, or throwing myself down and
> saying, "Go ahead," which he did, or saying, "I was going to
> tell." His response was, "Well, if you're going to tell, I might as
> well go ahead." I tried everything I could think of; for example,
> appealing to his morals as a brother. One time I remember
> holding a knife to myself. He got it away, always laughing. He'd
> force off my clothes, rub and suck my breasts, put his penis
> between them and rub. He would perform oral sex on me often.
> I remember sucking his penis once. He did not come in my
> mouth. He would rub his penis all over my vulva and press
> against my vagina. He never inserted it, just pressed against it.
> I kept a calendar during his senior year of high school. I had
> made it a "countdown" of when he'd move out upon gradu-
> ation with the numbers going down.

Sibling sexual abuse is a phenomenon that occurs in families across all
socioeconomic levels. This survivor's mother had completed several
years of college, and her father held a graduate degree from a university.

Another survivor wrote:

When it all started, usually both of my brothers approached me together, often while my parents were away in the evenings and they were left to baby-sit. They would drag me kicking and screaming up the stairs and usually lay me on the floor and pull my clothes off. They took turns fondling me and having me masturbate them. During all of this, they would make crude comments about my body. Sometimes they would ejaculate all over me. My father was a minister and my parents were often gone in the evening, so there was plenty of time for all this to happen. As the years went by, I became much more compliant and simply went with them when they approached me. It also became a matter of usually one or the other approaching me at a time.

A survivor from Kansas described the progression of her sexual abuse from an older brother:

He started the activity by fondling me and progressed to having me manually stimulate his penis. After the initial two incidents, I refused to cooperate further. He then began to expose himself to me when we were alone and try to force me to participate. My refusal led to a stage of terrorism, where he would chase me and threaten me.

A common tactic of perpetrators was to isolate the victim in order for the sexual abuse to occur. One respondent, an adult women, described how her older brother would know when to attack her.

He would always seem to know when I was alone and when no one could hear. I would always know when he entered a room when it would happen. He would make me terrified. I would think, "Oh, no, not again!" He'd try to compliment me in a sexual way. Complimenting a 4-to-6-year-old on her "great breasts" was not what I'd call a turn-on. He'd either undress me or make me undress myself. He would undress and make me touch his erection. I hated that because he'd force me to do it and would hold my hand against it to almost masturbate him. He never orgasmed, though. He'd touch me, almost like he was examining me. A few times he had oral sex on me. He attempted intercourse but that was difficult. He'd force my legs apart. I was always so scared because my muscles were so tight and my opening was so small. He never really could enter without severe pain. I would say he was hurting me, which he was, and I'd cry in hopes he'd stop. Sometimes he did. Other times he would force himself inside of me so that I would hurt for days.

Similarly a woman from Michigan wrote:

> One thing my brother always did was to isolate his victim. He was always saying, "Come over here. I want to show you something," or "Come on, let's go for a ride."

The continuing sexual abuse would often occur at night, when other family members were sleeping, as it did for this survivor:

> I would try to put off going to bed. I would try to cover up tight with my blankets. It didn't help. My brother would come into my room and touch me all over. I would pretend I was asleep. After he left I would cry and cry.

When sexual abuse from a sibling occurred at night, a common defense of the victims would be to feign sleep. Knowing she was powerless physically as well as emotionally against her attacker and that she could not resist, a victim would act as if she were sleeping. This behavior may also be viewed as a psychological defense against the emotional pain and suffering she experienced. It was as if she were saying, "If I am asleep, I won't be aware of what is happening. It won't hurt me as much."

Two survivors wrote:

> My brother would come into my room at night and fondle my breasts and genitals. He used to put his fingers inside me and would put his penis between my legs. He never tried to penetrate me with his penis. I always pretended to be asleep.

> Typically, my brother would sneak into my bed in the middle of the night and "experiment" on me. I would stir and try to scare him away by pretending to wake up but he was undaunted. He would wait until I seemingly fell back to sleep and start again—vaginal penetration or oral sex.

One survivor's sexual abuse began when she was 3 or 4 years old. Her brother, 13 years older, forced her to perform oral sex on him, wrenching back her head with his hand in her hair.

I had already learned that if I cried out in pain he would beat me worse so I had to remain silent until he left. The abuse continued through the years—sometimes in his car, sometimes in my room at night. I was terrified of him. I was terrified to go to my room at night. I wedged myself on the cold linoleum floor (cold Connecticut winters) between my bed and the wall trying to hide from him at night and stay awake so the nightmares wouldn't come. It was the family joke that I must keep falling out of my bed at night.

Most of the survivors in this research were women. But these are the comments of a man who was sexually abused by a brother:

My brother caught me masturbating once. That's when the sexual abuse began. At night he would have me fondle him, masturbate him, and fellate him, depending on what he wanted. He threatened to tell Mom about catching me masturbating if I didn't go along. The abuse went on about a year or two. It was always at night. He would lay on his back. A street light would shine across his body through the curtains, and he would call me to come "do" him. I felt like I was on stage with the street light and trapped in a bad part. I hated him immensely. Finally, after a year or so I told him he could tell whomever he wanted but I wouldn't do it anymore. The abuse stopped, but the damage was done. My feelings would haunt me into high school, college, and my marriage.

The continued sexual abuse often occurred in connection with physical abuse or the threat of violence if the victim did not comply with the perpetrator's intent. Emotional abuse would be used to make the victim feel that really it was her fault for what was happening. The comments of three survivors demonstrate this:

It usually started with my brother yelling at me. Then he would hurt me somehow—cut me, hit me, etc. Then he would overpower me to rape me. After this he always told me this was my fault.

I would be in my bed asleep. He would jump in the bed with me. I would try and push him out. I was just not strong enough and he would always keep a baseball bat or knife with him.

He would lay me down, put his big fist by my face and he would say, "If you scream, this is what you'll get." Then he would sexually abuse me.

The victims' attempts to stop the abuse and their helplessness in doing so are portrayed by the comments of this respondent from Arizona:

The sexual abuse was on a daily basis. I think my brother enjoyed it, and it became a regular habit. I would say no but my pleas never helped. I not only felt sorry for him but also for myself.

Similarly, another survivor wrote:

My brother would sneak into my room at night and put his hand down my pajama bottoms and rub my clitoris until I had an orgasm. Then he would leave. I was too scared to move and wasn't sure what was happening. My parents were usually out playing bridge when this occurred. As it progressed, however, sometimes he would sneak into my room when everyone was asleep. I locked my door, but he slit the screens and got in through the window.

Most of the incidents of sexual abuse presented so far have consisted of masturbation, oral sex, or intercourse. But other survivors' sexual abuse took the form of inappropriate touching or sexually slanted comments. Several survivors described this form of sexual abuse:

My brother, 2 years older, would commonly grab my chest where my breasts were developing and would twist. When I would ask him to stop he would say, "You love it and you know it."

When I was in my teens, my brother would say provocative things to me to see how I'd respond.

My brother would come up behind me and grab my breasts. He would verbally harass me and constantly make sexual references, even when we were older teenagers.

The feelings of the survivors as they recall their sexual abuse can best be summarized by the comments of two respondents:

It's too much to even put into words on paper.

I still feel so hurt and sad for that poor little defenseless girl. They raped her—she suffers still.

The latter comment reflects a psychiatric diagnosis often associated with incest or the sexual abuse of a child: multiple personality. The victim psychologically handles the abuse by denying that it really happened to her but delegates the trauma to someone else, to a different part of her personality (Bliss, 1986). The development of multiple personalities thus becomes a way of survival in the face of the severe trauma of sexual abuse and the overwhelming feelings resulting from it (Briere, 1989; Gelinas, 1983; Herman, Russell, & Trocki, 1986; Wilbur, 1984; Young, 1992).

In summary, several observations may be made about the typical experiences of sexual abuse by a sibling. The abuse most often occurred when the parents were away from the home and an older sibling was placed in charge, or during the night, when everyone was sleeping. Undoubtedly, sexually abusive incidents also occurred when siblings were off somewhere playing together, as in the woods, which was reported by several survivors. But it is important to note that most frequently sibling sexual abuse occurred in the family home. The implications of this information for the prevention of sibling sexual abuse will be discussed in a later chapter on preventing sibling abuse.

■ The Survivors' Responses

The survivors' immediate responses to sexual abuse by a sibling differed from their responses to sibling physical and emotional abuse. Victims of physical abuse were often unable to fight back due to limitations in size and strength compared with their perpetrators. Thus, they resorted to hiding and withdrawing into themselves to get away from the perpetrator and the hitting, slapping, and other forms of physical abuse. In cases of emotional abuse a typical response was to fight back verbally as aggressively and in turn to ridicule and call the perpetrator names. Generally, this was not effective and only served to further victimize the victim because the perpetrator intensified the abuse or shifted to other tactics.

But in cases of sexual abuse, none of the respondents reported that they fought back. Undoubtedly, some siblings do fight back against their sexual abuse by another sibling. Those who do are demonstrating their empowerment—their right and ability to say no—which may distinguish them from the survivors of sexual abuse who were not able to do so. An assertive verbal response can be an effective way to prevent sexual abuse.

A common response of sibling victims of sexual assault was to feign sleep. This response is also frequently reported by child victims of sexual assault by adult males within their household. These children too, "played possum" as a way of coping with the assault, lacking the ability to use force to ward off their assailant (Summit, 1983). This is a common response since children are often forced to cope with fears of the night by resorting to sleep or feigning sleep. Unfortunately, in courtrooms children are frequently attacked by attorneys and discredited by juries in the prosecution of sexual abuse cases because they made no protest or outcry. This only adds to their guilt and self-blame. Thus, the entire sexual assault situation—the traumatic incident as well as the investigation that follows—can be psychologically devastating for the survivor, especially a child.

A more frequent response of the victims was to acquiesce or submit to the sexual abuse. This response must be seen within the context of the abuse. First, the victims, especially young siblings because of developmental limitations, often were not aware of what they were doing when an older sibling engaged them in sexual play. Only after the event, sometimes many years later, when they began to experience shame and guilt for their involvement in the behavior, did they begin to feel like a victim. They frequently coped with their feelings of shame and guilt by blaming themselves for participating in the behavior, but in reality they may have had no other option, considering their lack of access to information or "empowerment" about sexual assault.

Second, sibling sexual abuse generally occurs within the context of threat. An older sibling threatens a younger sibling that if the parents are told, the victim will be harmed. Another threat is if the victim tells the parents, they will both be punished. The latter tactic leaves the victim feeling partly responsible for the sexual activity. Thus, the victim is frequently set up to pretend as if nothing has occurred, lest the victim experience retaliation from the perpetrator and from the parents for reporting the incident. As one survivor quoted earlier wrote:

> Once my mother was suspicious. She confronted my brothers and they denied it. She told them she would ask me. Then she

waited several days. During that time they told me I'd better not tell her or they'd get me into trouble.

Apart from victims of rape, some victims of sexual assault (occurring either on a one-time basis or over a period of time) are referred to as "accessory-to-sex" victims (Burgess & Holmstrom, 1975). In these situations, the offender has pressured the victim into being an accessory to sexual activity or into going along with sexual activity in any of several ways: the victim is told she will receive a reward of material goods (such as a present, candy, or money); the perpetrator tells the victim that it is all right to engage in sexual activity, misrepresenting moral standards; or the sexual activity is conducted under the disguise of friendship. A common factor in all these "accessory" situations is that the victims are unable to refuse to participate because of their circumstances and because of a level of cognitive or emotional development that prevents them from being able to make a decision.

Although the victim is pressured into remaining silent, however, this does not alleviate the emotional trauma associated with the sexual abuse. Rather, it forces the survivor to silently bear the anxiety, shame, guilt, and a host of other emotions alone. The only visible sign of this situation on the part of the survivor may be a tendency to withdraw, to want to be alone. Withdrawn behavior should thus be an important clue for parents, teachers, and other adults who are in contact with children that something is bothering the child that the child is not able to or dare not talk about. The withdrawn behavior may indicate that the child is attempting to repress the emotions surrounding a painful experience.

A survivor from Colorado repressed her sexual abuse for years, until she was pregnant:

> I had no recollection of the sexual abuse until I was pregnant with my daughter. I then started having very graphic nightmares about my brother raping me. I was about 3 or 4 years old in the dreams. He was on top of me, holding me down and forcing himself into me. I was crying and screaming at him to stop. He would say, "You know you like it." I thought I was a pervert to have those dreams, so I didn't tell anyone about them until when my daughter was about a year old. I was physically abusing her and I went to Parents Anonymous for help. The sponsor asked me if I had been sexually abused. I said I hadn't, but I told her about the nightmares. She said she thought it

really happened. With her support and encouragement, I asked
my sisters first. They said he had abused them, but there was
no penetration. Then I confronted him. I told him just exactly
what was in the dreams, down to the last detail. There was a
silence, then he said, "You are right, I did that."

Dr. Roland Summit (1983) has categorized the typical responses of
female children who are victims of sexual abuse by adults, generally
their father or another close male relative. He calls the typical response
the "sexual abuse accommodation syndrome." The syndrome is composed of five categories: (a) secrecy, (b) helplessness, (c) entrapment and
accommodation, (d) delayed, unconvincing disclosure, and (e) retraction. The first two categories refer to the vulnerable position in which
the victim has been placed. The sexual abuse occurs in the context of
secrecy between the perpetrator and the victim, the latter having been
cajoled or threatened to participate. The child generally is *helpless* to do
otherwise because of cognitive or physical limitations. Categories (3) to
(5) refer to a sequential process that frequently occurs for the victim.
Following an initial episode of sexual abuse, a victim experiences *entrapment*. If and when *disclosure* is made by the victim, it is often after the
abuse has continued to occur and is done with great emotional conflict
because of the risks and costs that may come to the victim. The disclosure may not be convincing because significant others may not believe
the victim's report and because the perpetrator denies it. The final
outcome for the victim often is *retraction*, as a way of retreat from the
chaotic aftermath of the disclosure. While this "sexual abuse accommodation syndrome" was devised to describe adult-child sexual abuse, the
present research indicates that it is also applicable to sibling sexual
abuse.

■ Sexual Curiosity

In this chapter respondents to the research have spoken out about their
sexual abuse by a sibling and how this abuse continued for many of
them throughout their childhood years. Some readers may react to the
survivors' account of their abuse by asking, "Isn't there also just sexual
curiosity between siblings?—for example, when two small siblings take
a bath together and look at and perhaps even touch each other's
genitals? Is everything that happens between siblings abuse?"

Obviously, not all behavioral interactions between siblings should be labeled "abuse." Although in a later chapter I specifically address the issue of distinguishing abusive behavior from normal behavior, sexual curiosity should briefly be discussed here because it does happen between siblings. Moreover, there may be considerable concern about this issue in the light of the frequent discussions in the media on the sexual abuse of children.

Sexual curiosity is normal. All children explore their own bodies, and to some extent and at some time they may engage in visual or even manual exploration of a sibling's body. This is one way that children discover sexual differences or verify what they have been told by their parents about the differences between boys and girls. If two small children explore each other's bodies, they are not thereby predestined to a life of emotional chaos and suffering. For example, Tim, age 4, was observed by a nursery school attendant showing his penis to Sue, who was the same age. The children became aware that the attendant had seen their behavior, and Tim's reaction was to blame Sue, saying she had told him to do this. Sue denied it. The nursery school attendant reported the activity to the teacher, who took the children aside and talked with them about their sexuality at a level that they could understand and reviewed with them an earlier discussion in which all the children had participated on the subject of good touches and secret touches.

Sexual activity may be viewed relative to the age and psychosocial developmental level of a child. For preschool-age children (ages 0-5) their patterns of activity include intense curiosity seen in taking advantage of opportunities to explore their universe. This may be expressed in the sexual behaviors of masturbation and looking at others' bodies. For primary-school-age children (6-10 years), activities include game playing with peers and continuing to seize opportunities to explore their universe. Sexual behaviors for this age group may include masturbation, looking at others' bodies, sexual exposure of themselves to others, and even sexual fondling of peers or younger children in a play or gamelike atmosphere. For preadolescent children (10-12 years) and adolescents (13-18 years), behaviors focus on individuation, including separation from parents and family and developing relationships with peers. For adolescents this includes practicing intimacy with peers of the same and opposite sex. Sexual behaviors for these developmental stages include masturbation, an intense interest in voyeuristic activities involving viewing others' bodies through pictures, films, or videos (some of which may be pornographic), or attempts at "peeking" in opposite sex locker/dressing rooms. Open-mouth kissing, sexual fondling, simulated intercourse, and intercourse involving penetration are sexual behaviors of these developmental stages (Sgroi, Bunk, & Wabrek, 1988).

Sexual activity among consenting participants probably presents the least risk of unfavorable consequences. But often young children may appear to consent but actually do not because they cannot anticipate unfavorable consequences from a behavior. In many instances what appears to be consent may actually be only passive consent or the inability to make a rational decision because of limited cognitive skills and life experiences.

There is a range of attitudes toward sexuality that may be identified in our society. Some adults are very uncomfortable with sexual issues and attempt to handle them with their children by pretending this area of life does not exist. Others advocate open sexual activity in the presence of children and even encourage children to engage in sexual activity. But neither approach guarantees healthy psychosexual development.

Because of the impact of sexual abuse by an adult, a peer, or sibling on a child's later adult psychosocial functioning, it is important for parents to take a proactive approach to sexuality with their children. Such an approach includes:

1. Providing children information about sex that is appropriate to their age and psychosocial development
2. Empowering children with the knowledge and ability to discriminate between good touches and secret touches
3. Providing an atmosphere where sexual concerns and problems can be discussed in the family

An analogy may help clarify this. A person can live his or her entire life crossing busy streets in the middle of the block, even dodging between cars in motion, yet never be hit by a passing automobile. But no wise adult would routinely engage in such behavior or teach their children to do so. The risk is too great. A safer way to cross a busy street is to go to the corner where a stop sign or traffic signal assists the pedestrian. Likewise, risk is involved in some sexual activity between siblings that might seem to be mere curiosity. Both siblings may not really be willing participants or be able to consent to the activity in which they are engaging. Parents can avoid that risk, just as people can avoid the risk of crossing a busy street in the middle of the block, by taking a proactive stance of giving children age-appropriate sexual information, teaching them the difference between good touches and secret touches, and setting a positive climate in the home for the development of a healthy sexuality for all family members.

■ Summary

Survivors' accounts of the sexual abuse they experienced from a sibling are tragic, filled with shame, guilt, embarrassment, and anger—emotions that still haunt many. Sexual abuse by siblings is a reality, and its impact on the lives of survivors is serious. Its seriousness requires that parents take steps to help children develop a healthy attitude toward sex, which includes the prevention of sexual abuse.

5   Parental Reactions
to Sibling Abuse

*My parents just ignored the hitting, punching, name calling, and
rude remarks of my brother toward me.*

                                         A sibling abuse survivor

In the previous chapters the survivors have spoken of their physical,
emotional, and sexual abuse by a sibling as children. Readers of these
chapters may be wondering: Weren't the parents aware of the abuse that
was occurring? If they were aware, what was their reaction to the abuse?
Didn't the parents do anything to stop the abuse? The answers to these
questions, provided by the survivors, are the subject of this chapter.

■   Parental Awareness

Were the parents aware of the abuse that was occurring between their
children? Each of the three sections of the questionnaire focusing on
physical, emotional, and sexual abuse by a sibling asked the following
question:

Were your parents aware of what was happening?
Yes _____ No _____ Unknown _____

Table 5.1 presents the responses of the participants to this question
according to the type of sibling abuse. Since each of the 150 persons who
responded to the questionnaire could answer any or all three parts of

Table 5.1 Parental Awareness of Each Type of Sibling Abuse

	Aware		Not Aware		Unknown		
Type	%	(n)	%	(n)	%	(n)	Total
Physical	71	(70)	10	(10)	19	(19)	99
Emotional	69	(81)	12	(14)	19	(22)	117
Sexual	18	(18)	56	(55)	26	(26)	99

the questionnaire dealing with physical, emotional, or sexual abuse, depending on the types of abuse they experienced, some individuals responded more than once to this question.

The data indicate that more parents were aware of physical and emotional abuse than were aware of sexual abuse. Seventy-one percent (70) of the survivors of physical abuse and 69% (81) of the survivors of emotional abuse felt that their parents were aware of it. This is understandable in the light of the fact that it would be difficult to hide physical abuse or its effects from the parents. Similarly, a child who is emotionally abusing a brother or sister through name calling, ridicule, or degrading comments is likely to engage in this behavior whether the parents were present or not. It would be difficult to hide physical and emotional sibling abuse from parents.

But only 18% (18) of the survivors, relatively few, indicated that their parents were aware of the sexual abuse. This finding is also understandable. Sexual abuse obviously occurs not in the presence of parents but when parents are away from home or during the night, when parents are sleeping.

The parents' lack of awareness of the sexual abuse was also often due to the inability of the victims to inform their parents about what was happening. One would think that children could surely tell their parents, but the data indicate the contrary. Many victims could not tell their parents for several reasons.

One reason is that at the time the sexual abuse was occurring, the victim often did not perceive it as abuse. The victim was not cognitively or emotionally mature enough to understand that it was abuse. This was especially true of young children. But the way the survivors in this research perceive the sexual activity now as adults, looking back on their childhood, is very different from the way they perceived it when they were children. For example, this is true of the survivor who was 7 years old during the first sexual incident with her older brother, quoted in an earlier chapter. He took her into the woods while their mother was working and "played dirty" with her by touching her on her breasts and genitals and making her do likewise to him. Afterward, he threatened to kill her if she ever told anyone. The survivor, now as an adult, recalled her reaction to the sexual abuse at the time:

> I didn't even realize what he was doing. To me it was like brushing my hair.

As an adult, however, this survivor's reaction to the abuse is very different. She is aware this was an abusive incident, the first of many. Looking back on these experiences, she is very angry that she was used by her brother. As a result, she experiences feelings of low self-esteem.

A second reason that children frequently did not tell their parents about sibling sexual abuse is that the abuse often occurred in the context of the abuse of authority. Some of the perpetrators, older brothers of the victims, were acting as baby-sitters for their younger sisters when they abused them sexually, as we have seen. The younger sibling had been instructed by the parents to obey the older brother. Recall the comments of two survivors:

> I remember a vague feeling that my brother was more important then me and I should keep quiet and do what he wanted.

> I was taught to do as people told me.

A third reason that children did not tell their parents was that the perpetrator threatened the victim with retaliation if he or she told, like the survivor who was abused by her brother in the woods. In the context of a physical threat, the victim was fearful that if the abuse were reported to the parents, the sibling perpetrator might act on the threat. Moreover, if the abuse occurred while the perpetrator was baby-sitting the victim, the victim feared that if left in the care of the perpetrator again in the future, the perpetrator would punish the victim for reporting the abuse.

Note the comments of survivors of sibling sexual abuse that occurred in the context of a threat, such as a male survivor who recalled:

> He would lay me down, put his big fist by my face and he
> would say, "If you scream, this is what you'll get." Then he
> would masturbate me.

And from this female survivor:

> I would be in my bed asleep. He would jump in the bed with
> me. I would try and push him out. I was just not strong enough
> and he would always keep a baseball bat or knife with him.

A fourth reason that victims did not tell their parents about the abuse
is that they blamed themselves for what happened. Some survivors in
this research spoke of experiencing pleasurable physical feelings during
the sexual encounters with a sibling. Because they derived sexual
pleasure from the experience, often of an autonomic nature, the survivors blamed themselves for contributing to the abuse. They were afraid
to report the activity to their parents, lest their abusive sibling in
self-defense tell the parents of their participation.

Moreover, to keep the victim from telling the parents, the perpetrator
often blamed the victim for not resisting the sexual advances. "You
could have stopped it (the sexual abuse), if you had wanted," perpetrators defensively would say as they attempted to shift the blame for the
abuse from themselves to the victim. Generally, the survivors participating in this research had not been "empowered" by their parents
about good touches and secret touches to effectively resist the sexual
advances.

Yet another reason why the victims did not tell their parents is that the
climate in the home made it impossible for them to report it. One
survivor did the best she could to communicate it under the circumstances:

> I remember every time my parents went out, I'd sit in my
> parents' room while they got ready and I'd ask them, "Do you
> really have to go out tonight? Can't you stay home?" That's as
> close as I could get to telling them or asking for their protection.

This survivor felt that her parents could have helped prevent the abuse
from occurring in the first place by creating a different atmosphere:

> Somehow they should have provided a family atmosphere
> in which their children—me at this point—could have ap-

proached them with the situation without being fearful of getting into trouble.

This survivor couldn't tell her parents about the sexual abuse she was experiencing because she didn't feel comfortable talking to her parents about such things. A climate had not been established in the home that allowed her to talk to her parents. She does not specifically say so, but her parents, though physically present, may have been psychologically absent from the home; this is, they were neither sensitive nor empathic to her needs. They may have been too busy and may not have taken the time to listen to their daughter.

▪ Parental Responses

How did the parents who were aware of the abuse occurring in their home respond? Did they try to do anything about it?

Some parents do intervene in the abuse and stop it. Undoubtedly, children growing up in such homes were not involved in the present research. These individuals do not identify themselves as *victims* or *survivors* of sibling abuse. Although they experienced abusive behavior from a sibling on a single occasion or even over a period of time, the response of their parents to the abuse was positive and effective. The behavior did not continue, and the incident or incidents did not become emotionally charged for the survivor and had less impact on the survivor's life.

Although some parents effectively respond to abuse and terminate the abusive behavior, the parents of the respondents to this research did not do so. They responded in ways that were not helpful to the victims, and in many instances their responses further victimized the victim. Parents responded to the abuse in various ways, according to the comments of the survivors. Different types of parental responses are identified.

Ignoring or Minimizing the Abuse

A very typical parental response to sibling abuse, especially to physical and emotional abuse, was to ignore or minimize it. They often excused the behavior on the basis that it was normal sibling rivalry. "Boys will be boys; children will be children," victims were told by their parents. While it is true that certain behaviors are accepted as appropriate to children because of the level of their maturity, the abuse of one sibling by another is not. Nothing excuses or justifies the abuse of one person by another.

A survivor from California, for example, told of her parents' reaction to her physical abuse from an older brother:

> They ignored or minimized the abuse. They told me, "Boys were boys and needed to clear their system."

She must have felt helpless at this excusing of her brother's behavior. Her parents minimized or ignored her brother's abusive behavior because they incorrectly assumed that all children engage in such behavior—even behavior with an abusive quality—as part of normal development.

Just as objects made of silver from time to time need polishing to bring out their true luster, so the term *sibling rivalry* must be reviewed and its meaning recast in the light of the existence of sibling abuse. (Chapter 8 discusses criteria for helping distinguish abusive sibling behavior from normal behavior or sibling rivalry.)

One respondent who was the frequent victim of an older brother's abusive behavior reported that her parents excused his behavior by saying, "He doesn't know his own strength." Obviously, this response did not help the victim; rather, it further victimized her. This inappropriate response was actually telling the victim that she would just have to accept the abusive behavior. No attempt appears to have been made to confront her brother about his behavior.

A 33-year-old woman reported that when she told her parents about the physical abuse she experienced from an older brother:

> My mother would say that my brother was not hitting me hard enough for me to complain. Or she would say that he is going through a stage and would outgrow it.

At the age of 8 this survivor was pushed down a flight of stairs by her brother. Subsequently, two to three times a week she was thrown to the floor and hit in the stomach or on the arms.

A 37-year-old man who is the survivor of an older brother's physical abuse described his parents' reaction:

I told them once and they didn't believe me, and they would leave me alone with him again. Then I really suffered for telling on him. I soon learned not to tell.

A woman from Canada got this reaction from her parents about the physical abuse she was experiencing from an older sibling:

My parents had no reaction to anything except denial. My mother may have made a token effort to stop it, but she was very ineffectual.

These comments illustrate that parents' ignoring or minimizing physical and emotional abuse does not make it go away. If anything, the perpetrator in essence is given covert license or permission to continue the behavior and further victimize the victim.

A survivor of physical abuse from a brother wrote:

My parents saw what my brother said and did to me as normal sibling rivalry and did not correct any of it. If they were around when it was occurring, they would just say we had to learn to get along better.

Another survivor described her parents' reaction:

They dismissed it as normal sibling rivalry and said it was probably half my fault. They were unwilling to become involved.

This survivor suggested what her parents could have done:

They could have talked to my brother to help him realize how hurtful his teasing and name calling was. If this did not work, they could have forbidden this kind of behavior and punished appropriately. Perhaps they could have been a better role model, also.

A woman from Kansas described her parents' reaction to the emotional abuse she experienced from an older brother:

My parents seemed to think it was cute when he ridiculed me.

A Tennessee survivor described the following reaction from her parents:

It wasn't abuse to them. It was normal. Our abuse of each other as siblings disturbed their own peace and so they'd yell or get in on it, too. Then, when Mom and Dad were not watching, the big boys would get even anyway and it would be worse, so I just as soon didn't want Mom and Dad "protecting" me or Mom and Dad getting into another fight with each other—a vicious, escalating, abusive cycle of insanity!

A respondent from Pennsylvania reported that her parents knew her older brother was emotionally abusive toward her but they "framed their reaction in such a way that it seemed okay." Her parents would tell her, "The smartest one keeps quiet. All kids fight." Another survivor wrote that when she reported being emotionally abused, her parents would tell her, "Sisters must love each other!" The survivor added in large letters, "GREAT!" as if to say, "What good did that do for me?" It is obvious from her comments that her emotional abuse by her sibling continued.

The parents of a respondent from Ohio accepted the emotional abuse she was experiencing from a younger sister: "They laughed it off."

A survivor from Arizona reported her parents' reaction:

Everything was always a joke to them. They laughed at my emotions. Usually their reply was to quit complaining—"You'll get over it."

An Indiana woman stated that her mother accepted the emotional sibling abuse because her mother had come from a home where even physical abuse was tolerated. Her mother excused the behavior by saying what she saw her children doing was not as severe as what she had experienced as a child.

Another survivor wrote that her parents ignored the emotional abuse she was experiencing from a sibling. She described the effect this had on her:

Both of my parents minimized my brother's angry, aggressive behavior, especially my mother, who I don't think knew what to do. I received little support from my parents. I often went to my mother for her to intervene, but she made minimal efforts. I soon began to feel very powerless as a child and felt that I had to just put up with my brother's abuse.

Some parents ignored or minimized the physically and emotionally abusive behavior because they themselves abused their children. They could not recognize what was occurring between the siblings was dysfunctional when they did not recognize the pathology of their own behavior toward their children. Actually, the siblings were modeling or repeating behaviors that they observed in and experienced from their parents.

A survivor from California wrote:

> My father was so emotionally abusive to us, especially to my brother, that he probably wouldn't have noticed that there was anything wrong with the way my brother treated me. My brother in essence was doing to me what was done to him.

Similarly, a respondent from Arkansas wrote:

> My parents didn't do anything to stop it. They didn't talk to me to help me understand it because they emotionally abused me too.

A New York survivor:

> My brother constantly belittled me, telling me how stupid, incompetent, ugly, useless etc. I was. But again he was only modeling our mother's behavior.

Three other survivors described similar emotionally abusive family interactions:

> My parents had no reaction to the emotional abuse I experienced. Such "put-downs" were relatively frequent on their part as well.

> My parents were abusive too so it was just part of everyday life.

> My parents, especially my mother, was the greatest one to emotionally abuse in the whole family. It seems my older brothers and sister copied her.

Some parents not only excused abusive sibling behavior but felt it was good for the victim. "It will make you tough," a father told his daughter when she reported that her two older brothers would relentlessly tease her to tears about being ugly.

Blaming the Victim

Other parents accepted the reports of sibling abuse when told to them, but they blamed the victim for what occurred. This parental response was reported frequently by sibling abuse survivors in this research as well as by survivors in other studies of sibling abuse (Laviola, 1992; Loredo, 1982). When parents blame the victim, the victim becomes a victim a second time, revictimizing the victim. The unfortunate outcome of this parental response is that perpetrators are absolved of responsibility for their actions and are given the implicit message that the behavior was appropriate or that the victim deserved what the perpetrator did. The perpetrator is in essence given license to continue the behavior. Blaming the victim also increases the likelihood for self-blame on the part of the victim as he or she internalizes the message of being responsible for the abuse that occurred.

The respondent who was tickled until she vomited reported that when she told her parents' about this form of abuse from an older sister, as well as repeated episodes of punching and shoving, her parents stated, "You must have asked for it." This is a typical response of parents as reported by the research respondents. Rather than examining what happened between the siblings, the victim is made to feel guilty for what occurred.

Many altercations between siblings that involve physically and emotionally abusive behavior may in fact involve the contributions of both persons. There is some truth to the cliché, "It takes two to tango." One theory about sibling abuse, the interactional theory of abuse, argues that the way some children interact with others may make them prone to becoming victims of abusive behavior. This theory does not blame the victim, because blaming the victim involves absolving the perpetrator of responsibility for the behavior and placing the burden of guilt on the victim. The interactional theory, by contrast, assumes that victims must be helped to understand that some aspects of their behavior may prompt or promote an abusive response from the sibling, but does not place responsibility on the victim. Analyzing the contribution of both siblings to situations that may result in abusive behavior is an integral part of the problem-solving approach to sibling conflict management, discussed at the end of this chapter.

This survivor was blamed for her sibling's abusive behavior:

I was hurt by the abuse I received from a younger sister, but my sister was not blamed or it was turned around that I had done something to cause it. She was never wrong.

Another respondent said that her parents would attempt to intervene when the siblings fought. The fighting generally followed episodes in which the survivor was teased with a pet bird of which she was deathly afraid:

My parents would usually break it up, but with me being the oldest I'd always get accused of causing the problem and be told I should set a better example and I wouldn't get hurt.

A 42-year-old woman quoted her mother's response when she reported the physically abusive behavior of two brothers, 5 and 8 years older:

Mom would say, "You should know better than to be there. You should know better, they don't."

A typical abusive situation and a parental response was described by a 33-year-old woman from Texas who was abused by an older brother and sister:

It started when I was 10 or 11. My sister would hit me and then my mother would hit me because she said I deserved it if my sister hit me. I always tried to be good, but a lot of times it seemed like for no reason this would happen. It was as if my mother was giving my sister the okay to treat me as she saw fit.

A survivor of sexual abuse by an older brother reported:

Most of the time the abuse was happening, I lived with my divorced mother. I'm not sure that she knew what was happening, but even if she did, I don't think she would have stopped it. Her philosophy was that you just took what men and life dished out to you and you didn't complain because you probably did something to deserve it. My mother treated all her daughters with disrespect and had none for herself, so my brother learned early on that he didn't have to respect us either. The abuse finally stopped because I ran away from home when I was 16 and never came back.

Another survivor reported being blamed for the abuse by her parents:

> My parents didn't know but they would have blamed me or at
> least made excuses for my brother. My mother would say, "Men
> are hunters, don't trust any, not even your own brother." But
> she meant it in general, not for her son, the "King."

A survivor from California was blamed by her parents for her sexual
abuse by her brother, who was 3 years older:

> When I hinted that I was having problems, they placed the
> blame on me, or they ignored it. My mother once walked in on
> us and beat me up. She told me I was a slut, that I deserved it.

A male survivor of sexual abuse from an older brother wrote that his
parents were not aware of the abuse, but he could anticipate what their
response would have been:

> Since I was the "good son" in the family, an excellent student,
> always helpful, never in trouble, I would have received all the
> blame and the target of their anger. They would have said that
> I should have known better and that I could have stopped my
> brother. He would have been yelled at, but would not have
> received the shame that I did.

Inappropriately Responding to the Behavior

The ways some parents responded to being told of the behavior were
ineffective and in some instances exacerbated the abuse.

A 44-year-old survivor who was physically abused from the age of 4 by
a brother 6 years older indicated that her parents initially didn't believe
her when she told them what he had done, for example, kicking and
throwing her pet rabbit and repeatedly physically abusing her. As an
adult now, looking back on what occurred in her childhood, she
feels that her parents didn't know how to stop her brother's abusive
behavior. His abuse apparently escalated because, as this respondent
reported, eventually her mother came to fear this boy as he grew
older and threatened her. Another respondent reported that her parents
would tell her three older brothers to stop physically abusing her, and
the behavior would stop for a short period of time, but soon resume.

Similarly, a respondent from Alaska wrote:

> My mom would tell my brother to stop abusing me—he was
> not allowed to hit girls—but it went in one ear and out the other.

He did not listen to what she said. She would get tired of me asking her to do something about it. She would just give up.

One can sense this mother's frustration at not knowing how to prevent her son's abusive behavior toward her daughter. Her intervention was not effective, and the usual methods of disciplining a child proved ineffective.

Another inappropriate response to sibling abuse in the family was to abuse the perpetrator in return. A young woman who was a victim of physical abuse from an older sister provides an example:

My parents would yell at her and pinch and bite her to "teach" her how it felt so she'd stop doing it. It only made it worse for me though. They'd clean my wounds and tell me a story to tell my teacher to explain my bandages and markings.

This approach appears to be built on the myth that giving perpetrators a dose of their own medicine will teach them to stop the behavior. Some parents use this form of behavior control with small children. They may bite a child who has bitten them or encourage a child who has been slapped to slap back. But this form of discipline establishes no new behavioral patterns for the child; rather, mimicking the negative or abusive behavior of the perpetrator reinforces this behavior in the child. Just as violence sometimes begets more violence, the violence of this form of discipline encourages continued violence. The perpetrator may become angrier as a result of this discipline and may be expected to ventilate this anger once again on the parent or the victim.

Another kind of inappropriate parental intervention that also uses violence to combat violence is the severe corporal punishment of the perpetrator. One respondent reported that when she told her parents about the physical abuse she was receiving from her older brother, her father beat her brother so badly that she resolved never again to tell her father. A two-stage process of self-blame resulted from her father's action. First, the survivor blamed herself for her brother's severe beating because she had reported his behavior to her father. Second, feeling guilty for what happened, she then blamed herself for the initial abuse from her brother, saying that perhaps in some way she may have caused her brother to treat her this way.

This respondent's parents' reacted with violence against the perpetrator, demonstrating the ineffectiveness of this reaction:

> My older brothers received a severe beating when I told my parents how they were abusing me. The severity of the beating, however, discouraged me from ever reporting again what happened because I wanted to avoid a more violent outcome.

Sometimes a victim's physical abuse and attempts to report it to parents set up further violence throughout the whole family.

> My father would never know about my abuse from an older brother and sister because my mother would never tell him for fear of what he would do. She would try to hide it from him. She would say, "Do not tell your father; do not get him started."

Similarly, a female respondent from California wrote:

> On a couple of instances my father did know about my abuse from an older brother when I cried out in pain. Once my father beat my brother in front of me. Once he yelled at my brother for hours about not hitting a woman. When my brother started crying, my stepmother went to comfort him. My father then hit her in the face for taking my brother's side.

Research on the effects of parental punishment of sibling aggression or fighting indicates that parents are more likely to punish the older sibling rather than the younger (Felson & Russo, 1988). This tendency to punish the older or more powerful sibling, the researchers found, generally results in more frequent aggression because the younger siblings do not hesitate to be verbally or physically aggressive, knowing the parents will identify with them and punish the older sibling. A more effective approach, the researchers found, is for parents to intervene in the fighting but not to engage in punishment. A problem-solving approach to conflict management, they found, is a more effective way to intervene in conflicts between siblings. In the problem-solving approach the parents together with the siblings experiencing the conflict discuss what has happened, determine how it occurred, and, most important, how the outcome of physical or verbal aggression can be avoided in similar situations in the future. The positive outcome of this approach is that the two antagonists leave the situation with new skills for avoiding conflictual behavior. These skills can not only be used in sibling relationships but also in peer relationships outside the home and in other relationships as the children grow into adulthood.

Some respondents reported that when they told their parents about the abuse they experienced, all the children were indiscriminately punished. Unfortunately, indiscriminately punishing all the children involved further victimizes the victim rather than protecting the victim from further abuse. A respondent from Louisiana received this reaction from her parents:

> If any of the siblings made me cry for some reason, and my parents became aware of it, we would all get whipped.

A survivor from Montana described her father's handling of abuse that occurred among the siblings in her family:

> Dad would yell at us and threaten us with a belt if we didn't shut up. Anger was not directed at my brother who abused me but at all the kids. I learned to cry silently because of my Dad. The belt was worse than my brother's abuse.

The parents of a respondent from Ohio were inconsistent in the way they responded to the emotionally abusive behavior three older brothers engaged in toward her. Sometimes her parents would tell her brothers to stop the behavior, and would even beat them, but at other times would do nothing. This response was obviously ineffective because the brothers experienced no firm, consistent message that their behavior would not be tolerated in the family.

Another inappropriate parental response to abusive behavior is provided by a survivor from Washington. When she reported her older siblings' abusive behavior of ridiculing and degrading her, the parents replied that her siblings were just jealous of her. They told her that God would eventually reward her for being good when they were so bad to her. This ineffective intervention only gave the perpetrators further license to continue their abusive behavior toward her.

A respondent from Tennessee, who described her home life as a "death camp existence," wrote that if her parents had known her brother was sexually abusing her,

> There would have been more beatings for everyone all around. Instead of a constant at random sort of violence, there would have been a concerted and pointed effort to make people even more miserable.

A survivor from New York did not tell her parents about the sexual abuse because of the consequences it would have for her mother:

> If my father had known, he probably would have beaten my brother and thrown him out of the house. My mother would have insisted that we both get counseling. She would have blamed herself. She would have thought my brother's problems stemmed from the emotional abuse he suffered from my father as an alcoholic.

Joining in the Abuse

Perhaps the saddest parental response, especially to emotional abuse such as name calling and ridicule, was to join the perpetrator in abusing the victim. The effect on the victims was devastating. The victims were further victimized by the very parents from whom they were seeking protection. The victim could turn for protection to no one else. The victims' crying and the sadness they felt is understandable.

Parents sometimes resort to emotionally abusive behavior in the form of ridicule and degrading comments as a way to supposedly motivate a child to make some change in their behavior. For example, parents may call a child a "slob" because of the way their room is kept or refer to an overweight child as "chubby." Unfortunately, such name calling or degrading comments rarely motivate anyone to change their behavior. Rather, it is destructive to a person's self-esteem.

A survivor from Ohio wrote that when her older sister emotionally abused her,

> My mother would pick up on it and also make fun of me.

A respondent from Arizona stated:

> When I was 6 and started school, the girls took me in the bathroom and put me in the toilet to wash me. Then, they called me "Stinkweed." I was crushed. When I got home, I talked about it. Even my whole family laughed at me and called me that daily. It still hurts. It is something I'll never forget. They still remind me of it.

Another reported that when her father observed her trying to protect herself from her sibling's physical assaults, he would perceive this as "fighting" and "Dad would join in and hit us harder."

Disbelieving That Abuse Was Occurring

When some survivors of sibling abuse, especially sexual abuse, reported the abuse to their parents, the parental response was disbelief. Again, the effect of this response was further victimization. The survivors became a victim of their parents' disbelief and failure to protect them, as well as of their perpetrator's continuing abusive behavior.

A respondent from New York was further victimized in this way when she reported her sexual abuse by her brother to her parents:

> When I tried to tell my father about it, he called my mother and brother into the room, told them my accusations and asked him if it was true. Naturally, he said I was lying and my mother stood there supporting him. Nothing happened except that I got beaten later by my mother for daring to say anything and for "lying." My brother then knew that from then on, there was nothing he couldn't do to me. He was immune from punishment. Never again did I say a word since to do so would have only meant more abuse from both of them. I concluded it was better to keep my mouth shut.

One man recalled that when he tried to tell his parents about his physical abuse by his brother, they refused to believe him. When his brother began to sexually abuse him, he knew it was hopeless to report it to his parents because he knew they would never believe him.

> When I tried to tell them about the beatings I was taking, they didn't believe me and they would leave me alone with him again. So when it came to the sexual abuse, I didn't think they would believe me.

As a result of his parents' failure to believe him and intervene in the abuse, he was locked into repeatedly being his brother's victim.

A study of factors that influence a mothers' belief of children reporting sexual abuse found that mothers are most likely to believe the report if the offender is an extended family member, such as a grandfather, uncle, or cousin (Sirles & Franke, 1989). Mothers believed their children in 92% of these cases. But when the offender was a biological father, 86% of the mothers believed their child's report. The proportion of mothers who believed the report fell to only 56% when the offender was a stepfather or live-in partner. These data indicate that parents may disbelieve or dismiss reports of sexual abuse when a close family member is reported to be the perpetrator.

The researchers found that the age of the child was also an important factor in whether or not the report of sexual abuse would be believed (Sirles & Franke, 1989). The younger the child was, the more likely the mother was to believe the report of sexual abuse. If the child was 2 to 5 years of age, 95% of the mothers believed the child's report of abuse. If the child was 6 to 11 years old, 82% of the mothers believed the report. If the child was a teenager, 12 to 17 years, only 63% of the mothers believed the report. The authors suggested several possible explanations for these findings. Younger children generally are not knowledgeable about sexual functioning, so that mothers may be more likely to believe their reports. Moreover, the relationship between a mother and a small child is generally very close. But teenagers are not so closely attached to their mothers. Teenagers are also more likely to falsify a report because they are knowledgeable about sexual functioning. If the mother knows her teenage child is sexually active, she is less likely to believe the report of sexual abuse. Sexual abuse victims who react to their sexual abuse by sexually acting out may be decreasing their chances of being believed by their mother when reporting sexual abuse.

Similarly, in a study of women who had been sexually abused as children, Benward and Densen-Gerber (1975) found that in cases where the victim has passively consented, "it was a rare mother who allied herself with the daughter by giving her emotional support or by moving to protect the daughter from future incidents" (p. 335). The more typical reaction was for the mother to not believe the daughter, to become angry with her or to blame her.

In situations of sexual abuse whether by an adult or a sibling, perpetrators' accounts of what happen often tend to be believed more than what the victim says (Sgroi & Bunk, 1988). Sexual abuse is the only crime in which the accused rather than the victim often is asked whether anything happened. It would be unthinkable to ask the person who is accused of robbery, larceny, murder, or assault if he or she did it, yet this routinely occurs in cases of incestuous child sexual abuse. This makes very little sense.

Indifference

Still another parental response to sexual abuse in the family was indifference. Some parents may not have known what to do. For others, their indifference may have stemmed from their overwhelming problems or from being under so much stress that they did not have the energy to look beyond their own problems. One respondent wrote:

> I told my mother about my oldest brother molesting me about 2 years after it happened and she asked me what I expected her to do about it. I never bothered to tell her about other things that happened because obviously she didn't care.

▪ An Effective and Appropriate Parental Response

Given these ineffective and inappropriate parental responses to the physical, emotional, or sexual abuse of one sibling by another, is there an effective and appropriate response? There may be no single effective response; a variety of responses may be appropriate, depending on the situation. One possibility is the problem-solving approach presented through the acronym S-A-F-E. This is a *safe* way to handle sibling conflicts. This model for problem-solving need not be used every time two siblings are involved in an altercation, but it is intended for use when a parent observes a *pattern* of abuse over a period of time or when a single emotionally charged or potentially abusive incident occurs. The model must be implemented at a level that children can understand and use, depending on their level of cognitive development. A dividend of parents using this model is that problem-solving rather than violence is being taught to children when any interpersonal conflict occurs whether with siblings or peers.

S = Stop the Action; Set the Stage for Problem-Solving

The first step in the problem-solving process is for the parent to stop the abusive action that is occurring whether it be physical in nature—hitting, slapping, punching—or emotional—name calling, ridicule, degradation. Ignoring the behavior will not make it stop. Rather, as research respondents reported, when parents ignored abusive behavior occurring between siblings, the perpetrator took this as a message that the behavior was appropriate and continued the abuse. Stopping the action means separating the siblings and may include sending the children to their rooms or to different parts of the house, if they share a room, or helping them become involved in an activity alone or with a friend rather than with the sibling with whom they are having a conflict. Engaging in problem-solving immediately at the time of the conflict generally is not wise. The situation usually is too emotionally charged for the rational process of problem-solving to occur. The siblings involved in the altercation, as well as the parent, may need some time to emotionally cool down. Letting a period of time, perhaps an hour or so, pass often helps defuse the emotionally laden situation. The parent may inform the sibling that in the evening after dinner as a family they are going to discuss what happened. Obviously, the statement sometimes used by a mother—"Wait until your Dad comes home," is inappropriate because it sets Dad up as the "great disciplinarian."

A = Assessment

The parent attempts in this step to appraise the situation on the basis of data or information. Data are the facts the sibling participants are able to provide about what occurred, the circumstances surrounding the incident, similar previous incidents, other persons who may have been involved, the role of each sibling in the incident, events leading up to the incident, and the impact of the incident on the victim.

When parents attempt to assess the facts of what happened in a highly emotionally charged altercation between siblings, children often intersperse their report with projections of blame or responsibility onto the other sibling; for example, "Tommy, hit me." "Mary called me a name." "Tim took my bicycle and then hit me when he brought it back." A way parents can cut through children's projections of blame onto each other is to insist that each child speak only in "I statements" when describing the incident. This means that each statement must begin with the word *I*. For example, "I hit Tommy back after he hit me." "I teased Mary and she called me a name." "I was angry at Tim when I found out he took my bike without asking me." The use of "I statements" forces children to focus on their own contribution to the altercation rather than project all responsibility onto their sibling. This makes sense because a child can take responsibility only for his or her own behavior. The levity that may arise in situations where only "I statements" are used also helps reduce the tension of the moment.

Although assessing the *facts* surrounding the incident are important, an equally important aspect of assessment is assessing the *feelings* of the participants. Although the destruction of a toy or being called a name might seem insignificant, the feelings attached to the incident may be far more important. Drawing out the feelings of the victim about the incident will help both the parent and the perpetrator realize the emotional impact of the incident on the victim.

Figure 5.1 presents a simple model for enabling children to put into words the feelings they are experiencing. Just as there are three basic colors—red, blue, yellow—and all other colors represent blends of these three basic ones, so some mental health professionals suggest there are four basic feelings or emotions—sad, glad, mad, scared—and all other feelings are blends of these four.

F = Find Out What Will Work

This step represents the essence of the problem-solving process. Assessing the facts and feelings of the altercation in which the siblings were involved, a parent may begin to see a pattern that has developed over time in the relationship between the siblings. While it may be easy for a parent to simply state what appears to happen repeatedly in the altercations between the siblings, it is better if the parent can help the siblings develop an awareness of the repeated behaviors that occur or the pattern that seems to underlie their altercations. If parents and children summarize in as brief a statement as possible what appears to happen in the siblings' altercations, it will facilitate the completion of this step of the problem-solving process. If the parent formulates the statement, the parent should check out the accuracy of the statement with the participants involved in the incident.

For example, Tim, age 8, took his younger sister's bicycle and rode it to a friend's house without asking for her permission to do so. Later, when he returned home with the bicycle, his sister, Jennifer, was very angry. The air became heavy as the siblings called each other names and hit and pushed each other. The children's mother, Mrs. Bray, decided to apply the problem-solving approach SAFE to this altercation between the two siblings because she had noticed during the past weeks that Tim

Figure 5.1. Four Basic Feelings

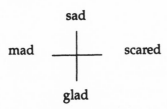

was repeatedly being inconsiderate of his sister's feelings. That evening after dinner when the family was finished eating, Mrs. Bray suggested the family discuss the altercation that had occurred between Tim and his sister, Jennifer.

In addition to Jennifer and Tim recounting the facts of what had happened earlier in the day that led up to their altercation, Jennifer was asked to identify which of the four feelings in Figure 5.1 summarized how she felt when Tim had taken her bicycle without permission. Jennifer pointed out that it made her mad.

Following an assessment of the facts and feelings of these altercations, Mrs. Bray gave this summary statement of the problem that she checked for accuracy with the two children: "These fights seem to occur when one sibling borrows without permission something that belongs to the other sibling; for example, today it was Tim using Jennifer's bike without asking her for permission to do so." The children agreed with the statement, and Tim recalled an earlier incident where he became very angry with his sister when she had come into his room and had taken his baseball glove without asking him.

After this analysis of the facts and feelings, the parents' and siblings' next task was to find out what would work to counter the problem that repeatedly occurred. Mrs. Bray approached this by asking the children, "What do you think we should do about this situation? Can we set up a rule that all of us can follow?" The discussion that followed culminated in the decision from the children that no one would borrow anything from another person without first getting their explicit permission.

Sibling conflicts often develop in families over tasks the children are to do such as loading or unloading the dishwasher, feeding the family pets, taking out the trash, and mowing the lawn. A helpful way many parents find to avoid the conflict over who is to do what and when is to set up a schedule posted for all to see, such as on the refrigerator door. Agreement is reached in advance by all concerned about who does what, when the task should be completed, and the consequences if the task is not done.

E = Evaluate the Results

The final step in the problem-solving process is monitoring or evaluating whether or not the plan set up in the previous stage is working. If problems arise, it may not be necessary to repeat the entire problem-solving steps but rather to diagnose what went wrong and to fine-tune the plan.

Initially, parents may react to the problem-solving process by asking, "Who has time to go through all this every time two of my kids are fighting?" The problem-solving process—SAFE—is not intended to be used every time two siblings have an altercation. It should be used when a *pattern* of behavior is observed or when a serious incident occurs. Moreover, the process does not take a great amount of time. The entire process can take place in 15 minutes.

The problem-solving approach is a model that parents can follow to positively resolve problems between siblings. It is not a panacea for all sibling problems. Implementing the problem-solving process does require effort on the part of both parents and siblings. Name calling, degrading comments, and even physical abuse are far easier. But the consequences of such behavior are costly, and they leave unresolved the underlying problem or problems that prompted the altercation. Fighting between siblings can be expected to continue and, in many instances, may escalate into more serious and abusive behavior.

An old adage states, "An ounce of prevention is worth a pound of cure." The problem-solving approach to sibling conflicts is that ounce of prevention that is worth far more than the pound of curing the effects of abusive sibling relationships.

■ Summary

A variety of parental responses to sibling physical, emotional, or sexual abuse have been identified in this chapter. Survivors frequently used the word *betrayed* to describe how they felt about their parents' response to the abuse they were experiencing from a sibling.

> I felt betrayed when I told them about what my brother did and they just ignored it.

> It was like a betrayal when I was blamed for my sister fighting with me. What could I do?

Such parental responses to sibling abuse often intensified the survivors' hurt and suffering.

An analogy may help in understanding and empathizing with the survivors in this situation. You are getting out of your car in the parking lot of a large shopping mall. A stranger approaches you, and when he is only a few feet from you, you notice he is holding a small gun in his hand. He demands your money. You give him your money. He takes it and immediately runs to a nearby car that was waiting for him. You notice a policeman is ticketing some cars that are parked illegally, only a short distance from where you are standing. You scream for help. The policeman looks up at you and sees your distress, but he goes back to ticketing the illegally parked cars and ignores you. You run into the nearest store to call the police. A few minutes later, the police arrive and you describe the crime. The policeman writes a few notes on his report form as you are talking. When you are finished, the policeman comments, "I really don't believe what you're saying. But if by chance it were true, you must have done something that caused that man to rob you."

The policeman first ignores you, then does not believe you, and finally blames you for the crime. Not only were you a victim of a crime, but now you are a victim of those who are supposed to help you; they have ignored you and blamed you for what happened. How do you feel?

Imagine the same scenario again, but this time the police officer to whom you report the offense is concerned about what happened and helps you report the crime. How do you feel?

The differences in feeling resemble the differences in feeling that siblings have when parents ignore or join in aversive behavior on the one hand or attempt to help them resolve the problem on the other. The problem-solving approach—SAFE—is one way to resolve problems that occur in sibling relationships.

6

Understanding
Sibling Abuse

*The abuse I experienced from my brother was the same as what my
dad was doing to my mother. Obviously, my brother learned how to
treat me by watching my dad.*

A sibling abuse survivor

In earlier chapters of this book, survivors have told how they were
physically, emotionally, or sexually abused by a sibling as a child.
They have described how they tried to cope with this abuse, and they
have reported their parents' reactions. The questions to ask now are:
How can the physical, emotional, and sexual abuse of one sibling by
another be explained and understood? What is the reason for the
behavior? Can a "theory of sibling abuse" be formulated that will assist
in understanding this social problem? It is important to understand
why sibling abuse occurs because only then can it be prevented and its
effects on the survivors treated.

In trying to understand the reasons for any behavior, whether it is
sibling abuse or other dysfunctional behavior, people often search for a
single, simple explanation. Even the way the question in the previous
paragraph was posed is inappropriate—"What is *the* reason" for sibling
abuse? This inappropriately formulated question sets up the search for
a single answer. The question was deliberately phrased that way to
demonstrate the problem that seeking a single, simplistic answer creates when the answer is very complex.

It would be as if someone asked, "What is *the cause* of juvenile delinquency?" Someone may answer, "Growing up in homes broken by divorce!" Although some research supports the view that children charged with juvenile offenses more often come from families that are not intact than from homes where a father and mother live together, many youngsters come from homes broken by divorce who are *not* juvenile delinquents. Thus, it is incorrect to say that divorce causes juvenile delinquency or to imply that this is *the* cause of juvenile delinquency. Someone else may argue that *the* reason for juvenile delinquency is the absence of adequate recreational facilities. Research may be cited to support the fact that teenagers who do not have acceptable and safe places to associate with their peers are more likely to get into trouble. Still, it is incorrect to state that this is *the one* cause of juvenile delinquency. Obviously, many adolescents who have no access to recreational facilities don't become juvenile delinquents. Each answer may be partially correct, but to seek *a single cause* for the problem of juvenile delinquency is inappropriate because *there isn't a single cause for the problem.*

When we search for single causes of human behavior, our answers are of little value and generally have little empirical support. Complex questions require complex answers. Human behavior, both functional and dysfunctional, is very complex. When reasons for human behavior are sought, generally

1. Multiple reasons must be considered, encompassing psychological as well as social factors.
2. These reasons may interact with each other in complex ways.
3. Our understanding of human behavior and the social environment may be inadequate to identify all the factors that account for certain behaviors. (Blalock, 1964)

This also applies to our attempt to understand the physical, emotional, and sexual abuse of one sibling by another.

In an attempt to explain and understand why sibling abuse occurs, the reasons are drawn from the survivors' own accounts of their abuse, their parents' responses, and the effect of the abuse on them. The reasons given here are not all-inclusive; additional factors that are not evident in the survivors' responses may be needed to explain sibling abuse. Thus, information on understanding sexual abuse drawn from other research will be presented for explaining sibling sexual abuse. Also, the various factors may interact in complex and different ways for different survivors.

The reasons for sibling abuse presented here are not excuses for the perpetrator's behavior. All persons are responsible for their behavior. Rather, they are attempts to understand the factors that contribute to the abuse so that the abuse can be stopped, the effects can be treated, and future sibling abuse be prevented. Although there is a trend to view problems in social functioning as addictions or diseases as described by Stanton Peele (1989) in *The Diseasing of America: Addiction Treatment Out of Control*, sibling abuse is not a disease and it is not an addiction. It is destructive behavior that was learned from somewhere and must be unlearned. Nonabusive behavior must replace the abusive behavior.

■ Abuse of Power

A commonality of all forms of sibling abuse—physical, emotional, and sexual—as well as of all types of family violence—child, spouse, and elder abuse—is the abuse of power. The abuse of power focuses on a more powerful individual abusing a less powerful one. In sibling abuse, as the comments of respondents indicated, this often was an older sibling physically or emotionally abusing a younger sibling. In many instances, power was associated with gender. Male siblings abused female siblings.

Although the abuse of power appears to be an act of the strong against the weak, actually these abusive acts appear to be engaged in by the perpetrator to compensate for his or her perceived lack of or loss of power (Finkelhor, 1983). For example, an older sibling may not be achieving academically as successfully as a younger sibling, so the older sibling resorts to name calling when referring to the younger sibling. Older siblings baby-sitting younger siblings attempt to order the younger siblings around, to get snacks for them, to go to bed early so that they can watch television alone. When older siblings are not successful in getting younger siblings to do their bidding, the former may resort to physically abusive behavior.

As stated earlier, the abuse of power frequently occurs along gender lines with males abusing females. Feminist theories of abuse focus on the abuse of power and control as basic to all types and forms of family violence, especially sexual abuse. The largest percentage of respondents to this research were women who had been physically, emotionally, or sexually abused by a brother. A persistent theme in their accounts is the dominance of a brother over his sister, or a brother's need to prove his masculinity in the way he interacted with his sister.

The roots of the need for males to exert power and control over females may be seen in the socialization of males. Historically, women were considered the property of men, which implied that men could treat women as they wished. Biblical literature, taken literally without regard to its historical context, reinforces a superior attitude in males; for example, women are instructed to be subject to their husbands. Male superiority has been evident historically in art and literature and continues in the popular media, such as in cartoons and television programs. The popular saying "A man is king of his castle" implied that a man could do whatever he wanted within the premises of his own home, including being abusive to his wife and children. (One of the first books exposing violence in American families was appropriately titled Behind Closed Doors [Straus et al., 1980].) The different socialization of boys and girls and the gender-role stereotyping that results can also be seen in gender-related toys, games, and sports. Boys are encouraged to play with what are viewed as "masculine toys," such as trucks and guns, whereas girls are encouraged to play with dolls and to mimic housekeeping activities (Zastrow & Kirst-Ashman, 1994). Society reinforces these views in adulthood, when males and females who do work requiring comparable skills and responsibility under comparable working conditions are paid differently. Women are likely to receive less compensation than men even though their job responsibilities may be the same (Bellak, 1982). Men and women also are socialized to display emotions differently. Men are not to cry or to verbalize their emotions (Goleman, 1995).

The effects of male superiority become clear in an analysis of spouse abuse (Walker, 1994). Men's violence toward their wives is often prompted by the false assumption that they must control their wives and dominate their activities. Diana Russell's (1986) *The Secret Trauma: Incest in the Lives of Girls and Women* reported on her study of 900 randomly selected women in California, which found that sexual assault by the victims' husbands occurred twice as often as sexual assault by persons unknown to the victim.

Likewise, the comments of female survivors of sibling abuse in this research reveal what appears to be an underlying assumption of their brothers: that they had a right to assert their will over their sisters. Physical force and verbal abuse were seen as appropriate ways to achieve this goal. In instances of sexual abuse, brothers tended to view their sisters as sexual objects rather than as individuals.

▪ Inappropriate Expectations

The most frequently cited cause of sibling abuse, generally of a younger sibling by an older sibling, was that the older sibling was in charge of the younger at the time the abuse was occurring. The older sibling was baby-sitting the younger, when the parents were away from the home at night or immediately after school before the parents returned home from work. Sibling abuse that occurs when an older sibling is in charge of a younger sibling may be designated as "inappropriate expectations," since the parents assume the older sibling can handle this responsibility and expect the older sibling not to abuse his or her role.

Inappropriate expectations are frequently associated with adult-child physical abuse as well. Parents who abuse their children physically are often those who treat their children as adults. They tend to lack understanding of the developmental stages of children and have unrealistic or premature expectations of their infants and children (Bavolek, 1989; Berg, 1976; Clark, 1975; Hawkins & Duncan, 1985; Kravitz & Driscoll, 1983). It is frustrating to such parents when their children are not able to comply with their expectations. This often results in abusive behavior.

Similarly, in sibling abuse, parents may expect an older sibling to be able to care for younger siblings in their absence. Unfortunately, however, some siblings in this position are actually not old enough to handle this responsibility. Other siblings may be old enough, but lack the knowledge or skills to serve as a substitute parent. The comments of survivors abused by siblings in their parents' absence documents this.

A 43-year-old woman from Massachusetts, when asked to describe her typical experience of physical sibling abuse, presented the following scenario:

> When my parents went out dancing or to my aunt's home on a
> Saturday night, my two older brothers baby-sat us six children.
> Not long after they left, my brothers would tell us to go to bed.

It was too early so we didn't want to go to bed. When we resisted, we were hit. I was punched and slapped by my oldest brother. If I defended myself by hitting back, my oldest brother would grab my wrists in the air as he screamed at me that he would hit me more. He would be telling me what to do and to go to bed. I would be crying hard even more and would go to bed.

This survivor told her parents what was happening, and they instructed her brothers to allow the younger siblings to stay up. But the abuse persisted and even escalated to sexual abuse. When the survivor was 10 years old, she told her parents that she had been sexually molested by one of the brothers. After this incident, the parents hired a baby-sitter when they went out for an evening.

Another respondent reported:

My mother would go to bingo leaving my sister (3 years older) in charge with specific chores to be done. She would make us do the work. If it didn't get done when she said, she would hit us with a belt. Leaving her in charge gave her every right to do whatever she wanted.

Another survivor wrote that a brother, 5 years older, would be left in charge when her parents went away for an evening.

He would constantly be telling me to do something for him, ordering me around like to change TV channels, get him a soda pop, make popcorn, get him a sandwich, etc. My refusal or sometimes just being too slow to comply would merit me being hit, usually open-handed but sometimes with a closed fist.

A respondent from Ohio described what occurred after her mother died and she would be left in the care of an older brother.

My father would go to work or out on a date and my brother would be watching TV. I would be in my room, and he would come to my room with a stick and some cord. He would beat me with the stick and then tie my hands behind my back and tie my feet together. If I screamed too loud he would put a scarf in my mouth or tie it around my mouth. Once he took a big pot of boiling water and poured it on my hand. He did so much to me, I've blocked some of it out of my mind.

Why do some older siblings use physical and emotional abuse as ways to control younger siblings left in their care? Why would older siblings make excessive demands on the younger siblings in the parents' absence?

One reason may be that the older sibling is modeling the behavior of the parents. Abusive behavior is often learned behavior. The older sibling may have learned from the parents his or her abusive tactics as a way to control a younger sibling. Physical and emotional abuse may have been the primary means the parents used to make their children comply with their wishes. Another reason may be that, in homes where parents did not use physical and emotional abuse, the sibling in charge was too immature to be able to understand how the parents motivated the children to comply with their expectations. Consequently, the sibling in charge resorted to physical and emotional abuse.

When older siblings abuse younger siblings by requiring them to respond to excessive demands, this reflects the inability of the older sibling to handle the responsibility of caring for the younger ones. It is appropriate to put an older sibling in charge when parents are away from the home *if the older sibling can handle the responsibility.* But the parents must set some standards for the sibling in charge, as well as for the younger ones. Parents must also be sensitive to complaints that younger siblings may make after being placed in the care of an older sibling. Insensitive responses on the part of the parents place the younger siblings in a very vulnerable position.

■   Modeling Parental Behavior

Respondents reported that the physically and emotionally abusive behavior they experienced from their sibling was no different from the way their parents treated each other. A survivor wrote:

> How could I expect my brother to treat me differently other than being physically and emotionally abusive when this is the kind of behavior we as kids saw our parents continually engage in toward each other?

A review of research on parents who are abusive toward each other reveals a high likelihood that the parents will be abusive also to their children (O'Keefe, 1995; Ross, 1996; D. Saunders, 1994). In domestic violence studies, about half the men who batter are reported to abuse their children. Slightly more than a third of the battered women on the average report they have been abusive to their children. To these findings, based on the current research, should be added the fact that in families where there is spouse and child abuse, it is highly likely that sibling abuse also is occurring. This can be explained in two ways. First, the children may be modeling their behavior after their parents' behavior. Second, research show that children who witness parental violence tend to have more behavioral problems than children not exposed to parental violence (Hughes, Parkinson, & Vargo, 1989; Jouriles, Barling, & O'Leary, 1987; O'Keefe, 1995; Suh & Abel, 1990). Sibling abuse may be one manifestation of such behavioral problems.

▪ Parents Overwhelmed by Their Own Problems

Another reason that the data suggest why siblings are physically, emotionally, and sexually abused by other siblings is that the parents are so overwhelmed by their own problems that they are not aware of what is happening between the siblings. The parents may not have the energy or the ability to handle the situation. Some of the parents were coping with alcohol problems, mental illness, and marital difficulties. These problems interfered with their ability to effectively intervene in the sibling abuse.

Drug and Alcohol Abuse

A survivor from Nevada described the chaotic conditions in her home when she was growing up:

> My mother was never home for 8 or 9 of my most important years. She probably wasn't aware of too much in our home as she was drinking. She'd stay away for weeks at a time and leave us there with my brother 10 years older.

A survivor from California described a similar situation in her childhood home:

My family was very chaotic. My father was an alcoholic. My
mother died when I was 11 years old. My father had many
lovers and was gone a lot of the time.

A survivor from Washington wrote that her mother could not control
her sister's abusive behavior toward her and that her father had problems of his own:

My father was always too drunk to take note of my abuse or
gone to the local tavern getting drunker.

A survivor wrote:

My parents were heavily into drugs when I was a child. As kids
we were left to ourselves to do what we wanted. Abuse from
the older siblings occurred frequently.

A large number of children in the United States are living in drug and
alcohol dependent families. The National Committee to Prevent Child
Abuse estimated that 10 million children in the United States are being
raised by addicted parents, and at least 675,000 children each year are
seriously mistreated by an alcoholic or drug-abusing caretaker (Bays,
1990). The national prevalence of cocaine addiction has been conserva-
tively estimated to be more than 2 million Americans, a significant
number of whom may be parents (Committee on the Judiciary, U.S.
Senate, 1990). Researchers found that 67% of the cases of serious child
abuse in a juvenile court sample involved parents who abused alcohol
or drugs. Alcohol abuse was found to be associated with physical
maltreatment and cocaine abuse with sexual maltreatment (Famularo,
Kinscherff, & Fenton, 1992). Another study that examined a sample of
206 cases of serious child maltreatment from a juvenile court found that
in 43% of the cases, at least one parent had a substantiated problem with
either alcohol or drugs (Murphy et al., 1991). Alcohol was the most
frequently abused substance (31% of families), followed by cocaine
(16%), heroin (12%), and marijuana (7%). In all, the use of hard drugs
was present in 22% of the families. Numerous other studies document
the relationship between drug and alcohol abuse and child abuse (Chaffin, Kelleher, & Hollenberg, 1996; Dore, Doris, & Wright, 1995; Muller,
Fitzgerald, Sullivan, & Zucker, 1994). In these families in which adult-
child abuse was occurring, there may likely have been sibling abuse also
taking place. The present research suggests that a relationship also
exists between parents who abuse drugs and alcohol and their children
engaging in abusive behaviors toward each other.

Mental and Physical Illness

Chronic mental or physical illness may so consume the energy of a parent that the children are left unattended, or in the care of an older sibling unable to adequately handle this role.

A respondent from Pennsylvania wrote:

> I don't think my mother knew how badly I was being hurt by my older sister, and I was afraid to tell her for fear of retaliation. She was busy trying to survive on practically nothing and deal with her own emotional problems, and probably she had systemic lupus then, even though it wasn't diagnosed for another 15 years or so, but I think she didn't *want* to know how bad things were because she was powerless enough to change her circumstances.

Stress-Related Issues

Some respondents wrote that their fathers were not involved in what was happening because they had to work two jobs to support a large family. Others reported that both parents had to work to support the family because one parent's job alone did not suffice.

Some parents may have been physically in the home but psychologically absent from the family. Holly Smith and Edie Israel (1987), of the Sexual Abuse Team in Boulder, Colorado, studied 25 cases of sibling incest that were reported to the team during a 3-year period. They found that a distinctive characteristic of the families in which sibling sexual abuse occurred was the distance or inaccessibility of the parents. Twenty-four percent of the fathers were described as physically present yet emotionally distant. These fathers verbalized a disinterest in parenting, a failure to attach and bond with their children, and a feeling of being sabotaged by their wives' relationships with the children. The fathers could not empathize with their children's needs and seemed so isolated that they didn't feel they had anything to contribute to the children's well-being. Some indicated that they had no knowledge of children's developmental stages and thus could not relate to the children. Many of the mothers also expressed similar feelings of being distant and inaccessible to their children, although not as much as the fathers.

Dysfunctional Families

Research suggests that adolescent sibling sexual abuse perpetrators often come from discordant families. Worling (1995) compared 32 adolescent male sex offenders who assaulted younger siblings with 28 males who offended against nonsibling children. Adolescent sibling-incest offenders reported significantly more marital discord, parental rejection, use of physical discipline, a more negative and argumentative family atmosphere, and general dissatisfaction with family relationships than their nonsibling sexual offender counterparts. The researcher suggested several possible explanations for the relationship between discordant families and sibling incest perpetrators. First, children who live with abusive and rejecting parents may turn to each other for comfort, nurturance, and support. As these children enter adolescence, a risk of sexualizing these relationships may occur. Second, intrafamilial offenders may be seeking some form of retribution within their families for the abuse and rejection that they have suffered. Third, the adolescents may be modeling their aggressive behavior toward their siblings after what they observe in their parents' relationship to each other as well as to their children. Fourth, although the research data did not suggest this, the sibling-incest offenders may be exposed to more sexualized behaviors in the home such as family nudity, pornography, or witnessing parental sexual acts.

A tendency exists to view a problem such as sibling abuse from an intrapsychic perspective; namely, that the problems results from the psychological dysfunctioning of the perpetrator. However, the occurrence of sibling abuse and the inability of some parents to effectively intervene must be seen in a much broader perspective. An ecological or social-situational perspective enables the problem to be seen in a more comprehensive perspective (Garbarino, 1977; Wiehe, 1989). An ecological or social-situational perspective views the family as a system within the larger social system of which it is a part. A mutual dependence exists between the family and its social environment, and interdependent interactions occur between the two systems. The psychosocial development of individual family members, as well as that of the family as a whole, occurs in the context of the physical, social, political, and economic characteristics of society. Thus, parenting cannot be viewed only from the perspective of psychological functioning. Rather, the external, sociological forces influencing each parent must also be considered. Dr. Jay Belsky (1980) of Pennsylvania State University stressed the importance of an ecological framework in understanding child maltreatment by adults, which relates also to the abuse of one sibling by another. Belsky conceptualized child abuse as a social-psychological phenomenon, affected by forces at work in the individual (ontogenic development), the family (microsystem), the community (exosystem), and the culture (macrosystem). For example, inadequate opportunities for vocational training may require parents to work two or even more unskilled jobs. Inadequate housing may prevent siblings of different ages and genders from having adequate privacy. Psychiatric hospitalization or outpatient treatment may not be available, or a person may be unable to pay for it. Latchkey programs for children who return home from school before parents return home from work may not be available. Under these circumstances, problems arise, affect the parents, and are in turn experienced by the children. This affects children's relationships to their parents and toward each other as siblings.

Thus, the problem of sibling abuse, as well as any of the other forms of domestic violence—child, spouse, elder abuse—has implications for the development and implementation of social policy. Healthy and sound psychosocial development for individuals and families occurs in the context of a society that provides basic support systems such as adequate housing, day care, latchkey programs, and mental health and social service programs that are accessible and available to all persons. Thus, while it may be easy to blame the perpetrator or the parents of the victims of sibling abuse for the problems occurring in the family, these individuals must be viewed in the context of society in which they were attempting to live and raise their families and the impact that deficiencies in this society had on them in their respective roles.

■ Contribution of the Victim

Another causal factor associated with sibling abuse is the victim's own contribution to the abuse, particularly to physical and emotional abuse. This causal factor is discussed in the literature on child abuse as the interactional theory of child abuse (Parke & Collmer, 1975).

When an adult abuses a child, the adult does not necessarily abuse all the children in a family. Frequently, the abuse is selective and directed at one specific child. Genetically determined physical and behavioral characteristics may make a child more prone to abuse. Certain children may also develop behaviors that may make them targets for abuse. In these cases, abuse often becomes cyclical and escalates. The child's behavior may prompt an adult to further abuse the child. This may reinforce the child's behavior, which in turn may prompt more emotional and physical abuse of that child. Research supports the hypothesis that the behavioral patterns of abused children tend to invite further abuse (Bakan, 1971; Patterson, 1982).

It is important to note that the interactional theory of child abuse *does not blame the child for the abuse.* Blaming the child implies that in some way the child deserved what occurred, but no one deserves to be abused. Rather, the interactional theory identifies and analyzes the factors contributing to the abuse for the purpose of helping prevent and treat this social problem.

The interactional theory of child abuse by adults also applies to sibling abuse. Certain siblings may be more prone to abuse by another sibling because of physical characteristics. In name calling and ridicule, as we have seen in survivors' comments, physical characteristics often become the target of the sibling's emotional abuse. Likewise, the behavior of some siblings may set up situations in which sibling abuse is more likely to occur. For example, when a younger sibling makes excessive demands on an older sibling for attention or the use of toys or clothes, this may provoke incidents of sibling abuse. Again, this is not to blame the younger sibling for the abuse; rather, it is to place responsibility on the parents to be aware of such provocations and to effectively intervene. Using the problem-solving approach, discussed earlier, may help determine goals and agreements about the privacy of possessions and about the respect siblings must show each other.

▪ Ineffective Interventions

Another cause of sibling abuse in some families is the inability of the parents to intervene and effectively stop it because they do not know how. This does not mean they are not interested in or concerned about the abuse. Rather, the way they attempt to stop the abuse is not effective, and consequently the abuse continues and in some instances escalates out of control. Behaviors such as verbal put-downs, name-calling, hitting, and slapping between siblings occur at some time in all families. It is not abnormal behavior, but effective intervention on the part of the parents generally stops the behavior. The parents may take the problem-solving approach with the children, which gives the message that the behavior should be avoided and will not be tolerated in the family. The parents' effective intervention also prevents the behavior from escalating into abuse.

Ineffective interventions, by contrast, do not give this message. The children are not instructed on how to avoid the abusive behavior. Where corporal punishment is used, such as giving the perpetrator a severe beating, the abuse may even escalate. The perpetrator becomes angry at the victim for reporting what happened and in retaliation increases the abuse of the victim. The victim may be forced not to report the abuse in the future for fear of retaliation.

The victim may also fear the consequences to the perpetrator, as did a survivor who told her parents about the physical abuse she was experiencing from her brothers:

My older brothers received a severe beating when I told my parents how they were abusing me. The severity of the beating, however, discouraged me from ever reporting again what happened because I wanted to avoid a more violent outcome.

A respondent from Tennessee did not tell her parents about her brother's abuse for a similar reason:

There would have been more beatings for everyone all around. Instead of a constant at random sort of violence, there would have been a concerted and pointed effort to make people even more miserable.

This latter comment illustrates two basic principles in the "theory of violence": that violence tends to evoke counterviolence, and that violence in one setting or relationship tends to spread to others (Glaser, 1986). When parents used severe corporal punishment or other violence as the means to intervene in sibling abuse, further violence occurred among the family members. Some respondents described the atmosphere of the home in which they grew up as a "battleground." A culture of violence developed in the family with all family members living in this atmosphere. Verbal and physical assaults become a typical pattern of interaction among family members—between husband and wife, and between parents and children. Researchers are becoming aware that often more than one type of violence occurs in a family, such as spouse abuse and child abuse (Sutphen, Wiehe, & Leukefeld, 1996). In families where both types of violence are occurring, drug and alcohol abuse are prominent. These are being referred to as "multiple abuse families." Survivors' comments to this research suggest that sibling abuse also is prevalent in these families:

> My parents were so busy abusing themselves and each other and us that it was a part of our everyday life.

> My mother abused me physically and emotionally also. She thought I deserved beatings from her and from my sister.

A 36-year-old woman from Indiana described life in her home as a child:

> My parents abused me as bad if not worse than my brothers did. I would miss weeks of school at a time because of bruises, black eyes, etc. I didn't think they would be able to stop my brothers from hurting me when they did it themselves.

The fact that physical abuse was also rampant in some families where sibling abuse was occurring supports the "intergenerational theory of abuse" that is used to explain the physical and emotional abuse of children by their parents. The intergenerational theory states that parents may abuse their children because they were abused themselves. In essence, the parents are modeling with their children the behavior they experienced from their own parents. (Other options, however, are available to the abused child as he or she grows up and becomes a parent. The child may chose not to be abusive because of their negative experience [Kaufman & Zigler, 1987]).

If it is true that victims of abuse may in turn abuse others, the existence of sibling abuse makes the proportions of abuse even more frightening. Applied to sibling abuse, the intergenerational theory of abuse implies that perpetrators of physical and emotional sibling abuse may potentially abuse their own children as well. Likewise, unless the survivors of abuse seek help, they may also be potential child abusers. The survivor of physical abuse by an older brother exemplifies this pattern of sibling abuse in a family:

> The worst fights started around the time I was in third grade. I got a lot of abuse from my older brother. Then I would turn around and abuse my sister. I would get her twice as hard as what I received. As we got older, it got worse.

Although some sibling perpetrators modeled their abusive behavior after that of their parents, not all siblings abuse each other because their parents abused them. Parental abuse is no more the single cause of sibling abuse than any other proposed single cause. All are only partial explanations. Indeed, only a minority of the respondents cited this as a factor in their abuse. Many respondents gave no indication that they had been abused by their parents. Rather, their abuse from a sibling appeared to be related to other factors.

■ Behavior Viewed as Normal

Some parents accept physical and emotional abuse between siblings as normal because they feel that the sibling perpetrator is "going through a phase." They excuse the behavior as appropriate for males, or they accept the behavior as "normal sibling rivalry."

A 46-year-old woman, who has received professional help for her emotional problems that she now realizes relate to her abuse from two older brothers when she was growing up, came to the following conclusion:

> I truly thought the abuse was normal until last year.

A survivor from Washington wrote:

> The abuse was considered normal behavior by my parents, who had no idea what normal might be. I might add that the physical abuse by my siblings was much less than the emotional and sexual abuse by them.

Sibling rivalry has been in existence for as long as brothers and sisters have been around. Literature is filled with examples of siblings attacking one another. The biblical story of Cain and Abel is just one example. The fact that sibling rivalry is so universal suggests to parents that sibling abuse is normal. *Sibling rivalry is normal; sibling abuse is not.* A careful distinction must be made between sibling abuse and sibling rivalry.

Why does rivalry between siblings occur? According to Adele Faber and Elaine Mazlish (1988) in *Siblings Without Rivalry: How to Help Your Children Live Together so You Can Live Too*, the presence of another sibling in the home casts a shadow on the life of the first child. The second and additional children are seen as threats to their well-being. A sibling implies there will be *less*—less attention from the parents, less time with the parents, less energy for meeting their needs. The first child may even think that the parents love the second child more. Thus, the new sibling implies a threat. Psychologist Alfred Adler referred to the birth of a second child as a "dethroning" of the first-born.

Viewing sibling rivalry from this perspective suggests ways parents can intervene to prevent sibling rivalry from becoming sibling abuse. Each child needs to be reassured that he or she is special, important, and loved. Faber and Mazlish stated that parents either intensify the competition between siblings or they reduce it. The hostile feelings between siblings can be driven underground or they can be expressed safely in the problem-solving approach to handling sibling differences. Fighting and abuse between siblings can be exacerbated or cooperation can be encouraged as a realistic alternative. Ineffective parental interventions, such as the use of corporal punishment, only exacerbate the abuse and place the perpetrator and victim more firmly in their respective roles.

A respondent from New York stated that sibling abuse does not occur in a vacuum but is a learned behavior. It may be learned from other children in school, from television, where violence often is portrayed as a way of conflict resolution, or from parents who use violence to settle differences. Another respondent:

> My mother was as abusive toward me as my brother was. He simply followed her behaviors. My mother, in a sense, gave him permission to abuse me.

Indeed, this mother as a role model may have inadvertently taught the brother how to abuse his sister. Similarly, when a parent resorts to beating the perpetrator after abuse is discovered, the parent is demonstrating an ineffective approach to conflict resolution—countering violence with violence.

■ Inappropriate Expression of Anger

Another reason one sibling abuses another is to express anger. A respondent from Indiana wrote:

> My oldest brother would come in from school agitated and start literally pushing me and my brothers around. If I spoke *at all*, I was threatened to "Shut my mouth." If I cried, he would slap me or shove me down.

A respondent from Texas described a similar situation in her home with two older brothers:

> My brothers always seemed mad. It never took very much to make them hurt me. It seemed to start if I made a mistake—that is, said something wrong, turned on the TV, or needed something. Then they would yell and call me names. Then it usually started with them hitting me with their fists. If time allowed they used other things, such as sticks, belts, glass, razors, knives.

Victims developed a keen sense of being able to detect the moods of their abusive siblings, especially when they came home from school. They became sensitive to the abusive sibling's becoming angry, even when the anger in no way involved them. From past experience they knew they had to "seek shelter," as if from an impending tornado, because they knew they could easily become the target of that anger. The sibling would often express his or her anger through verbal abuse at first, then would turn to physical abuse.

The way of handling anger is sometimes seen as "letting off steam." Ventilation of anger is viewed as a healthy way of dealing with these feelings in the popular press, on television, and in movies, as well as by some psychotherapists. This is referred to as the "ventilationist" view of anger (Berkowitz, 1973). The idea is that by ventilating one's anger, that anger is dissipated. Obviously, the target of ventilation should not be another person, such as siblings. Those who support the ventilation of anger generally suggest that the target be an inanimate object, such as a punching bag, a golf ball, or a football.

But other research indicates that ventilating anger does not dissipate it and in fact often has the opposite effect—it exacerbates or inflames the anger. Dr. Seymour Feshbach (1964), a psychologist at the University of Colorado, found that children who were encouraged to be aggressive as a way of ventilating their aggressive feelings did not subsequently demonstrate a lower rate of aggressiveness. On the contrary, they behaved in more hostile and aggressive ways than before. Other researchers report that marital couples who ventilate their anger by shouting and yelling at each other felt not *less* angry after doing so but *more* angry (Straus et al., 1980).

Carol Tavris's (1982) *Anger: The Misunderstood Emotion*—based on studies from the social and biological sciences, as well as on interviews—suggested that anger is a social transaction between two persons. Tavris argued that unfortunately the concept of anger has become so reified that it no longer is seen as a concept but as a concrete material object, and anger itself is viewed as a force or energy that warrants discharge. Tavris regards a cognitive approach to anger as more appropriate than the ventilationist approach. In the cognitive approach, individuals work out their differences by talking. The ability to think and to express thoughts and feelings, including feelings of anger, distinguishes human beings from animals. This ability must be used in the resolution of anger. The problem-solving approach to conflict resolution socializes even small children to work through their differences rather than merely ventilating their anger or "blowing off steam." The cognitive approach requires individuals to state how they feel when they are angry, what it is that makes them feel this way, and how an angry conflict might be prevented when it occurs again (Goleman, 1995). This is a much more effective way of handling anger than "letting off steam" or physically or verbally attacking another person. Parental support for cognitive approaches to handling anger encourages children to appropriately express anger for the purpose of conflict resolution, rather than to ventilate anger merely for the sake of getting it out of one's system.

▣ Influence of Television and Videos

Although participants in the research did not specifically mention the effect television and videos had on their perpetrators' abuse of them, research indicates that abusive behavior can be explained in part by perpetrators' modeling or imitating behavior seen on television, in videos, or in movies. This can occur in several ways:

1. Constant and repeated exposure to violence in the media may *instigate* aggressive behavior in the viewer, depending on the strength of the cue and the readiness of the observer to behave in that manner.

2. Repeated exposure in media programming may have a *disinhibiting* effect in that viewers may more readily engage in aggressive acts, modeling their behavior after what they saw on the television or movie screen.

3. Long-term exposure to violence in the media may have a *desensitizing* effect in that the violence alters the viewers' sense of reality with the result that viewers neither react with revulsion at the violence any longer nor perceive the violence as behavior to be avoided. (Eron, 1980; Eron & Huesmann, 1985; Leyens, Camino, Parke, & Berkowitz, 1975; Paik & Comstock, 1994; Phillips, 1983)

Research demonstrates that playing violent video games can influence children's interpersonal behavior (Irwin & Gross, 1995). In the research, children were found to model physically aggressive acts of the human-like video game characters in their play and in verbally and physically aggressive behavior toward other human beings. Such modeling or imitating of behavior seen in television, videos, and movies may be expected to occur also in sibling relationships.

▪ Factors Associated With Sexual Abuse

In addition to the factors identified from survivors' comments, a model proposed by Finkelhor (1984) for understanding adult-child sexual abuse provides additional information for understanding sibling sexual abuse.

Finkelhor's model for understanding adult-child sexual abuse is based on four preconditions that must be met before abuse can occur. The model incorporates both psychological and sociological factors. The preconditions include the following:

1. The potential perpetrator must have some motivation for sexually abusing a child.

2. The potential perpetrator must overcome internal inhibitions against following through on this motivation.

3. The potential perpetrator must overcome external barriers to following through on this motivation.

4. The potential perpetrator or some other factor must influence, undermine, or overcome a child's possible resistance to the sexual abuse. (Finkelhor, 1984, p. 54)

Precondition 1: Motivation to Sexually Abuse

Precondition 1 suggests that there are reasons for perpetrators' being sexually interested in their victim. Three reasons are suggested for adult perpetrators that may be applicable to sibling perpetrators: emotional congruence, an adult's sexual arousal from children, and blockage. Emotional congruence refers to the fact that an adult may find relating to a child emotionally gratifying. Some adults are more comfortable emotionally relating to a child than to peers because of their poor self-esteem, poor self-worth, or arrested psychological development (Groth, Hobson, & Gary, 1982a, 1982b). Likewise, a sibling perpetrator who generally is older than the sibling victim may be more comfortable relating to a younger sibling than to a peer. Sexual involvement may meet other emotional needs by providing the perpetrator with a sense of power, control, and security that can be achieved with a younger sibling but not with a peer.

Some adults are physiologically aroused by children. This may be true also for an older sibling's sexual interest in a younger sibling victim. Research suggests that males' sexual interest in children may be more widespread than generally thought and may not involve just a small, extremely deviant subgroup of the population. Briere and Runtz (1989) surveyed 193 male undergraduate students regarding their sexual interest in children. Twenty-one percent of the respondents reported sexual attraction to some small children. Of these, 9% described having sexual fantasies involving a child, 5% admitted to having masturbated to such fantasies, and 7% indicated some inclination to have sex with a child if they could avoid being caught. Why sexual arousal is evident or stronger in some adults as compared to others remains largely unexplained. Possible reasons include the sexualization of small children in the media, an offender's history of sexual traumatization as a child, and biological factors such as hormonal levels or chromosomal composition.

Blockage in adult-child sexual abuse refers to adults' inability to have emotional and sexual needs met in relationships with other adults. For sibling sexual abuse this may refer to the inability to meet sexual needs in peer relationships or through masturbation, prompting the individual to turn to a younger sibling who is easily accessible.

Precondition 2: Overcoming Internal Inhibitors

Internal inhibitions may be absent or must be overcome by the perpetrator in order for sibling sexual abuse to occur. Factors cited for a breakdown in inhibition in adult-child sexual abuse cases, which may also relate to sibling sexual abuse, include substance abuse, found in a large number of adult-child sexual-abuse cases (Rada, 1976); psychosis, found relatively rarely (Marshall & Norgard, 1983); and poor impulse control (Groth, Hobson, & Gary, 1982a, 1982b).

Feminist theories add that inhibitions against sexual abuse are lowered when society blames the victim rather than the perpetrator. Blaming the victim provides offenders justification for their behavior (Finkelhor, 1980; Rush, 1980). The view that the home is a man's private domain in which he has the privilege of doing as he wishes, including intrafamilial sexual abuse, may be extended to include older male siblings.

Precondition 3: Overcoming External Inhibitors

Whereas Preconditions 1 and 2 focus on the perpetrator's behavior, Preconditions 3 and 4 focus on the setting or social and cultural environment in which sibling sexual abuse occurs, as well as on the victim. Precondition 3 suggests that external inhibitors outside the perpetrator and child victim must be overcome in order for sexual abuse to occur. Parents are expected to provide a sibling with protection from sexual victimization. When parents are physically or psychologically absent, such as through death, divorce, illness, or extended periods of absence from the home because of employment, the likelihood of sexual abuse increases (Kaufman, Peck, & Tagiuri, 1954; Maisch, 1973). Many sibling sexual abuse survivors reported that their sexual victimization occurred in their parents' absence when an older brother was baby-sitting them after school before parents returned home from work or in the evening when the parents were away. Social and physical isolation of families, as well as the absence of privacy in sleeping arrangements, may also increase a victim's vulnerability (Summit & Kryso, 1978).

Precondition 4: Overcoming the Resistance of the Child Victim

The potential perpetrator must in some way influence, undermine, or overcome a sibling's possible resistance to the sexual abuse. A victim's emotional insecurity or affectional deprivation may make the victim vulnerable to attention and affection from a sibling perpetrator. Lack of sexual information also may increase a victim's likelihood of succumbing to a sibling's sexual advances. Finally, threats of physical harm that older sibling perpetrators use against younger sibling victims also may break down a sibling's resistance to sexual victimization.

■ Summary

Numerous factors cited by sibling abuse survivors have been identified that aid in understanding why sibling physical, emotional, and sexual abuse occur. A model developed for understanding adult-child sexual abuse has been applied to understanding sibling sexual abuse. Additional factors not suggested by the respondents to this research may also be identified through further research. As they are identified, a better understanding of the treatment and prevention of sibling abuse will emerge.

7

Effects of Sibling
Abuse on the Survivor

As an adult I continue to struggle with the effects of the abuse from
from my brother when I was a child—low self-esteem and the
inability to trust others.

A sibling abuse survivor

How does sibling abuse affect survivors as adults? "Time heals all wounds," runs an old adage, but the number of individuals seeking help from mental health professionals and joining support groups for the abused disproves this adage. Physical, emotional, and sexual abuse can have devastating psychological effects on survivors, whether the perpetrator of the abuse was an adult or a sibling, as research documents (Bagley & Ramsey, 1986; Beitchman et al., 1992; Briere & Runtz, 1990; Meuenzenmaier, Meyer, Struening, & Ferber, 1993; Moeller, Bachmann, & Moeller, 1993; Mullen, Martin, Anderson, Romans, & Herbison, 1996). The emotional pain the abuse causes never seems to completely go away, even though the survivor undergoes psychotherapy. Survivors learn to cope with the pain, but the remembrance of the abuse does not disappear.

I get so angry just thinking about how humiliating, degrading
this was. And my brother has been dead for 20 years.

Prior to discussing the effects that being physically, emotionally, or sexually abused by a sibling as a child had on the survivors as adults, some comments should be made about the effects of the abuse on the victims at the time the abuse was occurring or shortly thereafter. Several studies provide a description of the immediate effects of abuse by an adult on a child victim that would also be applicable to victims of sibling abuse. The behavior of 93 prepubertal children evaluated for sexual abuse and 80 nonabused children was examined using the Child Behavior Checklist approximately 4 months after the sexually abused children had been clinically seen for their abuse (Dubowitz, Black, Harrington, & Vershoore, 1993). The sexually abused children had significantly more behavior problems than the nonabused comparison group of children, including depression, aggression, sleep and somatic complaints, hyperactivity, and sexual problems. Similarly, in a study of school-aged children who had been physically abused as compared to a nonabused sample, the abused children displayed pervasive and severe academic and socioemotional problems (Kurtz, Gaudin, Wodarski, & Howing, 1993). The abused children performed poorly on standardized tests of language and math skills, received low performance assessments by teachers, and were more likely than their nonabused counterparts to have repeated one or more grades. A number of the children who were age 14 and up already had dropped out of school. The researchers felt that since physically abused children are often angry, distractible, anxious, and impulsive, it is extremely difficult for these children to learn.

The abuse can affect the survivor in the years immediately following the abuse rather than waiting until adulthood, as the survivors in the present research reported. For example, in a 17-year longitudinal study of 375 subjects who had experienced physical and sexual abuse before age 18 from a family member (mothers, fathers, siblings, stepparents, uncles, cousins), researchers found the abused subjects as compared to their nonabused counterparts demonstrated significant impairments in functioning both at ages 15 and 21, including depression, anxiety, psychiatric disorders, emotional-behavioral problems, suicidal ideation, and suicide attempts (Silverman et al., 1996).

Respondents to the present research were asked how they felt their childhood sibling abuse affects them as adults. They were asked to do this for each type of abuse they experienced—physical, emotional, or sexual. In this chapter, the survivors of sibling abuse tell how their lives as adults, in some instances, 30, 40, or more years later, have been affected by the abuse they experienced as children from a sibling.

■ Poor Self-Esteem

Nearly every respondent to the research, whether a survivor of physical, emotional, or sexual abuse, referred to poor self-esteem. From these responses, it would appear that low self-esteem is a universal effect of sibling abuse.

Indeed, low self-esteem appears to be an effect of all types of abuse—physical, emotional, or sexual—whether by an adult or a sibling. Research on the effects of parents' psychological maltreatment of their children has found that these children tend to feel unwanted, inferior, unloved, and inadequate—symptoms that can affect a person's psychological development (Cavaiola & Schiff, 1989; Cerezo & Frias, 1994; Garbarino et al., 1986; Kurtz et al., 1993; Vissing, Straus, Gelles, & Harrop, 1991). Similarly, for the respondents to this research, the sibling abuse they experienced as children left them feeling that they are in some way inferior, inadequate, and worthless.

> If someone says something hurtful or gets angry, I think they will stop loving me.

> I lack self-esteem and self-confidence. I cling to my husband and am afraid of a lot of things.

> The emotional abuse has severely affected my self-esteem as well as my ability to trust others.

> I am insecure of my abilities. I lack assertiveness for fear I might verbally be assaulted.

One woman was emotionally abused by an older brother and sister when she was growing up. They constantly belittled her and told her the family really didn't want her. She told her mother about the emotional abuse, but her mother would either ignore it or tell her older siblings to stop abusing her but then not follow through when they did not obey. This survivor says that now as an adult,

> I have little confidence in my ability to be genuinely liked or to do something correctly.

A middle-aged woman who as a child was emotionally abused by two older brothers stated:

> The abuse contributed to my low self-esteem and self-confidence. I still have difficulty accepting credit for successes. I have a

continuing sense of being worthless and unlovable despite evidence to the contrary.

Absolute feelings of worthlessness are expressed by another survivor:

> I feel unwanted, unloved. I feel like no one could love me. I feel no one needs or wants me. I feel like no one cares!

Among survivors who were emotionally abused in the form of name calling and degrading comments, poor self-esteem is reflected in the image they have of their bodies. As children, many of the names these survivors were called by their siblings focused on their physical characteristics such as their weight or their attractiveness.

A respondent who was repeatedly told she was ugly, too tall, and fat by an older brother wrote:

> I have a hard time believing I am a slender, attractive woman. At times I feel that I'm fat and ugly, but I know I'm not.

Similarly a survivor from Ohio:

> I grew up hearing how "fat" or "chubby" I was and grew up believing it. Now even when I'm thin, I feel fat.

Another survivor feels this way about herself:

> I have low self-esteem. I feel that I'm not smart. I feel that I'm fat and ugly.

A survivor who was called "cow" by a brother because of her weight problem is still affected by this emotional abuse as a 39-year-old woman:

> I think part of my weight and eating disorder problems are from believing I was a cow and cows are fat. I have a low self-image and self-worth, and at one time they were so low I didn't believe anyone would care if I was alive or not. I'm still on antidepressants.

A survivor of sexual abuse by an older brother:

> I have severe bouts of extreme self-hate.

Survivors of sexual abuse reported their feelings of worthlessness are often associated with feelings of guilt and shame, a combination that frequently ends in self-blame for their victimization. This survivor attempted to cope with her poor feelings of self-worth:

I felt dirty, so I sought baptism and religious experiences to cleanse me.

Although low self-esteem is an effect of sibling abuse, in reality it is not possible to separate poor self-esteem from the other effects of the abuse on the survivors' lives.

■ Problems in Relationships With the Opposite Sex

Women who were physically, emotionally, or sexually abused by a brother reported that the abuse affects their lives in their attitude toward males. These attitudes may be described as distrustful, suspicious, fearful, and even hateful. Female survivors of a brother's abuse experienced emotions that appear to have been transferred to men in general. This has significantly affected their ability to relate to men and especially to form intimate relationships with them. The abuse that some respondents experienced from a brother while growing up has influenced their decision not to marry.

I am uncertain of men's real intentions. I see them as a source of pain.

A 44-year-old woman from North Carolina was physically abused by a brother who threatened her with even more severe abuse if she ever reported his abusive behavior to their parents. She wrote that now,

I have no tolerance for men and I am afraid of them.

A respondent from Maine who was abused by an older brother was talking about this abuse later in life with her mother. Her mother confirmed that the brother had begun to abuse her when she came home from the hospital following her birth. This survivor described the effect the abuse has had on her life:

I continue to be constantly on alert toward certain men and have difficulty controlling my instinctive fear and anger that I feel.

A similar feeling was voiced by a respondent from Idaho:

Other than my husband, I am not comfortable in the presence
of any man in any given situation without knowing I have a
way out.

A 34-year-old single woman had been the victim of physical abuse by
an older brother and foster brother:

I do not trust men. I wish I could get along in life without them.

A California respondent:

I have a lot of fear of men and tend to use my mind and intellect
to push men away and intimidate them the same way I was
intimidated. I have a lot of difficulties in my relationships with
men. I tend to disagree a lot and to be very afraid/contemptu-
ous of a man's need for me.

A respondent from Chicago wrote:

I do not trust men. I fear them. I have been unable to marry. I
choose inadequate men to be involved with. I have a fear of
intimacy.

Female survivors of sibling abuse who have married feel the impact of
the abuse in their relationship with their husband. One survivor finds
it difficult not to view her husband as similar to her emotionally abusive
brothers:

I overreact to my husband's actions. Sometimes I doubt his
motives for doing things and accuse him of being like my
brothers. I learned not to trust men. I believed they were all evil.

An underlying fear and suspicion of men pervades the female survivors. The fear of entrapment by men that respondents repeatedly described may stem from the restraint under which their brothers held
them while physically abusing them. It may also stem from the entrapment they felt in their family when they pleaded in vain for protection
from their parents. As we have seen, survivors were often blamed for
what was happening, which may have further heightened their feeling
of entrapment.

Some survivors' discomfort with men has affected their religious life,
because in Judeo-Christian religious traditions, God often is depicted
in masculine terms. Masculine pronouns are generally used in Scrip-
tures and prayers to refer to God. Many respondents found it difficult

to conceptualize God as loving, kind, and good and yet also male, when their childhood relationships with males—their brothers and even fathers—could not be characterized as loving, kind, or good. A respondent, who was seriously physically abused by her only sibling, a brother approximately 4 years older, has extreme fear of men, and this fear affects her religious views:

> Prior to over 3 years of counseling, my concept of God was very warped. I saw Him as someone who was out to destroy or terrorize me.

For female survivors of sexual abuse by their brothers, the abuse has affected their ability to form intimate relationships with other males. A respondent from Louisiana wrote:

> I have difficulty trusting others in relationships. I am also very competitive with men and feel that I have to prove myself that I am equal.

A survivor from Washington:

> I feel angry with men, like all men will hurt you sexually. I feel like I owe them sex and I can use it to keep men. Sex is my tool.

A New Jersey survivor:

> Deep emotional or intimate relations with men are difficult. I feel like they are only trying to control me mentally and sex is just another form of male domination.

Another survivor is unable to relate to men:

> The emotional abuse I experienced from a brother has completely destroyed any possibility of closeness or intimacy with a man.

Another survivor:

> I have developed a very strong mind that I often use as a weapon with men to push them away. I am very vulnerable to intrusiveness and humiliation and so tend to either distance myself or pick men who are distant or nonintrusive. Yet all the men I have been with have a sadistic streak similar to my brother's abuse, only it doesn't show on the surface so much. My brother's abuse of me came out of a tremendous amount of pain so I tend to pick men who are in a lot of pain too.

Sibling abuse appears to have a similar effect on male survivors. A 36-year-old male found that his marriage is affected by the abuse:

> It ruined whatever self-esteem and self-worth I could muster. It drove me away from people in school thinking no one would like or love me if they knew the real me. This attitude is still prevalent today. This combined with the parental emotional abuse has just about ruined my life totally. It has affected my marriage immeasurably because I feel like if I get close, I'll get hurt. So, right now, 13 years into marriage, I honestly haven't got an intimate relationship.

A middle-aged male who had been physically abused by a brother 4 years older feels that the abuse has affected his marriage:

> I was a victim. As an adult, I created another victim. All the anger and resentment I had in me I took out on my wife. She took all she could take. She is now divorcing me. I've lost the best thing that ever happened to me.

▪ Difficulty With Interpersonal Relationships

Some survivors have difficulty relating not only to members of the opposite sex but to anyone, regardless of gender.

One woman wrote that the abuse she experienced currently affects her relationship with her own child. She said that "often she has been too hard" on her own son. She is one of several respondents who said she would have only one child so there would be no opportunities for sibling abuse in her family.

> It is hard for me not to repeat patterns of learned behavior. The verbal abuse is the hardest one for me to stop. I'm very aware of defending my boundaries. I'm still struggling with giving my son his own boundaries; however, my son and I have continued therapy to help us individuate. I'm too fearful of enmeshment and repeating earlier cycles to rely on my subjectivity to intercept what I'm too close to see. I doubt my parenting ability.

The difficulty that respondents have in interpersonal relationships is often related to their low self-esteem.

I do not stand up for myself. I accept things without questioning.

A physically abused survivor:

I still have a tendency to avoid conflict, back off, clam up.

Suspicion and distrust of others is evident in this survivor's comments:

I am afraid that everyone is going to abuse me in some way. I do not trust anyone. I feel in everything people say or do that they want to hurt me. I always want to take the blame for any mistake made or I feel that everyone is blaming me.

A respondent from Washington described the impact of the abuse on her interpersonal relationships:

I find it difficult to relate to others. I am not afraid of people or hate them. I find no desire to reach out to others socially or emotionally. Mostly, I simply want to be left alone except, of course, for my husband and two sons. We are extremely close and happy.

A middle-aged divorced woman from Maine who had been abused by a younger and older sister described these effects of her abuse:

I'm angry. I feel my self-esteem has been diminished. I act out in more sophisticated, socially acceptable ways. My anger is directed toward peers at work as though they were my sister.

A Washington resident was abused by an older sister:

It has made me *very* cynical—untrusting of those who attempt to get close quickly. I grew up feeling if your own family doesn't like or want you, who will?

Those survivors of emotional abuse who responded by verbally abusing the perpetrator in turn have felt the impact in the way they often communicate with other adults. One such survivor wrote

I still have an abusive tongue. My mouth is a big weapon. It keeps people at a distance.

The physical abuse experienced by some survivors has impaired their ability to have physical contact, even of a nonsexual nature, with other adults. Two adult women wrote:

I get very afraid and shrivel when anyone is physically forceful
with me—even if they are being playful or roughhousing, I get
terribly upset and tremble. When I'm frustrated, I tend to gently
or playfully slug the person. I have a hard time touching people
without it being a playful bop or light punch in the arm. When
I do hug someone, I'm very wimpy because I'm afraid my touch
will hurt them.

A 27-year-old woman who was physically abused by an older brother
and younger sister had difficulty as a college student with interpersonal
relationships. She ascribes these problems to the abuse she experienced
from a sibling as a child:

It took me until my 3rd year of college to really realize and get
under control my own rage when frustrated, to really act upon
not yelling at my roommates, threatening them, or throwing
adult temper tantrums.

Difficulties in interpersonal relationships impair the following survivor's ability to hold a job:

I believed my needs were not important. I believed I had
nothing to offer anyone. It is impossible for me to trust. Holding
on to a job has been very difficult. I expect friends, boyfriends,
employers to treat me as my brother did. I struggle in almost
all aspects of life.

The difficulty some survivors experience in their interpersonal relationships may take the form not of overt conflict with other adults but of
compensating for their poor feelings of self-worth. These individuals
seem to be trying too hard to please others, which interferes with their
ability to form good interpersonal relationships.

A survivor from the Midwest, who holds a graduate degree from a
university, was the target of emotional abuse from an older and younger
brother, partly because of her achievements in school.

Until I went into psychotherapy one year ago, I did *everything*
I could to be approved of by my family—worked all of the time,
spent money for their needs at special occasions, etc., just to
have them tell me I was okay. They continued to downgrade
my profession and my education. I was always trying to be
perfect and took all responsibility for my family. Unfortunately,
I married someone who had two adult children that treated me

as my brothers did and I went through the same dance for them too.

▪ Repeating the Victim Role in Other Relationships

A significant effect of sibling abuse is that survivors may as adults enter relationships in which they are revictimized. The survivors choose friends and mates that place them in situations where they again become victims. This phenomenon appears to relate to the survivors' feelings of low self-esteem and worthlessness. Their behavior gives the message to others that they are worthless and deserve to be used and abused, like the survivor who described herself as "a doormat" in her relationships with men.

Research on adult-child sexual abuse indicates that the survivors are also likely to continue being abused as adults (Faller, 1989; Herman & Hirschman, 1977; McGuire & Wagner, 1978; Summit & Kryso, 1978). Child sexual abuse survivors may internalize their victimization to the extent that they regard the abuse they experienced as normal. Thus, they may form dating relationships and choose mates who continue to abuse them as they were once abused. A similar phenomenon occurs among women who have been battered by their husbands. They frequently will leave one abusive relationship and enter into another, thereby continuing their role of victim (Walker, 1994).

A 35-year-old woman who was abused by an older brother reflected on the abuse and the impact it has had on her life as an adult. (Note also that she touches on the theme of power when discussing why she felt her brother abused her.)

> I now know that my brother hurt me because he needed something desperately from me that he felt he didn't have himself. He felt weaker than me. I tend to pick men now who are weaker than me and need a lot. Then I push them away. I also pick men who have a covert sadistic streak.

A girl abused by her brother or sister may grow up to marry a man who abuses her and she becomes a victim once again. A respondent from California wrote:

> It took me into my 30s before I began to see a pattern from the abuse I experienced from an older sister. I chose a first husband

who abused me. Also, I tend to constantly be doing too much
as if to make me feel better.

A respondent has experienced abuse as an adult, having been physically
abused by a sibling as a child:

> The abuse from my childhood made me think that was normal.
> It made me stay in an abusive adult relationship and think it
> wasn't so bad. It took a long, long time until I was able to call
> for the police to come to our home and then only after much
> counseling.

A respondent from Indiana had a similar experience:

> Being abused by someone I thought I was suppose to love set
> me up for further abuse from mates. I developed *very* unhealthy
> boundaries. I suffered through 3 years of abuse in my first
> marriage.

These comments indicate that being raised in an atmosphere of abuse
by a sibling, and in some instances also by a parent, may present a
message to the victim that abuse is normal behavior. Unless a child
abuse victim from a sibling or parent has a corrective emotional experience, such as visiting the homes of friends whose families do not abuse
each other, the child has no way of knowing that the abuse is not normal
behavior. A respondent voiced these feelings:

> The abuse I experienced as a child from a sibling made me think
> that was normal, that I deserved it. I still find myself getting
> into abusive relationships. The abuse I experienced made me
> not trust people. I have low self-esteem and feel shame.

Therapy and support groups for abuse survivors represent significant
opportunities to experience nonabusive interpersonal relationships.

■ Overly Sensitive

Sibling-abuse survivors, especially of emotional abuse, described themselves as being overly sensitive to the comments of others. This appears
to be due to the ridicule and degrading comments they experienced
from their sibling as children. It is as if they expect the ridicule and
degrading comments to continue from people in their adult life. Thus,

they look behind the positive messages they receive from others for hidden negative meanings.

> No matter what compliments I receive or deeds accomplished, I continue to feel like a hopeless, incompetent person. I am very sensitive to criticism. I do not trust others nor expect them to like me. So, I have few friends and seldom share my feelings with others. I am frequently depressed and have planned numerous suicide routes though never attempted any.

> I am *overly concerned* with what others think of me. I need constant reaffirmation and tend to read into everything something negative or critical of myself. I get really hurt when anyone says anything remotely insensitive or critical.

Another survivor is unable to handle criticism because of this:

> I would feel every mistake I made indicated what an awful person I was.

This survivor stated that only after therapy has she been successfully able to cope with her hypersensitivity and her poor self-esteem.

▪ Continued Self-Blame

Survivors of sibling sexual abuse often blamed themselves for the sexual abuse by a sibling. Survivors found themselves repeatedly thinking that they had allowed themselves to be sexually abused, even though in reality there probably was nothing at the time that they could have been done to prevent it, unless they had been empowered by their parents against sexual abuse. Unrealistically, some survivors now as adults continue to blame themselves.

A respondent from Idaho was made to feel responsible for her sexual abuse by an older brother and the impact it has left on her as an adult:

> I was told by several women and especially by my older sister that it was *my* fault because of the way I dressed and carried myself. I am very self-conscious now as an adult of how I dress. I do not like or wear short skirts. I prefer turtle necks and sweaters and high-necked blouses. I do not accept compliments very well from men, other than my husband.

One respondent at the age of 4 was paid a quarter by her older brother to perform oral sex. She complied largely out of fear that if she didn't he would hurt her.

> I have punished myself for 22 years for taking that quarter from him. I don't like myself.

A tendency to blame oneself for the abuse is also illustrated by a survivor from Arizona who stated that she feels guilty for not being able to prevent her traumatic childhood. This is an example of what mental health professionals call "stinkin' thinkin'": an absence of reality in how the survivor perceives what happened. The dissonance between what should have happened and what actually occurred is assumed by the survivor through self-blame, when in fact the circumstances were such that there was little the survivor could have done differently. The survivor, for example, had not been empowered by her parents to say no to sexual assault, and her parents did not protect her.

A parent blaming a victim for sexual abuse can be devastating, not only at the time the abuse occurs but also as the child grows into adulthood. Carolyn Agosta and Mary Loring (1988) are the cofounders of Ending Violence Effectively (EVE), a private Denver treatment center for survivors of violence, especially rape, child sexual abuse, and other forms of family violence. They have used their own experiences as survivors of sexual assault to aid other survivors. Over 1,200 survivors, ranging in age from 2 to 84 years, have participated in their treatment program. Agosta and Loring believe that the parental response of blaming the victim reinforces feelings of guilt in the survivor even in adulthood:

> The adult retrospective victim has an immense feeling of guilt and responsibility for her behavior as a child. "How could I have let this happen to me?" asked one woman, whose victimization began at the age of 5, when her uncle first raped her. Intellectually, survivors are able to see such thinking as ridiculous, but emotionally, they cannot accept their inaction and inability to protect themselves. They have difficulty accepting the total feeling of helplessness they experienced.
>
>   Further, as children, they were directly or indirectly told that they were responsible for what happened, either by the perpetrator, the person they told, or others around them. (pp. 119-120)

Research shows that feelings of self-blame and stigma (feeling ashamed, tainted) linger into adulthood for individuals sexually abused as children and may influence adult psychosocial adjustment by affecting the survivor's core beliefs about their worth as a person. Struggling with feelings of self-blame and worthlessness may result in heightened levels of psychological distress in adulthood (Coffey, Leitenberg, Henning, Turner, & Bennet, 1996).

■ Anger Toward the Perpetrator

Many survivors of sibling abuse reported that the abuse affects their lives as adults in the anger they repeatedly experience. For some survivors, this was a generalized form of anger, expressed in angry outbursts that could be provoked by various situations. For others, the anger was more specifically directed at men (bosses, male friends, mates) who remind them of their abuser. It is as if all men represent their male perpetrator to them and they perceive that all men will treat them as their perpetrator did.

How angry are the survivors specifically against their siblings who abused them? Each respondent was asked to rate their anger toward their sibling on a five-point Likert-type scale, where 1 meant "Not at all angry" and 5 meant "Very angry." Over half of the survivors of all three types of sibling abuse indicated they were very angry at their perpetrator. Although the highest rating on the scale was a 5, several respondents added higher numbers to the scale to show how intense their anger was toward their sibling perpetrator.

The survivors related their present anger to anger they felt in three phases in their life:

1. The anger they felt *as a child* for their abuse that they were often not able to express because of their parents' inappropriate response

2. A continual festering of the anger *throughout the adult years,* the source of which they often did not know until they sought professional help

3. The anger at their sibling they still experience *today* for the abuse they suffered

Although many respondents had sought professional help, their anger was still a factor with which they had to cope continually.

For some survivors, their anger is inappropriately directed to people in their daily life. A survivor from Maine wrote:

I have a tremendous amount of suppressed anger that erupts occasionally.

A survivor from New York has struggled over the years to control her rage that she has inappropriately directed at times to friends and associates:

I am afraid to think about having children. I'm afraid I may lose control one day and really hurt my own kids.

When the survivors describe how their abuse has affected their lives as adults, their intense anger can be understood. Many of the survivors have not been able to lead normal, emotionally healthy lives. Some have been victims of other types of abuse, which they associate with their sibling abuse. Others have spent an untold number of hours in therapy, some of which has been very painful as they have struggled with the effects of the abuse on their lives. Also their therapy has been extremely costly.

Some of the survivors, however, indicated that they were not at all angry at their perpetrators. Several explanations may be offered for this. One is that these survivors may have already completed psychotherapy and worked through their anger toward their sibling. This does not mean that they have forgotten what has happened to them, but they may have cognitively and emotionally made peace within themselves for the abuse they experienced.

Another reason that some survivors feel no anger toward their sibling may be that they are denying their anger. This may resemble emotional denials made by children of alcoholics. According to research, children who are victims of their parents' alcoholism learn early in life that it is not safe to experience their feelings of fear, embarrassment, loneliness, and anger (Black, 1981). These children learn they must engage in a pervasive process of denial to survive the problems and stress created by their parents' alcoholism. Consequently, they pretend to be happy, and they deny the reality of their emotional pain. For some, this denial process continues into adulthood and creates psychological problems in their everyday functioning. Therapists report that the denial of the emotional pain that children of alcoholic parents experience is frequently also a significant factor in deterring them as adults from seeking professional help for their resultant emotional problems. For some, this denial takes the form of blocking out most childhood memories. It is as if they can't remember what happened to them when they were a child.

Likewise, research on survivors of sexual abuse by adults, such as their fathers or other close family members, indicates that these survivors often have overwhelming feelings of anger toward the perpetrator, but that they respond to these feelings by denying them. It is as if the feelings are too painful to be recognized and must be denied (Blake-White & Kline, 1985).

A 38-year-old woman wrote:

> I'm realizing how sketchy my memories of my abuse are. I guess like most people, I've blocked out an awful lot of it.

Harriet Goldhor Lerner (1985), in her book titled, *The Dance of Anger*, described the way many women who are survivors of various types of abuse attempt to handle their anger:

> Most of us have received little help in learning to use our anger to clarify and strengthen ourselves and our relationships. Instead, our lessons have encouraged us to fear anger excessively, to deny it entirely, to displace it onto inappropriate targets, or to turn it against ourselves. We learn to deny that there is any cause for anger, to close our eyes to its true sources, or to vent anger ineffectively, in a manner that only maintains rather than challenges the status quo. Let us begin to unlearn these things so that we can use our "anger energy" in the service of our own dignity and growth. (p. 10)

Lerner asserted that anger is inevitable whenever a person is a victim, is taken advantage of, or is manipulated and used. Unfortunately, the ways people generally manage their anger is ineffective in the long run. These ineffective ways of managing anger include silent submission, ineffective fighting and blaming, and emotional distancing. They were evident in many of the comments of survivors of sibling abuse.

Lerner provided valuable advice for sibling abuse survivors (although her book is not specifically addressed to that audience). She suggested that survivors ask themselves two questions. The first is: What unresolved and unaddressed issues with an important other person, in this instance a sibling, are getting played out in your current relationships?

The anger that a sexual abuse survivor directs at someone else, such as a mate, child, or boss, may be anger that the survivor feels toward the perpetrator but is inappropriately transferring to other relationships.

The second question is: How is the misdirected anger being maintained or kept alive? Why do people persist in inappropriately expressing this anger at those around them, instead of at the perpetrator? Are there payoffs in doing so?

Judi Hollis (1985), in *Fat is a Family Affair*, described the relationship between anger and eating disorders. Some respondents to the present research noted that they have eating disorders and are bulimic or anorexic. Hollis feels that people with eating disorders use food to push down the anger within them that they are attempting to deny. On the outside the survivor may smile ingratiatingly, and seem not at all angry, but in reality they may be seething with anger. Besides avoiding anger, the survivor may also withdraw from other social contacts. A recurring cycle develops, in which the survivor uses food to gain pleasure and solace.

The survivor's anger at their sibling and in some instances at their parents make it difficult for them to maintain any contact with their families of origin. Many of the survivors have had very little contact with their families of origin because of the abuse and the painful feelings they still experience as a result of this. Survivors reported avoiding their families of origin because seeing the family reminds them of the abuse. Some survivors even experience panic attacks in the presence of their perpetrators at family gatherings (Gelinas, 1983).

A survivor of sexual abuse from four older brothers wrote:

> There is still a lot of resentment toward my parents for being so irresponsible. I blame them for some of the confused feelings I have regarding sex. In fact, I blame them much more than I do my brothers because my brothers were just victims as myself.

■ Sexual Dysfunctioning

An effect that survivors of sexual abuse by a sibling in particular noted is in their sexual functioning. Two kinds of reactions were reported: one was the avoidance of all sexual contact, and the other was sexual compulsiveness or promiscuity.

Some female survivors reported that because of their sexual abuse by an older brother, they have an aversion to sex, sometimes even in marriage. A respondent, whose sexual abuse began at age 8 and continued several times a week during her teenage years wrote:

> I've spent 8 years in therapy for sexual abuse. I still freeze up when I'm touched in the vaginal area, which makes sex *very* unfulfilling and has been a big factor in the break-up of my relationships.

Another survivor:

> I have been deeply affected by the sexual abuse from my brother. Even after years of therapy, it's hard for me to be truly open sexually with a man. I often experience shame and disgust around sex and tend to focus on the man's experience and pleasure rather than my own. I have a hard time initiating sex. I often experience myself as a sexual object to be used and contemptuously discarded by men.

Some survivors regarded their sexual abuse as a child as the reason for their inability to marry or their fear of marriage.

> I am scared every man is going to make sexual advances toward me. I am afraid of ever getting married because I am afraid my husband might abuse me.

> I feel uncomfortable with men, do not trust them, and wonder if I will ever be able to be married to a man of excellent character and moral quality and have a healthy home life.

A 35-year-old woman who feels that her sexual abuse as a child affected her adult sexual identity described being raped by an older brother several times a week. She told her parents about the sexual abuse, and when they confronted him, he denied it. The survivor's mother believed the brother and punished her for "lying." The survivor's sexual abuse by her brother intensified after this.

> The abuse made me so hate my body at so early an age that I became a transsexual and have lived as a man nearly all my adult life. I have yet to have surgery, but still hope to. The constant rejection of my body and self by my mother, and what is abuse but rejection at its worst, is, I have no doubt, the basis

of my transsexualism. And it wouldn't surprise me if it's behind
far more instances of transsexualism.

Other survivors' responses to their sexual abuse was of an opposite
nature: sexual compulsivity or promiscuity. Some respondents described their sexual compulsivity in their adolescent and later years. A
survivor from Tennessee wrote:

> I allowed others to take sexual advantage of me. I was sexually
> abused in my first marriage. I struggled for years with not
> knowing what normal, healthy sexual experiences were.

A respondent from Texas described her promiscuous behavior as an
attempt to punish men for her abuse by her brother:

> I became very sexually active after leaving home at 20, not
> wanting to have meaningful or strong relationships with any-
> one, but having sex with many men and never seeing them
> again so that they might have a feeling of being used and hurt.

Another woman responded to her sexual abuse as a child by becoming
promiscuous:

> I was promiscuous as a college student. I had extreme difficulty
> telling a man what I needed in a relationship. I felt I had to give
> a good performance. I had absolutely no self-confidence. I
> equated sex with love.

A female survivor from Indiana described the impact of being sexually
abused by a sibling:

> It resulted in profound confusion about intimacy, sexuality, and
> my own body. It prevented me from recognizing inappropriate
> behavior and left me open to later abuse by others. It prevented
> establishment of a firm sense of boundaries, so that I have
> difficulty respecting and protecting my boundaries. The result
> is I have spent my life either avoiding contact or in dysfunc-
> tional relationships. It resulted in a numbing of emotions to
> avoid the painful affect associated with the abuse.

Sexual acting out or promiscuity may be understood as the survivors'
unconscious effort to overcome and deny their feelings of powerlessness, shame, and rage that resulted from their childhood sexual exploitation. The traumas of childhood sexual abuse that contain elements of

distrust, secrecy, danger, and physical or emotional abuse are often recreated in the survivors' promiscuous encounters in adulthood.

The survivors' promiscuity may also be viewed as a confusion of the boundaries that delineate affection, sex, and abuse. This confusion, labeled as "traumatic sexualization," is the process of shaping a child's sexuality in developmentally inappropriate and interpersonally dysfunctional ways (Finkelhor, 1984). Examples of "traumatic sexualization" include a child being forced to engage in sexual activity that is developmentally inappropriate for the child's age, and a child being rewarded for sexual activity. The latter gives the child the message that sex can be used to get attention, privileges, and whatever he or she wants. Sexual abuse may also fetishize and give distorted importance to particular parts of the body.

A gay male survivor who was sexually abused by an older brother wrote that abuse has affected his sexual functioning as a homosexual:

> The abuse affected me in tremendous ways. I became a doormat. My early homosexual experiences were very passive on my part. I tried to make friends by doing things for them. I spent all my money and ended up with no friends. I have difficulty with the relationship I now have. I don't relate well sexually with him. I know now I need help to deal with the child inside me.

The findings of several studies on adults who were sexually abused as children support the comments of survivors of sibling sexual abuse in this research about sexual problems (Bagley & Ramsey, 1986; Briere & Runtz, 1987; Kinzl, Traweger, & Biebl, 1995). Briere (1984) and Meiselman (1978), using samples of adults who had been sexually abused as children and control groups of persons who had not been sexually abused, found the sexual abuse survivors had a higher percentage of sexual problems than the control group. Sarwer and Durlak (1996) investigated 359 married adult women who sought sex therapy with their spouses. A high percentage of these women had experienced sexual abuse as a child. The study also found that childhood sexual abuse involving physical force and penetration were predictive of an increased likelihood of sexual dysfunctioning. Studies also indicate that an unusually high percentage of both male and female prostitutes report being sexually abused as children (Blume, 1986; Janus, 1984; Silbert & Pines, 1983).

▪ Eating Disorders, Alcoholism, and Drug Abuse

Research shows a relationship between sexual abuse as a child and bulimia nervosa in adult women. Seventy-two women suffering from bulimia nervosa were compared with 72 matched controls who did not display bulimic symptoms (Miller & McCluskey-Fawcett, 1993). Rates of self-reported sexual abuse were significantly greater in the women diagnosed as bulimic. The researchers suggested the eating disorder may have developed in an attempt to cope with sexual victimization.

Some respondents to the research reported that sibling abuse has affected their adult lives in the form of eating disorders. A respondent who is a survivor of sexual abuse by both her brother and father associates her eating disorders with her abuse:

> I have an eating disorder—bulimic—and am at times anorexic. These have to do with the denial of needs and the shame and hate I have regarding taking things into my body.

In addition to eating disorders, 25% of the respondents to the research reported having a substance abuse (drug or alcohol) problem. Drugs and alcohol may play a self-enhancing or self-medicating role against feelings of low self-esteem and other psychosocial problems that survivors experience (Cavaiola & Schiff, 1989). One survivor wrote:

> I still tend to blunt my feelings or drown them in booze. I am in Alcoholics Anonymous.

Other research has indicated that there is a high incidence of sexual abuse in the histories of female drug abusers. Two researchers, Benward and Densen-Gerber (1975), interviewed 118 women who had been patients at Odyssey House, a psychiatrically oriented residential community treatment center for drug abusers. Of the 118 women interviewed, 44% (52) had been sexually abused by a blood relative or someone with close social ties to the victim and her family. Twelve percent of these abusive experiences were with a sibling. Forty-five percent of the abusive incidents occurred when the victims were 9 years old or younger; 73% occurred when they were 12 years or younger. The reactions of the women in that research are the same as the reactions of the survivors in this research. Both sets of survivors reported that the incident remains vivid in their childhood memories. As they grew older, they questioned whether adults, especially males, could be trusted to protect and care for them. Benward and Densen-Gerber feel that the girls who passively consented to the sexual encounter had the greatest psychological burden to bear. They could tell no one about what happened, and they attempted to mask how they really felt by pretending that nothing had occurred. These survivors reported feelings of confusion, humiliation, and guilt and described the incident as a bad dream from which they hoped to awaken.

Other studies indicate rates as high as 30% to 44% of substance abusers report incidents of childhood sexual abuse (Cohen & Densen-Gerber, 1982; Leonard & Blane, 1992; Pernanen, 1991; Rohsenow, Corbett, & Devine, 1988). For example, in a study of men admitted for treatment of alcoholism to the Alcohol Rehabilitation Department at Camp Pendleton Naval Hospital, 30% admitted during treatment that they had been sexually victimized during childhood (Johanek, 1988). Another study compared individuals who had been sexually abused by a family member with individuals who had not (Edwall & Hoffman, 1988). The study found that the incest survivors were more frequent users of both alcohol and stimulants than the nonincest individuals and that they were also more likely to have started their drinking before the age of 9.

Singer, Petchers, and Hussey (1989) found that adolescents with histories of sexual abuse and adolescents not known to have been sexually abused had significant differences in drug and alcohol use patterns. Their study found significant differences in the regular use of cocaine and stimulants between those who had been sexually abused and those who had not. Statistically significant differences also were found in the frequency of drinking, the frequency of drug use, the number of times drunk, and the number of times high on drugs. The data appear to suggest that mood-altering substances may help abuse survivors satisfy some of their interpersonal needs and may affect the way victimized individuals deal with their emotional difficulties.

▓ Depression

Respondents repeatedly referred to experiencing depression as adults, and they directly associated their depression with the sibling abuse they experienced as children. Research shows that depression is evident already in children shortly after abuse has occurred. In a sample of 39 girls aged 6 to 12 who had been referred for evaluation of suspected child sexual abuse, 67% of the children could be classified as experiencing symptoms consistent with a diagnosis of depression (Koverola, Pount, Heger, & Lytle, 1993). The severity of the abuse was not significantly correlated with the depression intensity scores. The effect of depression, if not noted in victims at the time of the abuse, was obvious for the survivors in adulthood, as the respondents to this research reported.

When asked how her sexual abuse by a sibling affects her as an adult, a 42-year-old woman responded:

Terribly! I have seriously considered suicide. I experience severe depression requiring medication.

Studies of adult survivors of childhood sexual abuse, not necessarily by a sibling, have reported high incidents of depression (Bagley & Ramsey, 1986; Sedney & Brooks, 1984). Researchers Briere and Runtz (1988) studied a nonclinical sample of 178 university women and found that approximately 15% had had sexual contact with a significantly older person before age 15. Those who had a sexual abuse history showed greater depressive symptoms than those who did not. Their depression may relate to a sense of powerlessness that they experienced at the time of the abuse and that they continue to experience into adulthood.

These survivors have been left with the feeling that they can do nothing about what occurred, such as the survivors of sibling abuse who told their parents but were not believed or whose parents ignored the situation. One such survivor felt this way both when her sexual abuse was occurring and when her parents failed to believe her:

If you can't trust and depend on your own family members, your siblings and parents, whom can you trust?

Feelings of powerlessness, hopelessness, despair, and depression continue to haunt the survivors into adulthood.

Respondents to the research were asked if they had ever been hospitalized for depression. Twenty-six percent (39) responded affirmatively. Because so large a proportion have been *hospitalized* for depression, it may be assumed that even more have sought help for depression on an outpatient basis.

Some survivors' depression was so severe, it led to suicide attempts. Thirty-three percent of the respondents reported having attempted suicide. Research shows a relationship between childhood sexual abuse and suicidality (Briere, Evans, Runtz, & Wall, 1988; Peters & Range, 1995). DeYoung (1982) found 68% of the women who had been sexually abused as girls had attempted suicide at least once, and 50% of those made more than one attempt. Briere et al. (1988) found that suicide attempts by adult survivors of childhood sexual abuse were made equally by men and women. In the present research, most of the survivors of sexual abuse by a sibling were women, but the impact on the male survivors appears to be equally severe.

Clinically, anger and depression are often seen as two sides of the same coin. Often depression is even thought of as anger that people turn on themselves rather than express to the object of the anger. Depression felt by survivors of sibling abuse may result from the anger that they feel toward their perpetrators, which they inappropriately turn on themselves. This is especially plausible for the several respondents who blamed themselves for the abuse they experienced and whose parents ignored their pleas for help. It appears that the only conclusion they could reach was that somehow they deserved to be abused.

▣ Posttraumatic Stress Disorder

Some survivors said they still experience anxiety attacks and flashbacks of their abuse by a sibling, symptoms of posttraumatic stress disorder, a psychosocial dysfunctioning experienced by individuals who have been traumatized. Anxiety attacks were reported by survivors when they were in situations with someone wanting to be intimate with them or in more general interpersonal relationships with peers and bosses. The anxiety seemed to be reminiscent for the survivor of encounters with their sibling perpetrator where they felt they could not escape from the physical or sexual abuse that was about to occur.

Survivors described flashbacks of their sexual abuse by a brother occurring especially when they were engaged in sexual activity.

> Until recently sexual intercourse was not very enjoyable. Well, I would enjoy it but could never achieve an orgasm. Sometimes sex would become so emotionally upsetting that in the middle

of it I would remember the past and the moment would be destroyed and I'd usually cry.

Another survivor wrote:

Sometimes I will be thinking about what my brother did to me and when my husband approaches me for sex, I will push him away. I find myself daydreaming about the whole nightmare of my sexual abuse. It's like it's still happening and never going to stop.

A survivor from Missouri:

I have a great deal of difficulty in my sexual relationship with my husband. Often I have had flashbacks during sex that are debilitating.

These flashbacks are sudden mental reenactments of the original sexually abusive incidents. They are similar to the flashbacks of Vietnam veterans and of many individuals who have experienced a severe traumatic event. Flashbacks are a symptom of a psychiatric diagnosis known as posttraumatic stress disorder (PTSD). The diagnosis depicts the psychosocial dysfunctioning experienced by individuals who have been traumatized.

Various types of trauma may evoke posttraumatic stress disorder, including serious threats to a person's life or integrity, threats or harm done to family members or friends, sudden destruction of personal property or the community in which one resides, and witnessing someone being seriously injured or killed as a result of physical violence or an accident. Mental health professionals are now adding to this list individuals who have been traumatized by sexual abuse (Patten, Gatz, Jones, & Thomas, 1989). The present research suggests that sexual abuse by a sibling can also create posttraumatic stress disorder in the survivors.

Research shows that a high number of individuals who experienced child sexual abuse also show the symptomatology of posttraumatic stress disorder. One hundred seventeen help-seeking adult survivors of childhood sexual abuse were assessed to determine the relationship between their sexual abuse and posttraumatic stress disorder. Seventy-two percent of the adult survivors of self-reported child sexual abuse met full *DSM-III* criteria for current and 85% for lifetime posttraumatic stress disorder, based on PTSD intensity scores (Rodriguez, Ryan, Rowan, & Foy, 1996). Other studies have reported a similar relationship between child sexual abuse and posttraumatic stress disorder with in some instances even higher rates (Beitchman et al., 1992; O'Neill & Gupta, 1991; E. Saunders, 1991).

Survivors of sexual abuse attempt to push the original event out of consciousness and try to forget it. They may enhance this denial with alcohol or drugs. But in posttraumatic stress disorder, the survivor reexperiences the stressful event—the abuse—that may have occurred over a period of time or as a single event, in various ways. The survivor may have flashbacks and may experience dreams in which the event is relived. When the survivor has experiences that in some way resemble the original trauma or symbolize what happened, such as having sexual intercourse or being alone at night, he or she may experience severe emotional distress. Survivors of childhood sexual abuse by an adult family member sometimes experience severe anxiety later in life at family gatherings when they are once again in the presence of the perpetrator. Sometimes even an after-shave lotion that smells like the one worn by the perpetrator at the time of the abuse can trigger a panic reaction in the survivors.

To avoid such discomfort, survivors who experience posttraumatic stress disorder often limit their contacts with others and withdraw. So, too, do some survivors of sibling sexual abuse in this research. They fear contact with men, they avoid sexual activity, and they avoid contact with their families of origin and with the sibling who abused them.

Parallels can be drawn between the experiences of survivors of sexual abuse and Vietnam veterans. The Vietnam veteran and sexual abuse survivor both complied with what was expected of them. For the veteran, it was to kill and for the sexual abuse survivor, it was to submit to the sexual molestation. Both were told that what they were doing was right and acceptable, even though they may have had doubts about what was being expected of them. The stress experienced by both in the situation in which they were placed was so severe that afterward they denied the events that had occurred or the emotions associated with the event (Blake-White & Kline, 1985).

A common effect of serious trauma is the absence of the very emotions that would be expected in someone who has experienced a stressful event. This effect is referred to as psychic numbing or emotional anesthesia. The psychically numbed person may feel detached or estranged from other persons and lose the ability to enjoy previously enjoyable activities. The numbness may be most pronounced in close relationships with other persons.

▪ Summary

Survivors of sibling abuse have been affected by the abuse in their adult lives in numerous ways, even though the abuse occurred many years before when the survivors were children. These effects include poor self-esteem, problems in relationships with the opposite sex and with others in general, repeating the victim role, being overly sensitive, self-blame for the abuse, anger, sexual dysfunctioning, the abuse of substances, depression, and symptoms of posttraumatic stress disorder.

8

Distinguishing Abusive Behavior From Normal Behavior

My sister's abuse of me was excused by my parents as normal sibling rivalry. I wonder if they think the low self-esteem I have as an adult as a result of the abuse is normal also.

A sibling abuse survivor

Many readers may empathize and even personally identify with the physical pain and emotional suffering experienced by the survivors of sibling abuse, especially in their adult lives. But others may react differently, with skepticism or uncertainty about the phenomenon of sibling abuse itself. Such readers may have no difficulty accepting certain behaviors as abusive, such as the physical assault of one sibling by another with a weapon, or the ridicule of one sibling by another and the parents' joining in. The rape of a younger sister by an older brother is obviously sexual abuse. But skepticism and uncertainty may linger over whether some of the other behaviors are really abusive. The difficulty is not a question of the truth of the survivors' reports; there would be little for the survivors to gain by falsifying responses to a research questionnaire. The uncertainty is in distinguishing abuse from normal interactions between siblings.

All siblings hit, slap, and punch each other. Siblings normally call each other names. Although to a lesser extent, it is not even extraordinary for

161

some type of sexual activity to occur between siblings. The critical question, then, is the distinction between normal sibling interactions and abusive behavior. How can one distinguish between harmful and harmless behavior?

Two brothers, ages 8 and 10, are playing. The younger brother puts a pair of toy handcuffs on his older brother's wrists behind his back, so he can't get out of them. He allows his brother to struggle while he goes into the house to get a snack. Is this physical abuse? A sister calls her brother a name, for example, "butt-head." Is this emotional abuse? A brother and sister aged 2 and 3 are taking a bath together. The brother notices the differences between his and his sister's genitals. He reaches over to check for sure if she really doesn't have a penis. Is this sexual abuse?

The purpose of this chapter is to identify criteria that can be used to distinguish normal interactions from abusive or potentially abusive behaviors. Prior to identifying the criteria, two other issues will be discussed: problems with using "Everyone does it" as a criterion, and the importance of identifying the specific behavior being analyzed.

A word of caution is in order regarding the criteria that distinguish normal sibling interactions from abusive behavior. These criteria should not be applied in an "either-or" or absolute manner. Human behavior is very complex and does not lend itself to easy scrutiny. Many shades of gray can be found in sibling interactions, and questions as to whether a specific behavior is abusive will remain. Considering the physical pain and emotional suffering survivors of sibling abuse experience, it would be wise to err in the direction of protecting the victim in cases of uncertainty.

■ "Everyone Does It"

Every parent is very familiar with a response that children frequently give when confronted about a behavior that does not meet parental approval: "Everyone does it!" This popular view may also be held by parents themselves when they are confronted with sibling abuse. Parents may observe that children continually fight and call each other names. They may recall their interactions with their own siblings when they were growing up. Parents may reach the conclusion that since all children apparently engage in these behaviors, they are normal and even harmless.

All children may, in fact, engage in these behaviors at some time and to some extent, but the fact that many siblings engage in certain behaviors does not justify it or remove its effects on the victim, especially if the victim is not a willing participant.

An analogy may clarify this. Only a few years ago many adults in the United States smoked cigarettes. Even though large numbers of adults smoked, this did not remove the effects tobacco had on human health, as documented in recent years. Thus, the fact that "everyone" did it did not make it appropriate behavior. In recent years, the negative effects of other behaviors that had been generally regarded as socially acceptable have also been identified, including fraternity hazing, drinking while driving, and the recreational use of drugs. The rationale that "everyone does it" certainly does not remove their negative effects.

■ Initial Task: Identify the Behavior

Before trying to distinguish normal and abusive behavior, the behavior must be identified. The specific behavior may be identified by isolating what is occurring from the emotions surrounding the behavior, such as anger, hurt, or shame. The following are three examples of sibling interactions, each of which illustrates a specific behavior.

Example 1: Two siblings, 2 and 4 years old, are constantly fighting over toys. When the 4-year-old chooses a toy with which to play, the 2-year-old chooses the same toy. A toy struggle ensues, and one of them, generally the 2-year-old, ends up crying.

Example 2: Sue is 14 years old. She is very angry with her parents for the limits they have set on her dating. Her parents require that she do no individual dating but only go out with boys in mixed groups. Also, they have established a weekend evening curfew of 10 o'clock. But Mitzi, Sue's 17-year-old sister, is allowed to go on dates alone with a boy to a movie or a school activity. Her weekend curfew is 11 o'clock. Sue is very jealous of Mitzi's privileges, and every weekend she reminds her parents about how unfairly they are treating her. Furthermore, the two girls wage a constant battle over this issue. Recently, the parents overheard Sue call Mitzi "an ugly bitch" after a discussion of their different dating privileges.

Example 3: A mother notices that her 4-year-old son is fascinated by his new baby sister when she is changing her diaper. He seems very curious about her genital area and is always present when diapers are changed.

What specific behavior is occurring in each of the previous examples? In the first example, the behavior is *fighting*; in the second, it is *name calling*, and in the third, it is *observation*, and although the example does not state this, the 4-year-old probably also is *questioning* the mother about the differences in genitalia that he is observing.

▪ Criterion 1: Is the Behavior Age-Appropriate?

The first criterion for distinguishing abusive behavior from nonabusive behavior is the behavior's age-appropriateness. Consider the first example: Is it appropriate for a 2-year-old and a 4-year-old to be struggling over toys? Yes, it is. The 2-year-old is probably simply mimicking his older sibling in play. With whatever toy his older sibling plays, he too wants to play. It is easier to do what "big brother" is doing and it is probably more fun, even though "big brother" doesn't feel this way.

Consider the second example. Jealousy and fighting over differences in privileges are quite age-appropriate between adolescents. They are both struggling with their own identities and attempting to try their wings outside the safe nest of their home. Sue, at 14, does not view herself as less mature than Mitzi and sees no reason why she shouldn't have the same privileges. But name calling is hardly an appropriate way for Sue to handle her anger, although not uncommon.

A word of caution at this point: Even though fighting and jealousy between siblings can be expected to occur, they should not be ignored. Nonabusive behavior can escalate into abusive behavior if effective parental intervention does not occur. Ignoring the behavior will not make it go away. Moreover, constant fighting between siblings is unpleasant, not only for those involved but for those around the behavior.

The critical question is how to intervene. For parents who are having difficulty handling dysfunctional sibling interactions, various avenues of assistance are available. Parent education courses are available to parents through community mental health agencies, churches, and other educational resources. Books that focus on sibling relationships are available at bookstores or public libraries. Examples of such books are *Siblings Without Rivalry* (Faber & Mazlish, 1988), *How to Talk So Kids Will Listen & Listen So Kids Will Talk* (Faber & Mazlish, 1982), *Help! The Kids Are at It Again: Using Kids' Quarrels to Teach People Skills* (Crary, 1997).

Consider the third example: Observation and questioning on the part of a 4-year-old are normal, as is sexual curiosity. The child who has never seen a vagina may be expected to ask why his sister is different. If the 4-year-old child wants to touch his baby sister's vagina, an effective parental response may be to differentiate for the child appropriate and inappropriate touches. This example highlights the importance of children having sexual information regarding appropriate and inappropriate touching relevant to their psychosocial development.

What is age-appropriate behavior? Age-appropriate behavior can be determined in several ways. Professionals with a knowledge of child development may help determine which behaviors are appropriate to a child's developmental stage. Books on child development may assist in making this determination (Vander Zanden, 1993; Zastrow & Kirst-Ashman, 1994). Determining what is age-appropriate behavior can also occur through parents' talking to other parents and sharing information on their children's behavior. The parents of a mentally retarded child, for example, told their friends that their 4-year-old would sometimes crawl on the floor and bark like a dog or meow like a cat. The parents saw this as an example of his retardation. The friends, however, pointed out that their 4-year-old child, who was not mentally retarded, frequently did the same thing. As a matter of fact, they said he had once asked if he could try eating out of a bowl on the floor like the family pets. Thus, the first set of parents learned that this was age-appropriate behavior for their 4-year-old.

On the other hand, some behavioral interactions between siblings are not age-appropriate and should be considered abusive. Consider the following examples. A 10-year-old boy destroys his 3-year-old sister's dolls by pulling out their hair, tearing off a leg or arm, or stabbing them with a knife. An 8-year-old girl composes a song about her younger brother who is overweight. The words make fun of him and call him "tubby." She sings it whenever she is around him and in front of his friends. A 14-year-old boy fondles the genitals of his 3-year-old sister behind a shed in the backyard.

These examples portray three behaviors: the destruction of toys, ridicule through name calling, and sexual fondling. In the light of the age of the participants, especially the perpetrators, these are not age-appropriate behaviors. A 10-year-old boy should have learned by then to respect the toys of other children and not to destroy them. Likewise, an 8-year-old girl may delight in some teasing, but in this instance the teasing is vicious in nature as it is done before her brother's peers. And a boy fondling the genitals of his younger sister is not appropriate behavior at any age. By the age of 14, a boy should be aware of sexual differences between boys and girls and between good touches and secret touches. Moreover, the fact that the behavior is occurring in a clandestine setting implies that the perpetrator has some awareness that the behavior is inappropriate. Also, the younger child is not mature enough to decide whether she wishes to participate.

■ Criterion 2: How Often and How Long Has the Behavior Been Occurring?

Fighting, name calling, teasing, and even some sexual exploration occur between siblings at some time or another and may be considered normal sibling rivalry or simple sexual curiosity. But frequency and duration of the behavior may turn a nonabusive behavior into an abusive behavior. When fighting, name calling, teasing, and sexual exploration occur frequently over a long period of time, the behavior becomes abusive, especially if the perpetrator is admonished to stop but doesn't.

This does not mean that a single occurrence of a potentially abusive behavior between siblings, such as sexual activity, should be minimized. In some instances sexual abuse by a sibling is only a single occurrence, but its effects on the survivor are serious and affect the individual into adulthood. Recall the survivor who at the age of 4 was paid a quarter by her older brother for performing oral sex and who complied largely out of fear of retaliation:

> I have punished myself for 22 years for taking that quarter from him. I don't like myself.

Thus, frequency and duration should not be used as the *only* criteria in determining whether a behavior is abusive.

How long is too long and how frequently is too frequently? Unfortunately, a definite period of times or number of occurrences would be helpful, but such a pat answer is not available. The use of common sense is the best way to answer these questions. When a parent begins to feel uncomfortable about a behavior, the time has come to intervene. For example, when fighting between children who are watching television begins to grate on parents' nerves to the point that they want to go into another room, it has gone on too long. This is especially true if it is a behavior *pattern* that occurs over a period of time. Ignoring dysfunctional sibling behaviors will not necessarily make them disappear.

▣ Criterion 3: Is There an Aspect of Victimization in the Behavior?

A *victim* is someone who is hurt or injured by the action or actions of another. They are unwilling, nonconsenting objects of abusive behavior. The respondents to the research who were abused by a sibling think of themselves as *victims* of their sibling's actions. They vividly recalled what they had experienced 10, 20, and 30 years before. They were victims—the targets of their sibling's physical assaults, the butt of their ridicule, or the object of their sexual abuse.

An individual in the victim role may be a dupe or may have been placed in a gullible position by the other person. Many of the respondents, especially those sexually abused by a sibling, had been placed in the victim role because of their powerlessness. They were duped or enticed to participate in sexual activity, were threatened, or were taken advantage of because of their age. These victims often had little choice but to acquiesce to their sibling's sexual demands because they felt there was nothing else they could do, or they were not mature enough to realize what was happening.

A victim, an unwilling participant, may not even be able to give or withhold consent. The fact that a victim participates in an activity does not mean that this participation was voluntary. A child may be unable to verbally consent to an older sibling's sexual advances because he or she is simply too young. For example, a 2-year-old child is not able to protest her older brother's sexual explorations. Likewise, a mentally retarded or emotionally disturbed adolescent who is the continual object of jokes and ridicule by a sibling may not be able to fend off these verbal assaults.

The question of whether an individual is being victimized can often be determined by assessing how the perpetrator gained access to the individual. If access was gained through game playing, trickery, deceit, bribery, or force, the person who is the object of the behavior is a victim. For example, a 4-year-old girl is bribed with candy to go to a tree house that her brother and his friends have built in the backyard. When she gets there, she is asked to remove her panties and expose herself. An older brother constantly acquires money from a younger sibling on the pretense that the coin size determines its value. In both instances the sibling is a victim and the behavior is abusive.

Another indication of victimization is the emotions surrounding a behavior that the sibling feels. A sibling called a name by another sibling may experience embarrassment or hurt. Sometimes the use of a name is not offensive to the individual who is the target. A husband and wife, for example, may call each other names that out of context would be offensive but that in context are terms of endearment. The emotional reaction of the person who is being called the name may be an important clue to whether he or she is being put into a victim role.

Individuals who have been targets of abusive behavior may not realize their victimization until long after the act. A prepubertal young child who is sexually abused by an older sibling may not realize the consequences of the activity in which she is involved. She may become aware of her victimization only after she experiences sexual dysfunctioning in her relationships with the opposite sex or other problems-in-living.

Victims commonly blame themselves for their victimization. Many of the respondents to the research not only blamed themselves for what happened but were blamed by the perpetrator or their parents. A parallel may be drawn to wives abused by their husbands. A wife may excuse and thereby tolerate her husband's abusive behavior by telling herself that she deserved his anger because she didn't have dinner on time or she was not sensitive to his wishes. That she is a victim may not become clear to her until she joins a group for abused wives and realizes that she cannot always please her husband, that his expectations are unrealistic, and that his actions are abusive. Sibling abuse victims, too, may have difficulty realizing their victimization if their parents blame them and do not protect them.

■ Criterion 4: What is the Purpose of the Behavior?

Another criterion to consider in distinguishing abusive behavior from normal behavior is the motivation of one sibling to engage in a behavior with another sibling. What is the purpose of the behavior?

In most instances of emotional abuse by a sibling, the purpose is to belittle the victim with name calling or ridiculing. This is destructive behavior and thereby abusive. If the victim provoked the perpetrator, both individuals are engaging in abusive behavior and are placing themselves in their roles of victim and perpetrator. Obviously, there are more appropriate ways for siblings to settle differences between themselves. Taking a problem-solving approach would be an effective way to stop abusive behavior between siblings.

When an older sibling, generally a male, sexually abuses a sibling for the purpose of achieving sexual gratification, the purpose of the behavior is not observation but sexual pleasure. For example, respondents to the research reported perpetrators receiving sexual satisfaction, such as through masturbation, by viewing or touching a younger sibling's genitals. In most instances of sexual abuse reported by respondents to the research, the individual who was the target of the behavior was victimized and the behavior was age-inappropriate. Such behavior must be regarded as abuse.

Sexual exploration with the intent of sadism or suffering is also abusive behavior. An older sibling may insert objects into the anus or vagina of a younger sibling with the intention of seeing the sibling suffer. The perpetrator may or may not masturbate. But, again, the activity sets one sibling up as a victim.

In some incidents of sexual abuse, an additional person besides the sibling perpetrator may be involved. Children may be requested or forced to engage in sexual activity because it gives a third party sexual gratification. An older sibling, for example, may encourage two younger siblings to engage in sexual play while the older sibling watches. Or one sibling may encourage another to physically or emotionally abuse a third sibling. In these instances, the behavior is abusive because of the purposes of the co-perpetrator.

A word of caution on the purpose the behavior serves for the perpetrator: Children are frequently not able to conceptualize the purpose of behaviors in which they engage. When parents ask a child who has done something with serious consequences, "Why did you do that?" the child often responds, "I don't know." Although partially defensive, the response may also indicate that cognitive limitations prevent the child from identifying why he or she did something. Children may not yet perceive cause and effect; rather, they engage in behavior at an impulsive level with little thought for the consequences. Nor have children had the range of experiences that enable them to anticipate consequences, especially undesirable consequences. In other words, they lack the maturity to look beyond their own behavior to the consequences.

▪ Supplementary Questions

The following questions may also help in distinguishing abusive behavior from normal behavior:

- In what context did the behavior occur?
- What preceded the behavior?
- What was the victim's contribution to what occurred?
- Was the perpetrator imitating something he or she had seen?
- Was the behavior planned or spontaneous?
- Has the behavior ever occurred before?
- How did the victim feel about what occurred?
- What was the perpetrator's reaction to what occurred?
- Has the perpetrator been confronted in the past about this behavior?

▪ Summary

The criteria and supplementary questions that have been suggested can be used singularly or in conjunction with each other to distinguish abusive from normal behavior. Examining abusive and normal behaviors between siblings in the light of these criteria is not a simple issue. Human behavior includes many gray areas. These criteria may serve as general guidelines for appraising sibling interactions. If the criteria indicate that a behavior is normal but a parent feels discomfort about the behavior, the safest approach may be to regard the behavior as potentially abusive and to intervene appropriately.

9	Preventing Sibling Abuse

Parents must first be made aware of sibling abuse. My parents were in total denial that what my brother was doing to me was abuse.
A sibling abuse survivor

How can sibling abuse be prevented? What specifically can be done? One way to determine how to prevent sibling abuse would be to ask the survivors to identify the best ways of preventing sibling abuse. Respondents to the research were asked to make one suggestion on how to eliminate sibling abuse. The survivors suggested eight ways that sibling abuse can be prevented:

1. Build awareness.
2. Listen to children and believe them.
3. Provide good supervision to children in the absence of parents.
4. Encourage openness about sex.
5. Give children permission to own their own bodies.
6. Seek help if sibling abuse is occurring in the family.
7. Violence-proof the home.
8. Reward good sibling interactions.

▪ Build Awareness

Nearly every respondent commented that "parents must be made aware of sibling abuse—that it can occur in any family and that it can be a serious problem." We may depersonalize sibling abuse by saying to ourselves that these are not people we know. "Abuse like this only happens in families that one reads about in the newspaper—families in trouble with the law, living in substandard housing, families where the parents are drunk all of the time and the kids are on drugs."

Sibling abuse may well be more likely to occur in multiproblem or highly dysfunctional families. But the only families wholly exempt from sibling abuse are those with only one child. It was not possible to determine the socioeconomic background of the respondents' families, but the parents of the survivors were quite well educated. Forty-three percent of the parents had attended college or gone further in their education. The families were moderately religious (meaning that some were not at all religious and some very religious). Thus, an above-average socioeconomic level and religious beliefs do not necessarily guarantee that sibling abuse will not occur in a family. A survivor from Texas who wrote about the importance of religion in her family experienced great emotional pain nonetheless.

> My problem and others is that we come from religious, "looking good" families on the outside but where there was a lot of pain and dysfunctioning on the inside.

Awareness that sibling abuse potentially can occur in any family is a first step toward preventing it. Mental health professionals must be sensitive to the fact that sibling abuse can and does occur, and they must be aware of the symptoms in the victims such as constant fighting or shy, withdrawn behavior by a child who clings to the parent. Mental health professionals must also ask about sibling abuse in adults they counsel for emotional problems. Adult survivors themselves may not link their behavioral, emotional, or sexual problems with the sibling abuse they experienced as a child. Making this link may help them understand and cope with their problems. Unfortunately, mental health professionals' lack of awareness of sibling abuse often prevents them from asking the right questions of their clients. (Of course, not every client who is experiencing problems-in-living is a survivor of sibling abuse.)

A survivor from New Mexico put it this way:

> We must first acknowledge that the problem of sibling abuse can occur—not minimize it or deny it. Once the potential for the problem is acknowledged, then appropriate steps can be taken to prevent the problem.

To build awareness of sibling abuse, individuals and families must be educated about sibling abuse. Local, state, and national organizations that work to prevent child abuse must add sibling abuse to the types of abuse they are fighting. Now that the survivors of sibling abuse have begun to speak out, sibling abuse must be added to child, spouse, and elder abuse. The methods these organizations employ, such as the media and abuse-prevention programs in schools, need to be modified to include sibling abuse.

But the educational process about sibling abuse must be done at many different levels and be done by a variety of individuals. Consciousness must be raised to be sensitive, alert, and aware of the problem. The educational process must be done by many different groups, such as families, schools, churches, the military, and business organizations. A survivor who grew up in a military family laments the support that the military could have provided:

> We were a military family. The military was in *total* denial of alcohol or other domestic problems of their enlisted people. They provided *no* mental health or social support systems to their families.

Teachers can sensitize others to the unrecognized problem of sibling abuse, as can the clergy, physicians, nurses, social workers, psychologists, and psychiatrists.

The process of education can occur in a variety of ways. Business organizations can include brief articles on sibling abuse in their newsletters that are circulated to personnel. Children may be introduced to the subject through social studies and health classes at school. Clergy can refer to it as a social problem affecting families. The public media can cover the subject when doing programming on social issues. Only as individuals and families are made aware of the problem of sibling abuse can it begin to be prevented and treated.

▓ Listen to Children and Believe Them

The survivors frequently lamented their parents' reaction to the abuse they experienced: "If only my parents would have listened to me! If only they had believed me when I told them what was happening!"

In the research mentioned earlier, mothers tended not to believe reports of sexual abuse when they involved a close family member and if the victim was not a small child (Sirles & Franke, 1989). For example, mothers tended to believe a report of sexual abuse if it involved an uncle but not if it were the husband. Adolescents were believed less frequently than preschool-age children. Siblings reporting abuse by another sibling to their parents may also not be believed because parents find it difficult to accept that a member of their immediate family is perpetrating the abuse. Moreover, the parents may have witnessed the abusive behavior, and the behavior of the victim may induce them to disbelieve or ignore the report, or to blame the victim for what happened.

Research shows that children rarely falsely accuse an adult of sexual abuse. When the cases of 287 children who alleged they had been sexually abused were reviewed, only 28 or less than 9% of them could not be substantiated (Cantwell, 1981). In a review of 88 psychiatric papers on children sexually abused by adults published between 1971 and 1978, not a single false accusation was reported (Goodwin, Sahd, & Rada, 1982). Of 64 children seen in emergency rooms who reported being sexually abused, staff concluded that no sexual assault had occurred in only 4 (Peters, 1976). In situations where the report could not be documented, the researcher felt that the family was pressuring the survivor to retract the statements. Although these studies are based on the reports of children who were abused by an adult, their conclusions may be applicable to the reports of children who were sexually abused by a sibling.

A survivor from Canada who was physically, emotionally, and sexually abused by an older brother during most of her childhood documents parental inaction and disbelief from her own personal experience:

> My parents could have believed me when I told them about the abuse or they could have tried to stop it. My parents had no reaction but denial.

A man from Connecticut who had been the victim of physical abuse by two older brothers experienced this as well:

> I would tell my mother about the way my brothers were treating me, but she always brushed it off. I really don't think she cared what they did. At least that's the message I got from her. It didn't pay for me to tell her my troubles.

A survivor from Kentucky who was sexually abused by an older sibling when her parents were away from home advises parents to listen to their children:

> Please listen to your children, even between the lines. I remember every time my parents went out, I'd sit in my parents' room while they got ready to go out and I'd ask them, "Do you really have to go out tonight? Can't you stay home?"

This survivor was trying to give her parents a message, but they really weren't listening.

"Listen between the lines," this survivor urged. In the 1940s, a book was written for psychotherapists, titled *Listening with the Third Ear* (Reik, 1948), whose central message was that to be a good psychotherapist one had to develop the ability to hear what clients were saying and feeling behind their verbal message. Therapists needed a "third ear" to really hear what clients were trying to communicate. Carl Rogers addressed this theme in many of his writings and emphasized that therapists must develop the ability to listen very sensitively to their clients and to empathize with them, to crawl into the client's skin and feel what the client is feeling.

Professionals can teach parents to develop these same skills. In a family therapy session, let us say, a child tearfully reports that his sibling repeatedly hits him and calls him names. The parents quickly brush off the comment or ask what the child did to provoke such behavior. But if the child is hurting, the therapist should encourage the child to discuss what is happening. Professionals can then teach parents to feel, to understand, and to experience what the child is experiencing as well. That is empathy—the ability to feel with someone what they are feeling and experiencing. Parents might complain that the process of empathizing takes too much time, but an empathic response needn't take any more time than a nonempathic one. Adults must develop a sensitivity to what a child is saying or feeling so that the child gets the distinct message that someone is concerned and cares, and if necessary something will be done about the problem.

As professionals help parents learn to respond sensitively and with empathy to children, the parents will begin to see patterns in their children's behavior. They may recognize that a younger sibling is constantly the butt of jokes of an older sibling or that one sibling is repeatedly ridiculed by another sibling because of a personality trait or physical characteristic. When an awareness of behavior patterns develops, appropriate interventions can be made.

The survivor who asked, "Do you really have to go out tonight? Can't you stay home?" was, in her own way, trying to tell her parents something. She could not come out and say what she wanted to say—that it was not safe for her when her parents left. If the parents had been listening with their "third ear," they would have explored what the child was trying to tell them, and perhaps the abuse could have been prevented.

Adele Faber and Elaine Mazlish (1982) suggest some excellent ways that parents can really listen to their children in their very practical book, *How To Talk So Kids Will Listen & Listen So Kids Will Talk*, including cartoons, parent-child dialogues, and exercises. Parents can use these techniques to analyze the ways they typically communicate with their children and the things that may prevent them from hearing what their children are trying to tell them.

Listening to children requires an atmosphere in the home in which the children can talk to the parents, or "open communication." Most children have no one else to talk to about things that are bothering them. Recall the comment of the survivor from Connecticut whose mother gave him the feeling that she really didn't care what his older brothers were doing to him. If as a young boy he felt his mother wasn't interested in his problems, why should he feel comfortable telling his rabbi, priest or minister, a school counselor, or any other adult? Why should he feel they would be interested in him if his own parents weren't?

Essential to open communication is the responsible handling of secrets. Many parents have difficulty with handling secrets. In most instances, children should be told they need not keep secrets from their parents, no matter who told them to do so—another adult, a brother, or a sister—even if the person has threatened to harm them, their pet, or something they own. A parent should assure the child that if he or she reveals a secret, they will be protected and no harm will come to them. The child's secret may be that he or she is being abused by a sibling.

While listening to children, parents and professionals should be alert for signs of physical, emotional, or sexual abuse. Following is a list of such signs; however, caution must be raised that these symptoms can be indicators of other problems-in-living for a youngster, other than just abuse:

- Feelings of worthlessness; low self-image and self-esteem.
- Bruises or marks on the body that the child excuses or cannot explain.
- Withdrawal—preferring to be alone rather than with siblings or friends, living in fantasy.
- A sense of sadness or depression that may be evidenced in low energy level or withdrawal.
- Clinging behavior.
- Fear of being left in the care of a sibling.
- Sexual self-consciousness; feelings of shame about the body.
- Lack of knowledge of sexual behavior or misinformation.
- Persistent and inappropriate sexual play with peers, toys, or self.
- Shyness, fearfulness, mistrustfulness.
- Overly compliant behavior at home or at school.
- Sudden change in school performance.
- Nightmares or other sleep disturbances.
- Unexplained fears.
- Regressive behaviors such as bedwetting, soiling.
- Talking about suicide; a suicide attempt.
- Genital or anal injury or bleeding.
- Genital itching or pain.
- Torn or stained clothing.

The list is not exhaustive; there may be other symptoms of sibling abuse, especially sexual abuse. Virtually any change in a child's normal behavior may be an important warning signal to parents that something is bothering a child. That "something" may be abuse by a sibling.

Numerous respondents reported that they couldn't tell their parents about the sibling abuse. The atmosphere in the home, that is, the relationship of the parents to the children was such that the child would not feel comfortable reporting the incident. Some survivors were afraid they would not be believed and would even be blamed for what happened. Such poor communication processes in which parents don't listen to or talk with their children may be due to the fact that the parents are away from the home, either at work or involved in other activities.

Even when parents are physically at home, they may be psychologically absent. But even though working parents may have fewer clock hours available for parenting, the hours they do spend with their children can be *quality* time in which an atmosphere of care, concern, and understanding is foremost. In a healthy, nurturing environment, sibling abuse cannot develop and grow.

■ Provide Good Supervision to
   Children in the Absence of Parents

The number of children who care for themselves after school or in the evening has grown over recent years due to the dramatic increase in the number of mothers who work full-time. The high divorce rate and the increasing number of mothers with sole responsibility for their children has forced parents to rely on substitutes to care for their children. The maturity of the child who is the caregiver in these situations, and the nature of the interaction between the caregiver and the child, are significant variables for the effectiveness of this arrangement. If the maturity level of the caregiver (older sibling) is inadequate, and if the interaction of the caregiver and child (younger sibling) is dysfunctional, sibling abuse can potentially occur.

The most frequent time for sibling abuse to occur was when the parents were away and the victim was in the care of an older sibling. The survivors repeatedly indicated that the sibling in charge did not know how to handle this responsibility. A survivor from Florida wrote:

> Parents should wake up and realize that just because a child may be the oldest doesn't mean they can take care of the younger children. My folks would always leave us with my older sister. This is when I and my other brothers and sisters suffered. My sister felt she could do anything she wanted to us. She did.

It may be appropriate for an older brother or sister to act as a baby-sitter when the parents go away for an evening, but the parents must provide an environment in which this sibling can appropriately and effectively act as a substitute parent. Optimally, parents should discuss with the sibling in charge, as well as with the other siblings, the rights and responsibilities of each; for example, how long and what television programs they can watch; the foods they may eat; appliances they may use, such as the stove; when their bedtime occurs; and other important items. Equally important, parents should evaluate how effectively the older sibling handled his or her responsibilities while they were gone. They should discuss the arrangement with all the children and if necessary, change their expectations of the sibling in charge and of the other siblings.

Latchkey programs provided in many communities throughout the United States are a vital resource for parents who must work and cannot be at home when the children return home from school. Without such programs, parents may inappropriately send young children home under the care of a sibling who may not be able to handle this responsibility. Communities have been successful in establishing latchkey programs for children in schools or in churches located near a child's home.

Some communities have established telephone support services for children who are home alone after school. Staffed by volunteers, the services can handle a wide range of children's problems, including problems in their relationships with peers and siblings. Although data on the use of these lines to help with sibling abuse are not available, children may be able to use them to discuss sibling-related problems.

Community child-care agencies sometimes offer courses on baby-sitting that older siblings may attend before assuming responsibility for younger siblings. This much needed educational service, however, is rare. Many adults appear to assume that children can step into a substitute parental role with no instruction. Unfortunately, this is potentially a source of problems, including sibling abuse.

■ Encourage Openness About Sex

Encouraging openness about sex does not mean encouraging nudity in the home or discussions of the parents' sexual activity. Indeed, those would likely encourage abuse rather than prevent it. Rather, encouraging openness means fostering a climate in a family where sexual issues and problems can be discussed without discomfort.

In an open climate, sexual issues are discussed when appropriate, and children are given sexual information that is appropriate to their age and understanding. Appropriate terms are used for body parts and body functions. Providing such a climate may be uncomfortable for some parents, but excellent materials are available to assist parents in this important role. Such instructional information in the form of books, pamphlets, and videos are available from various publishing companies (which frequently are willing to send sample copies for review purposes), through the public library, from pediatricians, from school counselors, and from community health departments. The criticism is sometimes made that sex education prompts children to inappropriately engage in sexual activities, but there is no research to support this mistaken notion. More likely, the opposite occurs. Children who do not have adequate or correct information about their sexuality are more likely to turn to sources that present unhealthy views of sexuality, such as pornography, and then may be tempted to experiment by abusing a sibling.

A friend recently described how his parents told him the facts of life when he was a young boy. His mother returned one day from a shopping trip while he was playing in his room. She called to him from the kitchen and told him she had purchased a book for him. He ran downstairs to the kitchen to get the book. When he arrived in the kitchen, his mother told him the book was in the drawer of a table in the living room. He couldn't understand why his mother would buy a book for him and then put it in a drawer. When he opened the drawer, he saw that the book was about sex. He recalled having the feeling that this was a book that should not be read when others were present and that there was something very secret and mysterious about sex (most of which he already knew). Obviously, his mother was not being open about sex in a positive, helpful way to her son.

Creating an open climate about sexuality is not a one-time event in which a parent sits down with a child, somehow tells them the facts of life, and feels this parental responsibility has been accomplished. Sexual information must be imparted at different times in a child's life, appropriate to the child's age and maturity. Sexual information should be appropriate to the age of the siblings with whom the child interacts, as well. For example, when an older sibling enters puberty, younger siblings may need additional information appropriate to their age to help them understand the physical developments the older sibling is experiencing.

An open and positive attitude about sex also implies that individuals have a right to privacy, or times and places where they can be alone.

While children may have to share a bedroom, they can have some privacy in the arrangement of furniture within the room. Parents must also set rules or expectations about privacy for the bathroom.

An openness about sex also implies that parents respond appropriately when sexuality is debased in films, videos, and television programs; in sexually slanted innuendos that one sibling may make toward another; and in sexually oriented jokes. The survivors of sexual abuse indicated that their parents' failure to confront these factors, especially the sexual innuendos of one sibling toward them, helped establish a family climate in which sexual abuse could be tolerated. The respondents appear to have been saying that since their parents allowed these unhealthy aspects of sexuality to exist in the family, the perpetrator sibling perceived that the sexual abuse of another sibling might be tolerated. This especially was true for older brothers who sexually abused a younger sister.

Creating an open climate about sex in the family is part of a parent's nurturing role. Just as small plants are nurtured with light, water, and food, children are nurtured by providing them with an atmosphere in which they develop wholesomely, including their sexuality, an essential part of their life.

■ Give Children Permission to Own Their Own Bodies

Children have a right to own their own bodies: they have the right to be hugged, kissed, and touched in appropriate places on their bodies in an appropriate manner by appropriate people. The converse is equally true: Children also have the right not be hugged, kissed and touched in inappropriate places on their bodies in an inappropriate manner by inappropriate people. Thus, children must be given permission to own their own bodies and to say no to inappropriate touches. This involves a process of education.

During recent years, in response to the increasing awareness of the sexual abuse of children, numerous programs have been developed to help children learn how to protect themselves from being sexually victimized. An important emphasis in these programs is empowering them to say no to approaches that may lead to sexual abuse. This is giving children permission to own their bodies. Children are taught, for example, to distinguish between good touches and secret touches. Good touches are the normal physical contacts that family members have with each other, such as a parent hugging a child leaving for school or kissing a child at bedtime. Good touches may also include a father "roughhousing" with a child (when both want to participate). Secret touches are touches of a sexual nature or the touching of body parts that an individual considers to be private, such as a brother touching his sister's breasts. Secret touches may also include tickling that continues after a child has said to stop. In essence, children must be taught that their bodies are their own property of which they have control.

Programs to prevent physical abuse are generally aimed at helping the *perpetrator* relate in a nonabusive manner. By contrast, programs to prevent sexual abuse are aimed at helping the *victim* learn behaviors to resist sexual abuse. This difference is due largely to the fact that potential sexual abusers tend not to be open to efforts to prevent sexual abuse and often do not view themselves as needing help. Sexual abuse victims are also often older than victims of physical abuse, and preventive instruction can therefore more effectively prevent sexual abuse. Finally, sexual abuse plays on children's lack of knowledge about sexual functioning. If children are appropriately informed about their sexual functioning, sexual abuse often can be prevented.

Numerous resources are available for educating children against sexual abuse, such as films, videos, cartoon strips, coloring materials, and other media geared to children's interests. Although these materials are focused on educating children against abuse by adults, they can be adapted to include the sexual abuse of children by a sibling. Mental health professionals who work with sexually abused children repeatedly indicate that the sexual abuse could often have been avoided if the victims had had some basic information, such as their right to say no to sexual advances, or the ability to distinguish between good touches and bad touches.

For information on effective programs to prevent sexual abuse that have been used in schools, churches, scout troops, and similar organizations, readers should contact the National Committee to Prevent Child Abuse (NCPCA) (322 S. Michigan Blvd., Suite 1600, Chicago, IL 60604; Tel.: 312-663-3520) for the name, address, and phone number of their nearest state chapter office. NCPCA, a nationwide network of agencies dedicated to preventing the physical, emotional, and sexual abuse of children, has chapters in all 50 states. A booklet titled *An Approach to Preventing Child Abuse* is available, as well as a publication titled *Database of Films and Videos on Child Abuse Prevention and Related Issues*. The latter publication contains a listing of numerous films and videos that can be used in prevention programs, where they are available, the cost, and a brief synopsis of each.

The Committee for Children (2203 Airport Way South, Suite 500, Seattle, WA 98134-2027; Tel.: 1-800-634-4449) publishes a catalog, available at no cost, of a wide range of materials in English and Spanish for the prevention of child abuse and youth violence, including curricula, videos, and training materials. Its video for children of grades 2-6, *Yes, You Can Say No*, has received nine major awards, including an Emmy. It focuses on 10-year-old David, who is being sexually exploited by a once-trusted adult. David's friends find out what is happening and demonstrate to him, as well as to those watching the video, how he can effectively handle the situation by making an assertive response. Also, a set of curricula on child abuse prevention for preschool through eighth grade, titled *Talking About Touching*, is available from the Committee for Children. These curricula teach children the skills they need to protect themselves against exploitation using the three new Rs. They are "Recognize," "Resist," and "Report."

Excellent books are available that can be used to teach children how to avoid becoming victims of sexual abuse. These books may be available at the public library, through a state office of the NCPCA, or at a bookstore that offers children's literature.

Efforts to prevent child sexual abuse must begin early in a child's life. Yet one study found that only 29% of 521 parents of children ages 6 to 14 in the Boston metropolitan area had had a discussion with their child specifically related to the topic of sexual abuse (Finkelhor, 1984). Only 22% of these discussions made mention of possible abuse by a family member. Most of the parents believed the optimal age for discussing sexual abuse with a child was around 9. For many of the survivors of sibling abuse who tell their stories in this book, the age of 9 would have been too late: They were already victims by the age of 9. Most of their parents just didn't view them as potential victims of sexual abuse. Many parents assumed any potential perpetrators were unrelated adults, not siblings or even family members.

Similarly, a researcher found from interviewing 20 sexually abused girls, ages 10 to 15, that they were provided with little or no sex education or information about sexual abuse (Gilgun, 1986). Neither parents nor schools provided this information. The researcher described their abuse as occurring in a knowledge vacuum. Because of their lack of knowledge, the victims did not understand what was happening. They lacked even an adequate vocabulary to discuss what had happened. The author concluded that providing information about sexuality and child sexual abuse must begin at an early age. The provision of this information is not a one-time event but a process that occurs over a period of time relative to a child's psychosexual developmental stages.

Many parents also fail to educate their children about sexual abuse because they fear this may be frightening to them. But parents educate their children about many dangers such as animals, automobiles, and appliances without frightening them. Other parents are reluctant to educate their children about sexual abuse for fear they will become distrustful of adults. Research evaluating the impact of these preventive programs does not support these views (Finkelhor, Asdigian, & Dziuba-Leatherman, 1995; Miltenberger & Thiesse-Duffy, 1988; Nibert, Cooper, & Ford, 1989).

Research has documented that preventative programs effectively provide knowledge to children about sexual abuse and how to avoid becoming a victim (Binder & McNeil, 1986; Kenning, Gallmeier, Jackson, & Plemons, 1987; Nibert et al., 1989). This type of instruction, if effective in group settings such as at school, can surely be equally effective in the setting of a parent-child relationship.

▪ Seek Help If Sibling Abuse Is Occurring in the Family

Imagine that you are uncomfortable with the way one child treats another in your family. An older brother is continually making fun of his younger sister. As parents you have talked to him about his behavior, but he persists in thinking of new and different ways to irritate her. The problem does not get any better.

You may be tempted to look the other way and say the problem will resolve itself, but this doesn't generally happen. Often a family's first reaction to the thought of seeking professional help is that this is admitting defeat. Unfortunately, some people subscribe to the idea that seeking help means admitting weakness or defeat. But not all individuals are born with the knowledge and skills necessary to handle all problems in life, including physical, emotional, and sexual development, interpersonal relationships with other adults, job responsibilities, finding a mate, continuing a marital relationship, being a parent, and on and on. To assume they are is a terribly big expectation.

Think of this example. Your car needs repairing. Why don't you simply lift up the hood, or jack up the car and fix it? Obviously, you can't. You don't have that knowledge. You aren't born with it; you must acquire it. Being instructed in car repair means tapping into the knowledge of a mechanic by watching the mechanic or by taking a course on car repair. Another analogy: You decide to plant a garden for fresh vegetables and herbs, but you've never turned over a shovelful of soil in your life. Until you get some guidance from an expert in gardening, you won't be an effective gardener. You may have some basic knowledge about gardening, but you aren't born with sufficient knowledge to produce a garden without problems.

But yet when it comes to living, especially parenting, many seem to feel they should have been endowed from birth with the knowledge of how to be excellent parents and tackle any problem that may come up. This is just simply not true.

One reason some people associate seeking professional help with admitting defeat is that many professionals were taught some bad psychology early in their formal education. The early child development field emphasized the importance of the environment on the development of a child; that is, on the way the parents nurture a child rather than on the child's genetic inheritance. Unfortunately, an overemphasis resulted in the impression that children are born like a *tabula rasa* or clean slate, and that how they turn out is the responsibility or "the fault" of the parents. More recent research has shown that children come into the world with genetic differences that affect their behavior, such as different temperaments (Thomas & Chess, 1977).

Thus, two children from the same family may be very different individuals. The first child, for example, may have been easy to get along with from the day the parents brought the child home from the hospital. But the ways they approached the child around feeding, setting limits, and making choices do not seem to work for the second. If the parents find themselves saying, "That kid sure has a mind of its own," they are correct. The child does have a mind of his or her own and a very different temperament, which may require them to relate to the child in a different way. The parents may need professional help.

Where should parents go for help? Agencies and mental health professionals that provide counseling services are listed in the yellow pages of the phone directory under the heading "Marriage and Family Counselors." Both private therapists in practice as well as social agencies offer these services; the latter generally charge a sliding fee based on a family's income. Agencies generally do not charge as much for their services as private therapists because the agencies are subsidized by public tax funds or United Way contributions. A family that wishes to use a private therapist should inquire if the fee is covered by their health insurance.

The ad in the phone book or a telephone call can provide information about the credentials of a private therapist. If licensing of counselors is required in the state, ask if the therapist is licensed. One may also inquire if a therapist is a member of a professional association such as the American Association of Marriage and Family Therapists (AAMFT), the American Psychological Association (APA), or the National Association of Social Workers (NASW). When contacting a family counseling agency, a person may inquire if the agency is a member of the Family Services Association of America (FSAA), an association whose member agencies must meet certain professional standards.

A final note: A family should not seek professional help for a child who is having problems with the intent that the child is going to be "fixed." Although the child is the focus of the attention, he or she is simply the one who is expressing the stress that other family members are also experiencing. A family that seeks professional help for one member can expect the entire family to be involved in family therapy. Involving all the family members can give the counselor an understanding of what is happening in the family, so that the family can begin to make some changes. A family is a social system, just as an automobile is a physical system consisting of the ignition, engine, brakes, and steering mechanism. If one part of that system is not working or working ineffectively, the entire system is affected. If one family member is experiencing stress and taking it out on another, the entire family is affected. In families where sibling abuse has been a problem, for example, effective treatment of the problem must involve the family as a unit rather than just the perpetrator and victim.

Seeking professional help is a sign of strength, not weakness. Parents are telling their children that they love them when they say, "We know you are not happy. We are concerned. We love you, and we want to do something about this, and we are. Let's get some help as a family."

▪ Violence-Proofing the Home

We live in a violent society. Simply turn on the television, read the newspaper, or run down the titles of current movies, and you will see that our society is very violent. Violence permeates every area of our lives, including our families.

Obviously, one person cannot turn society around to make it less violent. But each of us can make a contribution toward decreasing violence in our own lives and where our lives touch those of others. Families can violence-proof their homes. Just as a room can be sound-proofed, efforts can be made to violence-proof a home and the family occupying the home.

This can be done in several ways. First, we must develop a sensitivity to the violence that enters our homes through television and videos. Parents can screen the programs their children watch. Violence begets violence; it spreads; it reproduces itself. It can act as a stimulus to violent behavior in family relationships. As one survivor of sibling abuse put it:

> Kids mirror what they see whether it be on television, in the movies, or even in a book. If as adults we aren't alert to what kids are being exposed to, how can we expect them to behave any differently from the "Rambo images" they are watching?

Another important way adults can help reduce violence is to be sensitive to how children, in particular siblings, treat each other. Verbal put-downs of one sibling by another are often the prelude to physical abuse. Put-downs that are gender associated can be a prelude to sexual abuse, in which a brother inappropriately assumes the right and the power to dominate and abuse a sister. Parents and other adults have the responsibility to help children feel good about themselves but not at the expense of other children or siblings. Parents may need to first eliminate verbal put-downs in their relationship to each other since siblings sometimes treat each other in ways that mimic the ways the parents relate to each other.

Nor should pushing, shoving, hitting, and other acts of violence go unnoticed. Children can be given the message by adults in authority, in a nurturing context, that these physical abuses are unacceptable forms of behavior, whether at home or away from home. Adults supervising groups of children, such as in religious classes or at a scout meeting, can be sensitive to how children are physically and emotionally treating one another. Taking a child aside privately and in a nurturing way informing the child that abusive behavior is not acceptable can be a positive and corrective experience for a child. If a child is not told otherwise, he or she may assume that hitting, slapping, belittling, and ridiculing are acceptable in relationships with peers and siblings.

▪ Reward Good Sibling Interactions

Adults who supervise children, especially parents, often find their conversations with children heavily loaded with the word, *Don't*: "Don't write so messy." "Don't leave your papers lying around." "Don't come into the house with your dirty shoes." "Don't hit your sister." "Don't call your brother names." The negative behaviors that children engage in come to our attention immediately, while we may overlook or take for granted the positive or prosocial behaviors.

When children are interacting in a positive way, verbal note should be made of this with children. A parent may say, "Michael, I noticed how nicely you played this afternoon with your little sister. I'm really proud of you." Or a teacher might say, "I notice how nicely you and your sister get along." Positive behaviors that are reinforced encourage a child to continue them. Reinforcing positive behaviors give children positive feelings about themselves, which helps them to develop good self-esteem. When parents reward positive behaviors between siblings, children will prefer positive to the negative behaviors that have the potential of becoming abusive.

▪ Summary

The physical, emotional, and sexual abuse of siblings can be prevented in ways that include the following:

- Be aware of sibling abuse and the various ways it can occur.
- Listen to children; believe children. They may be trying to give a message that they are being abused by a sibling.
- Provide good supervision for children in the absence of their parents.
- Establish an open climate in the home in which children have adequate information about sex and can ask questions about their sexuality that may be bothering them.
- Give children permission to own their own bodies by teaching them the difference between good and secret touches and by empowering them with the ability to say no to secret touches.
- Seek professional help if sibling abuse is occurring.
- Violence-proof our homes.
- Reward good sibling interactions.

Treatment of
Sibling Abuse Survivors

*I have finally sought help for the emotional problems stemming from
my sexual abuse as a child by an older brother. Therapy is helping to
bring some sense into my life.*

A sibling abuse survivor

Although the treatment of sibling physical, emotional, and sexual
abuse survivors in essence does not differ from the treatment of
survivors of adult-child physical, emotional, and sexual abuse, several
factors relative to mental health professionals working with sibling
abuse survivors will be discussed in this chapter.

■ Uncovering Sibling Abuse

Numerous sibling abuse survivors who read the author's first book on
the subject have written expressing appreciation that the author's research has brought the problem of sibling abuse out into the open. Two
words that many survivors used when expressing their appreciation for
the research on sibling abuse were that the research "validated" or
"affirmed" for them that what they experienced from a sibling as they
were growing up was not sibling *rivalry* but *sibling abuse*. A survivor
from Montana wrote:

> I am a *sibling abuse* survivor and can now say that after having found your book in the library and having read it, I have looked for years in the literature for something written about the way my older brother treated me and even today as an adult continues to do so. Even a therapist I went to for a short period of time denied what I experienced was really abuse but "just a bad case of sibling rivalry." Your book affirms for me that I am an abuse survivor, and I am now in meaningful therapy with a group of other survivors.

Another survivor from Florida:

> I just read your book and had to write and say thank you for writing it. I am 27 years old and have been waiting for 20 years for someone, anyone, to acknowledge that sibling abuse exists! Parents, friends, school counselors, and nurses didn't believe me, because "these things just don't happen." I felt many of the statements in the book could have been made by me. Maybe I'll have the nerve some day to send a copy to my parents, who still don't believe me, don't remember anything about the abuse, and wonder why I don't speak with my brother. After all, as they say, "it was so long ago and was never that bad anyway." Few people can understand the double effect of the abuse and the failure to be validated in one's feelings and reactions. I have been made to feel that I am to blame for the results that the abuse has had on my life because people think the abuse didn't really happen.

These comments have been reproduced so that mental health professionals can become aware of the confusion that exists between sibling rivalry and sibling abuse, and even worse, the denial that sibling abuse does occur. This confusion and denial is found not only with parents of victims but even with mental health professionals to whom some survivors turn for treatment of the effects of their abuse from a sibling.

Perhaps what these comments most importantly demonstrate is the need for mental health professionals to be aware that sibling abuse does exist. Evidence of sibling abuse may occur, for example, in family therapy sessions where a therapist, focusing on problems affecting the family as a whole, may overlook and fail to explore the aversive behaviors that are occurring between the siblings. Also, in cases of spouse and child abuse, according to the theory that violence is a learned behavior, exploration of the relationship of the siblings toward each other should occur because the children may be modeling, in their relationship to their siblings, the behavior that the parents are engaging in with each other and with the children.

Therapists should keep in mind, in their assessment of clients' problems, that sibling abuse can be an etiologic factor for problems-in-living some adults may be experiencing and for which help is being sought. How should an assessment to determine if sibling abuse occurred be done? A therapist might be tempted to directly ask, "Were you ever physically, emotionally, or sexually abused by a sibling?" Experience shows, however, that such a direct question in many instances provokes a defensive denial. Individuals are reluctant to state they are victims of abuse unless the abuse has been very blatant. Also, as the comments of survivors indicate, survivors often do not identify the aversive treatment they experienced from a sibling as abuse, and since some survivors blame themselves for the abuse they experienced, they are reluctant to state they were victimized by a sibling.

A more indirect but effective way to assess whether or not sibling abuse occurred is for a therapist to ask a client to first describe *pleasant* memories they have of their childhood associations with their siblings. Following an eliciting and discussion of these memories, the therapist should ask the client to describe *unpleasant* memories of childhood associations with their siblings. The unpleasant memories provide the therapist the opportunity to explore selected memories in depth with the therapist, assessing whether or not these memories are indicative of abuse. The latter assessment can be made using the criteria discussed in Chapter 8 for distinguishing sibling rivalry from sibling abuse:

1. Were the behaviors age-appropriate?
2. How long and how often did the behavior occur?
3. Was the client a victim of the sibling engaging in the behavior?
4. What purpose did the behavior serve?

Such an assessment allows the therapist to determine if physical, emotional, or sexual sibling abuse occurred and if there may be an association between these abusive behaviors experienced by the client and the problems-in-living that the client is currently experiencing. The identification of effects of sibling abuse discussed in Chapter 7 may assist the therapist in the latter task.

◼ A Differential Effect of Sibling Abuse

Numerous effects of sibling abuse reported by survivors are identified in Chapter 7. However, a significant difference in the context in which sibling sexual abuse occurs as compared to adult-child sexual abuse may create a differential effect in adult survivors. The context in which sibling sexual abuse occurs is usually that of a threat. Recall the comments of survivors in earlier chapters who reported that their older brother threatened to harm them in various ways or to make their sexual victimization look as if it were their fault, if the victimization became known to the parents. On the other hand, because most perpetrators of adult-child sexual abuse, whether intra- or extrafamilial, are known to the victim, the context in which the sexual abuse occurs usually involves the victim implicitly trusting the perpetrator because of the loving relationship between the two persons, such as a grandfather and his granddaughter, or because of the authority role of the perpetrator, such as the scout leader and a scout. The loving relationship context may be reinforced by the perpetrator giving the victim gifts, such as candy, special favors, or privileges. This violation of trust that occurs in adult-child sexual abuse significantly affects the survivor's ability to trust others (Agosta & Loring, 1988).

As stated earlier, sibling sexual abuse generally occurs in the context of a threat. The victim becomes entrapped in the desire to please the perpetrator or the victim feels that she must comply for the sake of her own safety (Summit, 1983). The outcome of this scenario for adult survivors of sibling sexual abuse frequently is self-blame for allowing oneself to become entrapped. There initially may be a denial that sexual abuse occurred or a reluctance to discuss the victimization because the survivor is embarrassed that she allowed the sexual abuse to occur. (Thus, the manner in which sibling abuse is assessed, as discussed earlier, is important to the information the therapist can gather.) Regarding the survivor's self-blame for the sexual abuse, in reality she may have had no choice but to comply because developmentally speaking she cognitively did not understand what was happening, was operating under a threat, or had not been empowered by her parents to prevent sexual victimization.

An effect of this context of fear in which sibling sexual abuse occurs may influence the adult survivor not so much in terms of the inability to trust others but rather in terms of a fear of others, especially individuals who represent power or authority, such as teachers, employment supervisors, and others in positions of authority. One adult survivor of sexual abuse reported that she changed jobs and in some instances even cities where she lived over six times in the space of a few years. Her fear of authority and her need to please her superiors at work was so intense that she misinterpreted any criticism as failure and reacted with fear with the result that she would defensively take flight and seek other employment and even residency. She reported that until she sought therapy for the effects of the abuse, she was not aware of the intense fear that she was living under that pervaded many of her adult interpersonal relationships.

■ Substance Abuse

Numerous survivors of sibling abuse reported that they were experiencing problems with drugs and alcohol as an effect of their abuse. Although the participants in this research were adults (average age, 37), the problem of substance abuse may have started much earlier in life considering the participants experienced their abuse as young children. Research reports a significant relationship between adolescent chemical dependency and a history of abuse. For example, a review of 250 cases at a rural midwestern chemical dependency treatment center revealed 70% of the patients demonstrated some history of abuse, with a rate of 27% having experienced child/adolescent physical abuse and 9% sexual abuse (Potter-Efron & Potter-Efron, 1985). Other studies have likewise found high rates of abuse in chemically dependent adolescents (Cavaiola & Schiff, 1989; Harrison & Hoffman, 1987).

Therapists treating chemically dependent adolescents may wish to pay close attention in their assessment to the possibility of abuse. This abuse may have occurred at the hands of a parent, another adult, or even a sibling. Cavaiola and Schiff (1989), in their study of chemically dependent adolescents who were abused, provide valuable insight for mental health professionals treating such clients:

> While alcohol and drugs may play a self-enhancing role in chemical dependence, it appears that for the abused chemically dependent adolescent, the self-enhancement or self-medicating role of these chemicals is short-lived. In these adolescents the chemical dependence is the first layer of defense; it must be

removed before an attempt can be made to work through the repetitive trauma of abuse. This work is similar to working with a burn victim or multiple surgical case because of difficult scarring and adhesions. The therapeutic work is long-term and enduring in nature. (p. 333)

The authors also caution that chemically dependent adolescents do not readily reveal that they have been abused. The authors report that, on the average, the abused adolescents did not disclose the specifics of their abuse trauma until approximately the 4th week of residential chemical dependence treatment. The abuse and chemical dependency wreaked havoc on the adolescents' self-esteem. The struggle for appropriate self-esteem, sobriety, and recovery from victimization can be a lifelong process for these adolescents (Cavaiola & Schiff, 1989).

■ Stages of Therapy

Several distinct stages are identified that survivors go through in therapy for the sexual abuse they experienced from an adult as a child (Sgroi, 1989). These stages may be very similar for sibling abuse survivors, with slight modifications due to the context in which the abuse occurs, as discussed earlier. The stages are:

1. Acknowledging the reality of the abuse
2. Overcoming secondary responses to the abuse
3. Forgiving oneself (ending self-blame and punishment)
4. Adopting positive coping behaviors
5. Relinquishing survivor identity

These stages do not necessarily occur in an orderly fashion with one following the other but may occur in a cyclical manner with repetitions or survivors reworking aspects of an earlier stage later in therapy.

Acknowledging the Reality of the Abuse

As discussed earlier, this is perhaps the most critical aspect of sibling abuse because of the denial from significant other persons in the survivor's life that the aversive behaviors that he or she experienced from a sibling as a child was really abuse. Following exploration of these behaviors from a sibling, the therapist's validation or affirmation of them by labeling them as abusive can free up emotional energy for survivors to begin to cope with the effects of the abuse on their adult lives.

Various protective coping mechanisms are used by survivors to deny the reality of the abuse they experienced (Sgroi & Bunk, 1988). These mechanisms consume enormous amounts of emotional energy, which, after validation of abuse occurs, can be directed to problem solving and more effective coping strategies. These protective coping mechanisms include distancing oneself from emotions associated with the abuse such as fear, shame, or anger; continually giving and caring for others but not allowing oneself to accept nurturance—often seen in a constant activity or "busyness" in life; denying the seriousness of the abuse they experienced or even denying the events themselves; and self-blame for what occurred.

Overcoming Secondary Responses to the Abuse

Sgroi (1989) in this stage of recovery distinguishes denial of abuse at the time of the event from contemporary denial occurring in therapy. In contemporary denial, the survivor continues to excuse what occurred as abuse. In sibling abuse, support for this denial may occur from the perpetrator and family members of the survivor if the latter shares with them that he or she is seeking therapy or asks the perpetrator to apologize and assume responsibility for his or her behavior. Group therapy is helpful to survivors in this recovery stage because survivors, drawing on their own personal experiences in going through this therapeutic stage, can confront each other about the defensive mechanisms they are engaging in.

Forgiving Oneself

In this stage of the therapeutic process, if survivors are able to forgive themselves for the abuse that occurred and relinquish self-blame, a freeing-up process occurs. Sgroi (1989) identifies specifically how this process occurs in the context of group therapy:

(a) The survivor receives acceptance of the validity of her or his childhood victimization and current responses to it.

(b) Caring from others is also received, coupled with a message that the survivor is viewed by other members of the group as good and not blameworthy or deserving of punishment for the abuse experienced.

(c) The survivor receives feedback from group members regarding their self-blaming and self-punishing behaviors.

(d) Observations and concrete suggestions for self-blaming behaviors and substituting self-affirming behaviors are also received by the survivor in the context of the group members' wishes that the survivor will choose to stop practicing self-punishment.

(e) The survivor additionally experiences forgiveness from group members for the childhood sexual victimization and current secondary responses to it. (p. 124)

This stage in the therapeutic process represents a recognition that the survivor has become a self-abuser and now is ready to move away from that emotional state.

Adopting Positive Coping Behaviors

Exploration focuses on alternative ways to handle the effects of the abuse. For sibling abuse survivors, this may include a recognition of the futility of getting family members and especially the perpetrator to recognize that what the survivor experienced was abuse. Respondents to the research reported their frustration in trying to get their perpetrator to acknowledge responsibility for his sexual abuse of them and finally concluding that distancing themselves from the perpetrator and even other family members who were supportive of the perpetrator's denial was a more effective way of coping with the abuse.

Relinquishing Survivor Identity

Sgroi (1989) states this stage can be summarized in the following comment a survivor may make who has successfully completed the therapeutic process:

I am a human being, a person with strengths and weaknesses, good qualities and faults; a person who makes mistakes but also has useful and positive accomplishments. I was sexually abused when I was a child and that is an important part of my history. But that was then; this is now, and I no longer need to identify myself as a survivor. Instead, it is more accurate for me

simply to identify myself as a person and a self—no more and
no less. (p. 128)

■ Evaluation of Treatment

The results of a study of what survivors experienced as helpful or not
helpful when seeking help for problems-in-living stemming from their
sexual abuse may assist therapists in their work with sibling sexual
abuse survivors. Thirty women who had experienced incest in childhood or adolescence participated in the study (Armsworth, 1989). One
third of the women had experienced sexual abuse from a brother. The
women were from the Midwest and had sought help from school
counselors, agency counselors, psychiatrists, psychologists, social
workers, ministers/priests, pastoral counselors, psychoanalysts, and
support/therapy groups. The evaluations of their therapy were divided
into two categories:

1. Helpful interventions and practices
2. Harmful interventions and practices

Helpful Interventions and Practices

Four interventions and practices were found helpful by the survivors:

1. Validation
2. Advocacy
3. Empathic understanding
4. Absence of contempt or derision

Therapists who validated their client's sexual victimization were rated
as helpful to the therapeutic process. The researchers commented:

> Validation of the trauma experience . . . restores at least a partial
> sense of control to the victim mitigating to some extent the
> feelings of helplessness and powerlessness that accompany
> victimization experiences. In addition, validation of a life event
> provides an explanatory base for connecting past experience
> with present functioning and problems. (Armsworth, 1989,
> p. 556)

As stated earlier, sibling abuse survivors frequently are seeking valida-tion for the abuse they have experienced. For some survivors parents and even therapists have denied what they experienced from a sibling was abuse. Also, sexual abuse victims most frequently endure their victimization alone in fear, shame, secrecy, and confusion. Child victims are also often given the responsibility of caring for others while ignoring their own needs. Therapist assurance that the therapy is for the client and that the therapist is concerned about the client's well-being may represent a significant corrective emotional experience for the client. Sexual abuse represents a narcissistic wounding of the victim. Experi-encing empathy from the therapist can help survivors in a restoration of a sense of self and the development of a capacity to view what they have experienced with compassion rather than guilt and self-blame.

The disclosure of sexual victimization often occurs over time with a survivor's sending out feelers regarding how the admission of victimi-zation will be received by another person or even by a counselor. Many survivors are not believed when reporting their sexual victimization or are overtly or covertly blamed for the abuse.

> While the response of the professional to the disclosure of details of brutality, abuse, or coercion may be one of horror, seeing the past events from the perspective of the client is a necessary condition in helping abuse victims. The response of the professional is crucial. (Armsworth, 1989, p. 557)

Harmful Interventions and Practices

Four categories of harmful interventions and practices were identified by incest victims who sought help from a variety of counselors:

1. Lack of validation of the client's experience
2. Blaming the victim
3. Negative, rejecting, or absent responses from the therapist
4. Exploitation or victimization of the client

The first three categories have been addressed in the previous section from the perspective of what the survivors felt as helpful interventions and practices. Regarding exploitation or victimization, sexual abuse survivors are a high-risk group for sexual victimization by therapists because the dynamics in therapy are similar to those that are present in incest (Armsworth, 1989). These include a difference in power between the therapist and client, possible regressive behavior on the part of the client in the presence of the authority figure of the therapist, client neediness for attention but yet being highly vulnerable, and the possibility of the client relating to the therapist at a sexual level as part of a repetition compulsion or earlier confusion of affection and sex. Also, a therapist who exhibits little self-awareness through lack of training or poor impulse control may experience arousal from dealing with sexually explicit or taboo information when treating sexual abuse survivors (Armsworth, 1989).

■ Summary

Although the treatment of sibling abuse survivors in essence is similar to the treatment of survivors of adult-child physical, emotional, and sexual abuse, several factors unique to sibling abuse may affect the therapeutic process and mental health professionals must be aware of them. These include a tendency for survivors to not recognize the aversive behavior they experienced from a sibling as abuse and consequently to excuse the behavior or blame themselves for the abuse. The context of threat in which sexual abuse occurs in sibling abuse may also differentially affect the survivor as compared to adult-child sexual abuse where the context in which the abuse occurs involves entrapment and enticement.

A Final Word

Perhaps you became interested in this book because of the title. You may have seen yourself in the title. You may have been abused as a child—not by a parent or other adults, but by a sibling. As you read how the survivors were physically, emotionally, or sexually abused by a sibling, you may have said to yourself, "That's me! That was what life was like for me as a child."

If so, you are not predestined for a life of emotional pain and suffering. You may be at peace with the abuse and your sibling who perpetrated the abuse. Regardless of how this was resolved for you, it is good it was.

Unfortunately, for others this may not be true. You may be experiencing the effects of the abuse referred to by the survivors—low self-esteem, feelings of worthlessness, depression, substance abuse, difficulties in interpersonal relationships. If this is happening in your life and you see yourself in the survivors' comments in these pages, you are encouraged to seek help. Reread the pages in Chapter 9 on seeking professional help. Why prolong your suffering? Help is available, if only you reach out for it!

For still others, abuse may not have been a part of your life. But you may be asking, "How can we stop this senseless abuse—child abuse, spouse abuse, elder abuse, and now sibling abuse?" Only through your personal involvement in preventing the problem can the abuse of one individual by another be stopped. There are numerous ways to become involved—as volunteers with local agencies working in domestic violence, at spouse abuse shelters, at day-care centers for children from abusive homes, in support groups for those who have been abused, and in countless other ways. Contact a social agency in your community that works in the field of domestic violence. This could mark the beginning of your involvement in helping bring family violence to an end in our society.

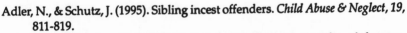

References

Adler, N., & Schutz, J. (1995). Sibling incest offenders. *Child Abuse & Neglect, 19,* 811-819.

Agosta, C., & Loring, M. (1988). Understanding and treating the adult retrospective victim of child sexual abuse. In S. Sgroi (Ed.), *Vulnerable populations* (Vol. 1, pp. 115-135). Lexington, MA: Lexington Books.

Armsworth, M. (1989). Therapy of incest survivors: Abuse or support? *Child Abuse & Neglect, 13,* 549-562.

Bagley, C., & Ramsey, R. (1986). Sexual abuse in childhood: Psychosocial outcomes and implications for social work practice. *Journal of Social Work and Human Sexuality, 4,* 33-47.

Bakan, D. (1971). *Slaughter of the innocents.* San Francisco: Jossey-Bass.

Battered families: A growing nightmare. (1979, January). *U.S. News & World Report,* 60-61.

Bavolek, S. (1989). Assessing and treating high-risk parenting attitudes. In J. Pardeck (Ed.), *Child abuse and neglect: Theory, research and practice* (pp. 97-110). New York: Gordon & Breach.

Bays, J. (1990). Substance abuse and child abuse: Impact of addiction on the child. *Pediatric Clinics of North America, 37,* 881-904.

Becker, J., Kaplan, M., Cunningham-Rathner, B., & Kavoussi, R. (1986). Characteristics of adolescent incest sexual perpetrators. *Journal of Family Violence, 1,* 85-97.

Beitchman, J., Zucker, K., Hood, J., DaCosta, G., Akman, D., & Cassavia, E. (1992). A review of the long-term effects of child sexual abuse. *Child Abuse & Neglect, 16,* 101-118.

Bellak, A. (1982). Comparable worth: A practitioner's view. In *Comparable worth: Issue for the 80's: A consultation for the U. S. Commission on Civil Rights* (June 6-7, 1982), pp. 75-82.

Belsky, J. (1980). Child maltreatment: An ecological integration. *American Psychologist, 35*, 320-335.

Benward, J., & Densen-Gerber, J. (1975). Incest as a causative factor in antisocial behavior: An explanatory study. *Contemporary Drug Problems, 4*, 323-340.

Berg, P. (1976). Parental expectations and attitudes in child-abusing families (Doctoral dissertation, University of Southern California, 1976). *Dissertation Abstracts International, 37*, 1889B.

Berkowitz, L. (1973, July). The case for bottling up rage. *Psychology Today*, 24-31.

Berne, E. (1967). *Games people play*. New York: Grove Press.

Binder, R., & McNeil, D. (1986). *Evaluation of a school-based sexual abuse prevention program: Cognitive and emotional effects*. Paper presented at the annual meeting of the American Psychiatric Association, Washington, DC.

Black, C. (1981). *It will never happen to me*. New York: Ballantine.

Blake-White, J., & Kline, M. (1985). Treating the dissociative process in adult victims of childhood incest. *Social Casework, 66*, 394-402.

Blalock, H. (1964). *Causal inferences in nonexperimental research*. Chapel Hill: University of North Carolina Press.

Bliss, E. (1986). *Multiple personality, allied disorders and hypnosis*. New York: Oxford University Press.

Blume, E. (1986, September) The walking wounded: Post-incest syndrome. *SIECUS Report, 15*(1), 5-7.

Brassard, M., & Gelardo, M. (1987). Psychological maltreatment: The unifying construct in child abuse and neglect. *School Psychology Review, 16*, 127-136.

Briere, J. (1984). *The effects of childhood sexual abuse on later psychological functioning: Defining a post-sexual abuse syndrome*. Paper presented at the Third National Conference on Sexual Victimization of Children, Washington, DC.

Briere, J. (1989). *Therapy for adults molested as children: Beyond survival*. New York: Springer.

Briere, J., Evans, D., Runtz, M., & Wall, T. (1988). Symptomotology in men who were molested as children: A comparison study. *American Journal of Orthopsychiatry, 58*, 457-461.

Briere, J., & Runtz, M. (1987). Post-sexual abuse trauma: Data and implications for clinical practice. *Journal of Interpersonal Violence, 2*, 377-379.

Briere, J., & Runtz, M. (1988). Symptomatology associated with prior sexual abuse in a non-clinical sample. *Child Abuse & Neglect, 12*, 51-59.

Briere, J., & Runtz, M. (1989). University males' sexual interest in children: Predicting potential indices of "pedophilia" in a nonforensic sample. *Child Abuse & Neglect, 13*, 65-75.

Briere, J., & Runtz, M. (1990). Differential adult symptomatologies associated with three types of child abuse histories. *Child Abuse & Neglect, 14*, 357-364.

Burgess, A., & Holstrom, L. (1975). Sexual trauma of children and adolescents: Pressure, sex, secrecy. *Nursing Clinics of North America, 10*, 551-563.

Caffey, J. (1946). Multiple fractures in the long bones of infants suffering from chronic subdural hemotoma. *American Journal of Roentgenology, Radium Therapy and Nuclear Medicine, 56,* 163-173.

Cantwell, H. (1981). Sexual abuse of children in Denver, 1979: Reviewed with implications for pediatric intervention and possible prevention. *Child Abuse & Neglect, 5,* 75-85.

Cavaiola, A., & Schiff, M. (1989). Self-esteem in abused chemically dependent adolescents. *Child Abuse & Neglect, 13,* 327-334.

Cerezo, M., & Frias, D. (1994). Emotional and cognitive adjustment in abused children. *Child Abuse & Neglect, 18,* 923-932.

Chaffin, M., Kelleher, K., & Hollenberg, J. (1996). Onset of physical abuse and neglect: Psychiatric, substance abuse, and social risk factors from prospective community data. *Child Abuse & Neglect, 20,* 191-203.

Clark, K. (1975). Knowledge of child development and behavior interaction patterns of mothers who abuse their children (Doctoral dissertation, Wayne State University, 1975). *Dissertation Abstracts International, 36,* 5784B.

Claussen, A., & Crittenden, P. (1991). Physical and psychological maltreatment: Relations among types of maltreatment. *Child Abuse & Neglect, 15,* 5-18.

Coffey, P., Leitenberg, H., Henning, K., Turner, T., & Bennet, R. (1996). Mediators of the long-term impact of child sexual abuse: Perceived stigma, betrayal, powerlessness, and self-blame. *Child Abuse & Neglect, 20,* 447-455.

Cohen, F., & Densen-Gerber, J. (1982). A study of the relationship between child abuse and drug addiction in 178 patients: Preliminary results. *Child Abuse & Neglect, 6,* 383-387.

Cole, A. (1990). *Brother-sister sexual abuse: Experiences, feeling reactions, and a comparison to father-daughter sexual abuse.* Unpublished doctoral dissertation, Union Institute, Cincinnati, OH.

Committee on the Judiciary, United States Senate (1990, May). *Hard-core cocaine addicts: Measuring and fighting the epidemic.* Washington, DC: U.S. Government Printing Office.

Corson, J., & Davidson, H. (1987). Emotional abuse and the law. In M. Brassard, R. Germain, & S. Hart (Eds.), *Psychological maltreatment of children and youth* (pp. 185-202). New York: Pergamon.

Crary, E. (1997). *Help! The kids are at it again: Using kids' quarrels to teach people skills.* Seattle: Parenting Press.

Demos, J. (1986). *Past, present and personal.* New York: Oxford University Press.

DeYoung, M. (1982). *The sexual victimization of children.* Jefferson, NC: McFarland.

Dore, M., Doris, J., & Wright, P. (1995). Identifying substance abuse in maltreating families: A child welfare challenge. *Child Abuse & Neglect, 19,* 531-543.

Dubowitz, H., Black, M., Harrington, D., & Vershoore, A. (1993). A follow-up study of behavior problems associated with child sexual abuse. *Child Abuse & Neglect, 7,* 743-754.

Edwall, G., & Hoffman, N. (1988). Correlates of incest reported by adolescent girls in treatment for substance abuse. In L. Auberbach Walker (Ed.), *Handbook on sexual abuse of children* (pp. 94-106). New York: Springer.

Eron, L. (1980). Adolescent aggression and television. *Annals of the New York Academy of Sciences, 347,* 319-331.

Eron, L., & Huesmann, L. (1985). The role of television in the development of prosocial and antisocial behavior. In D. Olweus, M. Radke-Yarrow, & J. Block (Eds.), *Development of antisocial and prosocial behavior* (pp. 285-314). Orlando, FL: Academic Press.

Eron, L., Huesmann, L., Lefkowitz, M., & Walder, L. (1972). Does television violence cause aggression? *American Psychologist, 27,* 253-263.

Faber, A., & Mazlish, E. (1982). *How to talk so kids will listen & listen so kids will talk.* New York: Avon.

Faber, A., & Mazlish, E. (1988). *Siblings without rivalry: How to help your chldren live together so you can live too.* New York: Avon.

Faller, K. (1989). Characteristics of a clinical sample of sexually abused children: How boy and girl victims differ. *Child Abuse & Neglect, 13,* 281-291.

Famularo, R., Kinscherff, R., & Fenton, T. (1992). Parental substance abuse and the nature of child maltreatment. *Child Abuse & Neglect, 16,* 475-483.

Farrell, L. (1985, April). The touching truth about tickling. *Mademoiselle, 54,* 56.

Felson, R., & Russo, N. (1988). Parental punishment and sibling aggression. *Social Psychology Quarterly, 51,* 11-18.

Feshbach, S. (1964). The function of aggression and the regulation of aggressive drive. *Psychological Review, 71,* 257-272.

Finkelhor, D. (1979). *Sexually victimized children.* New York: Free Press.

Finkelhor, D. (1980). Sex among siblings: A survey of prevalence, variety, and effects. *Archives of Sexual Behavior, 9,* 171-193.

Finkelhor, D. (1983). Common features of family abuse. In D. Finkelhor, R. Gelles, G. Hotaling, & M. Strauss (Eds.), *The dark side of families* (pp. 17-27). Beverly Hills, CA: Sage.

Finkelhor, D. (1984). *Child sexual abuse: New theory and research.* New York: Free Press.

Finkelhor, D., Asdigian, N., & Dziuba-Leatherman, J. (1995). The effectiveness of victimization prevention instruction: An evaluation of children's responses to actual threats and assaults. *Child Abuse & Neglect, 19,* 141-153.

Finkelhor, D., & Baron, L. (1986). Risk factors for child sexual abuse. *Journal of Interpersonal Violence, 1,* 43-71.

Finkelhor, D., Hotaling, G., Lewis, I., & Smith, C. (1990). Sexual abuse in a national survey of adult men and women: Prevalence, characteristics, and risk factors. *Child Abuse & Neglect, 14,* 14-28.

Freud, A. (1946). *The ego and the mechanisms of defense.* London: Hogarth.

Garbarino, J. (1977). The human ecology of child maltreatment: A conceptual model for research. *Journal of Marriage and Family, 39,* 721-735.

Garbarino, J., Guttman, E., & Seeley, J. (1986). *The psychologically battered child.* San Francisco: Jossey-Bass.

Garbarino, J., & Vondra, J. (1987). Psychological maltreatment: Issues and perspectives. In M. Brassard, R. Germain, & S. Hart (Eds.), *Psychological maltreatment of children and youth* (pp. 25-44). Elmsford, NY: Pergamon.

Gebhard, P., Gagnon, J., Pomeroy, W., & Christenson, C. (1965). *Sex offenders: An analysis of types.* New York: Harper & Row.

Gelinas, D. (1983). The persisting negative effects of incest. *Psychiatry, 46,* 312-329.

Gilgun, J. (1986). Sexually abused girls' knowledge about sexual abuse and sexuality. *Journal of Interpersonal Violence, 1,* 309-325.

Glaser, D. (1986). Violence in the society. In M. Lystand (Ed.), *Violence in the home: Interdisciplinary perspectives* (pp. 5-32). New York: Brunner/Mazel.

Goleman, D. (1995). *Emotional intelligence.* New York: Bantam Books.

Goodwin, J. (1982). *Sexual abuse: Incest victims and their families.* Boston: John Wright.

Goodwin, J., Sahd, D., & Rada, R. (1982). False accusations and false denials of incest: Clinical myths and clinical realities. In J. Goodwin (Ed.), *Sexual abuse: Incest victims and their families* (pp. 17-26). Boston: John Wright.

Groth, N., Hobson, W., & Gary, T. (1982a). Understanding sexual offense behavior and differentiating among sexual abusers: Basic conceptual issues. In S. Sgroi (Ed.), *Vulnerable populations* (Vol. 1, pp. 309-327). Lexington, MA: Lexington Books.

Groth, N., Hobson, W., & Gary, T. (1982b). The child molester: Clinical observation. In J. Conte & D. Shore (Eds.), *Social work and child sexual abuse* (pp. 129-144). New York: Haworth.

Harrison, P., & Hoffman, N. (1987). *Adolescent residential treatment intake and follow up findings* (CATOR 1987 Report). St. Paul, MN: CATOR.

Hart, S., & Brassard, M. (1987). A major threat to children's mental health: Psychological maltreatment. *American Psychologist, 42,* 160-165.

Hart, S., Germain, R., & Brassard, M. (1987). The challenge: To better understand and combat the psychological maltreatment of children and youth. In M. Brassard, R. Germain, & S. Hart (Eds.), *Psychological maltreatment of children and youth* (pp. 3-24). New York: Pergamon.

Hawkins, W., & Duncan, D. (1985). Perpetrator and family characteristics related to child abuse and neglect: Comparison of substantiated and unsubstantiated reports. *Psychological Reports, 56,* 407-410.

Herman, J. (1981). *Father-daughter incest.* Cambridge, MA: Harvard University Press.

Herman, J., & Hirschman, L. (1977). Father-daughter incest. *Signs: Journal of Women in Culture and Society, 4,* 735-756.

Herman, J., Russell, D., & Trocki, K. (1986). Long-term effects of incestuous abuse in childhood. *American Journal of Psychiatry, 143,* 1293-1296.

Hollis, J. (1985). *Fat is a family affair.* New York: Harper/Hazelden.

Hughes, H., Parkinson, D., & Vargo, M. (1989). Witnessing spouse abuse and experiencing physical abuse: A "double whammy"? *Journal of Family Violence, 4,* 197-209.

Irwin, A., & Gross, A. (1995). Cognitive tempo, violent video games, and aggressive behavior in young boys. *Journal of Family Violence, 10,* 337-350.

Janus, M. (1984, September). On early victimization and adolescent male prostitution. *SIECUS Report, 12*(1), 8-9.

Johanek, M. (1988). Treatment of male victims of child sexual abuse in military service. In S. Sgroi (Ed.), *Vulnerable populations* (Vol. 1, pp. 103-113). Lexington, MA: Lexington Books,

Jouriles, E., Barling, J., & O'Leary, K. (1987). Predicting child behavior problems in maritally violent families. *Journal of Abnormal Child Psychology, 15,* 165-173.

Justice, B., & Justice, R. (1979). *The broken taboo: Sex in the family.* New York: Human Sciences.

Kaufman, I., Peck, A., & Tagiuri, L. (1954). The family constellation and overt incestuous relations between father and daughter. *American Journal of Orthopsychiatry, 24,* 266-279.

Kaufman, J., & Zigler, E. (1987). Do abused children become abusive parents? *American Journal of Orthopsychiatry, 57,* 16-192.

Kempe, H., Silverman, F., Steele, H., Droegemueller, W., & Silver, H. (1962). The battered-child syndrome. *Journal of the American Medical Association, 181,* 17-24.

Kenning, M., Gallmeier, T., Jackson, T., & Plemons, S. (1987). *Evaluation of child sexual abuse prevention programs: A summary of two studies.* Paper presented at the National Conference on Family Violence, Durham, NC.

Kinzl, J., Traweger, C., & Biebl, W. (1995). Sexual dysfunctions: Relationship to childhood sexual abuse and early family experiences in a nonclinical sample. *Child Abuse & Neglect, 19,* 785-792.

Koverola, C., Pount, J., Heger, A., & Lytle, C. (1993). Relationship of child sexual abuse to depression. *Child Abuse & Neglect, 17,* 393-400.

Kravitz, R., & Driscoll, J. (1983). Expectations for childhood development among child-abusing and nonabusing parents. *American Journal of Orthopsychiatry, 53,* 336-344.

Kurtz, P., Gaudin, J., Wodarski, J. & Howing, P. (1993). Maltreatment and the school-aged child: School performance consequences. *Child Abuse & Neglect, 17,* 581-589.

Laviola, M. (1992). Effects of older brother-younger sister incest: A study of the dynamics of 17 cases. *Child Abuse & Neglect, 16,* 409-421.

Leonard, K., & Blane, H. (1992). Alcohol and marital aggression in a national sample of young men. *Journal of Interpersonal Violence, 7,* 19-30.

Lerner, H. (1985). *The dance of anger.* New York: Harper & Row.

Leyens, J., Camino, L., Parke, R., & Berkowitz, L. (1975). Effects of movie violence on aggression in a field setting as a function of group dominance and cohesion. *Journal of Personality and Social Psychology, 32,* 346-360.

Loredo, C. (1982). Sibling incest. In S. Sgroi (Ed.), *Handbook of clinical intervention in child sexual abuse* (pp. 177-188). Lexington, MA: Heath & Co.

Maisch, R. (1973). *Incest.* London: Andre Deutsch.

Marshall, P., & Norgard, K. (1983). *Child abuse and neglect: Sharing responsibility.* New York: John Wiley.

Masson, J. (1984). *The assault on truth: Freud's suppression of the seduction theory.* New York: Farrar, Straus & Giroux.

McGuire, L., & Wagner, N. (1978). Sexual dysfunction in women who were molested as children: One response pattern and suggestions for treatment. *Journal of Sex and Marital Therapy, 1,* 1-15.

Meiselman, K. (1978). *Incest: A psychological study of causes and effects with treatment recommendations.* San Francisco: Jossey-Bass.

Meuenzenmaier, K., Meyer, I., Struening, E., & Ferber, J. (1993). Childhood abuse and neglect among women outpatients with chronic mental illness. *Hospital and Community Psychiatry, 44,* 666-670.

Miller, D., & McCluskey-Fawcett, K. (1993). The relationship between childhood sexual abuse and subsequent onset of bulimia nervosa. *Child Abuse & Neglect, 17,* 305-314.

Miltenberger, R., & Thiesse-Duffy, E. (1988). Evaluation of home-based programs for teaching personal safety skills to children. *Journal of Applied Behavior Analysis, 21,* 81-87.

Moeller, T., Bachmann, G., & Moeller, J. (1993). The combined effects of physical, sexual and emotional abuse during childhood: Long-term health consequences for women. *Child Abuse & Neglect, 17,* 623-640.

Mullen, P., Martin, J., Anderson, J., Romans, S., & Herbison, G. (1996). The long-term impact of the physical, emotional, and sexual abuse of children: A community study. *Child Abuse & Neglect, 20,* 7-21.

Muller, R., Fitzgerald, H., Sullivan, L., & Zucker, R. (1994). Social support and stress factors in child maltreatment among alcoholic families. *Canadian Journal of Behavioural Science, 26,* 438-461.

Murphy, J., Jellinek, M., Quinn, D., Smith, G., Poitrast, F., & Goshko, M. (1991). Substance abuse and serious child mistreatment: Prevalence, risk, and outcome in a court sample. *Child Abuse & Neglect, 15,* 197-211.

Navarre, E. (1987). Psychological maltreatment: The core component of child abuse. In M. Brassard, R. Germain, & S. Hart (Eds.), *Psychological maltreatment of children and youth* (pp. 45-56). New York: Pergamon.

Nibert, D., Cooper, S., & Ford, J. (1989). Parents' observations of the effect of a sexual abuse prevention program on preschool children. *Child Welfare, 68,* 539-546.

O'Brien, M. (1991). Taking sibling incest seriously. In M. Patton (Ed.), *Family sexual abuse: Frontline research and evaluation* (pp. 75-92). Newbury Park, CA: Sage.

O'Keefe, M. (1995). Predictors of child abuse in maritally violent families. *Journal of Interpersonal Violence, 10,* 3-25.

O'Neill, K., & Gupta, K. (1991). Post-traumatic stress disorder in women who were victims of childhood sexual abuse. *Irish Journal of Psychological Medicine, 8,* 124-127.

Paik, H., & Comstock, G. (1994). The effects of television violence on antisocial behavior: A meta-analysis. *Community Research, 21,* 416-539.

Parke, R., & Collmer, C. (1975). Child abuse: An interdisciplinary analysis. In E. M. Hetherington (Ed.), *Review of child development research* (pp. 509-590). Chicago: University of Chicago Press.

Patten, S., Gatz, Y., Jones, B., & Thomas, D. (1989). Posttraumatic stress disorder and the treatment of sexual abuse. *Social Work, 34,* 197-203.

Patterson, G. (1982). *Coercive family process.* Eugene, OR: Castalia.

Peele, S. (1989). *The diseasing of America.* Lexington, MA: Lexington Books.

Pernanen, K. (1991). *Alcohol in human violence.* New York: Guilford.

Peters, J. (1976). Children who are victims of sexual assault and the psychology of offenders. *American Journal of Psychotherapy, 30,* 398-421.

Peters, D., & Range, L. (1995). Childhood sexual abuse and current suicidality in college women and men. *Child Abuse & Neglect, 19*, 335-341.

Phillips, D. (1983). The impact of mass media violence on U.S. homicides. *American Sociological Review, 48*, 560-568.

Potter-Efron, R., & Potter-Efron, P. (1985). Family violence as a treatment issue with chemically dependent adolescents. *Alcoholism Treatment Quarterly, 2*, 1-5.

Rada, R. (1976). Alcoholism and the child molester. *Annals of the New York Academy of Science, 273*, 492-496.

Reik, T. (1948). *Listening with the third ear*. New York: Grove.

Rodriguez, N., Ryan, S., Rowan, A., & Foy, D. (1996). Posttraumatic stress disorder in a clinical sample of adult survivors of childhood sexual abuse. *Child Abuse & Neglect, 20*, 943-952.

Rohsenow, D., Corbett, R., & Devine, D. (1988). Molested as children: A hidden contribution to substance abuse? *Journal of Substance Abuse Treatment, 5*, 13-18.

Ross, S. (1996). Risk of physical abuse to children of spouse abusing parents. *Child Abuse & Neglect, 20*, 589-598.

Royse, D. (1995). *Research methods for social workers*. Chicago: Nelson-Hall.

Rush, F. (1977). The Freudian cover-up. *Chrysalis, 1*, 31-45.

Rush, F. (1980). *The best kept secret: Sexual abuse of children*. Englewood Cliffs, NJ: Prentice Hall.

Russell, D. (1986). *The secret trauma: Incest in the lives of girls and women*. New York: Basic Books.

Sarwer, D., & Durlak, J. (1996). Childhood sexual abuse as a predictor of adult female sexual dysfunction: A study of couples seeking sex therapy. *Child Abuse & Neglect, 20*, 963-972.

Saunders, D. (1994). Child custody decisions in families experiencing woman abuse. *Social Work, 39*, 51-59.

Saunders, E. (1991). Rorschach indicators of chronic childhood sexual abuse in female borderline patients. *Bulletin of the Menninger Clinic, 55*, 48-71.

Sedney, M., & Brooks, B. (1984). Factors associated with a history of childhood sexual experience in a non-clinical female population. *Journal of the American Academy of Child Psychiatry, 23*, 215-218.

Sgroi, S. (1989). Stages of recovery for adult survivors of child sexual abuse. In S. Sgroi (Ed.), *Vulnerable populations* (Vol. 2, pp. 111-130). Lexington, MA: Lexington Books.

Sgroi, S., & Bunk, B. (1988). A clinical approach to adult survivors of child sexual abuse. In S. Sgroi (Ed.), *Vulnerable populations* (Vol. 1, pp. 137-186). Lexington, MA: Lexington Books.

Sgroi, S., Bunk, B., & Wabrek, C. (1988). Children's sexual behaviors and their relationship to sexual abuse. In S. Sgroi (Ed.), *Vulnerable populations* (Vol. 1, pp. 1-24). Lexington, MA: Lexington Books.

Silbert, M., & Pines, A. (1983). Early sexual exploitation as an influence in prostitution. *Social Work, 2*, 285-289.

Silverman, A., Reinherz, H., & Giaconia, R. (1996). The long-term sequelae of child and adolescent abuse: A longitudinal community study. *Child Abuse & Neglect, 20*, 709-723.

Singer, M., Petchers, M., & Hussey, D. (1989). The relationship between sexual abuse and substance abuse among psychiatrically hospitalized adolescents. *Child Abuse & Neglect, 13,* 319-325.

Sirles, E., & Franke, P. (1989). Factors influencing mothers' reactions to intrafamily sexual abuse. *Child Abuse & Neglect, 13,* 131-140.

Smith, H., & Israel, E. (1987). Sibling incest: A study of the dynamics of 25 cases. *Child Abuse & Neglect, 11,* 101-108.

Steinmetz, S. (1977). *The cycle of violence: Aggressive and abusive family interaction.* New York: Praeger.

Straus, M., Gelles, R., & Steinmetz, S. (1980). *Behind Closed Doors: Violence in the American home.* Garden City, NY: Anchor.

Suh, E., & Abel, E. (1990). The impact of spousal violence on the children of the abused. *Journal of Independent Social Work, 4,* 27-34.

Summit, R. (1983). The child sexual abuse accommodation syndrome. *Child Abuse & Neglect, 7,* 177-193.

Summit, R. & Kryso, J. (1978). Sexual abuse of children: A clinical spectrum. *American Journal of Orthopsychiatry, 48,* 237-251.

Sutphen, R., Wiehe, V., & Leukefeld, C. (1996). *Dual violence families: The relationship between spouse abuse, child abuse and substance abuse.* National Conference on Child Abuse & Neglect, Washington, DC.

Tavris, C. (1982). *Anger: The misunderstood emotion.* New York: Simon & Schuster.

Thomas, A., & Chess, S. (1977). *Temperament and development.* New York: Brunner/Mazel.

Vander Zanden, J. (1993). *Human development.* New York: Knopf.

Vissing, Y., Straus, M., Gelles, R., & Harrop, J. (1991). Verbal aggression by parents and psychosocial problems of children. *Child Abuse & Neglect, 15,* 223-238.

Walker, L. (1994). *Abused women and survivor therapy: A practical guide for the psychotherapist.* Washington, DC: American Psychological Association.

Wiehe, V. (1989). Child abuse: An ecological perspective. In R. Pardeck (Ed.), *Child abuse and neglect: Theory, research and practice* (pp. 139-147). New York: Gordon & Breach.

Wilbur, C. (1984). Multiple personality and child abuse: An overview. *Psychiatric Clinics of North America, 7,* 3-7.

Worling, J. (1995). Adolescent sibling-incest offenders: Differences in family and individual functioning when compared to adolescent nonsibling sex offenders. *Child Abuse & Neglect, 19,* 633-643.

Young, L. (1992). Sexual abuse and the problem of embodiment. *Child Abuse & Neglect, 16,* 89-100.

Zastrow, C., & Kirst-Ashman, K. (1994). *Understanding human behavior and the social environment.* Chicago: Nelson-Hall.

Index

About the Author

Vernon R. Wiehe is Professor in the College of Social Work at the University of Kentucky at Lexington. After he received a master's degree from the University of Chicago, he did postgraduate work in the Program of Advanced Studies in Social Work at Smith College. He received his doctorate from Washington University in St. Louis. He is the author of numerous articles in professional journals as well as the following books: *Perilous Rivalry: When Siblings Become Abusive; Working with Child Abuse and Neglect; Intimate Betrayal: Understanding and Responding to the Trauma of Acquaintance Rape;* and *The Brother/Sister Hurt: Recognizing the Effects of Sibling Abuse.* Dr. Wiehe has appeared on numerous television and radio talk shows discussing family violence, including *Phil Donahue* and *Sonya Live.* He is a frequently cited author on the subject of family violence.

9356537R0

Made in the USA
Lexington, KY
19 April 2011